Risk, Trust and Welfare

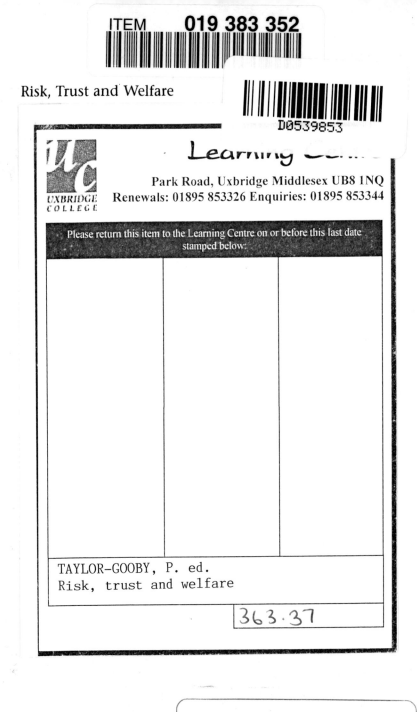

Also by Peter Taylor-Gooby

CHOICE AND PUBLIC POLICY

DEPENDENCY CULTURE (*with Hartley Dean*)

EUROPEAN WELFARE FUTURES (*with Vic George and Giuliano Bonoli*)

EUROPEAN WELFARE POLICY: Squaring the Welfare Circle (*with Vic George*)

FROM BUTSKELLISM TO THE NEW RIGHT

MARKETS AND MANAGERS (*with Robyn Lawson*)

POLITICAL PHILOSOPHY AND SOCIAL WELFARE (*with Raymond Plant and Harry Lesser*)

PUBLIC OPINION, IDEOLOGY AND THE WELFARE STATE

SOCIAL CHANGE, SOCIAL WELFARE AND SOCIAL SCIENCE

SOCIAL THEORY AND SOCIAL WELFARE (*with Jen Dale*)

THE END OF THE WELFARE STATE? Responses to Retrenchment (*editor, with S. Svallfors*)

THE PRIVATE PROVISION OF PUBLIC WELFARE (*with Elim Papadakis*)

Risk, Trust and Welfare

Edited by

Peter Taylor-Gooby
Professor of Social Policy
University of Kent

palgrave

in association with
ECONOMIC BELIEFS AND BEHAVIOUR
AN ESRC RESEARCH PROGRAMME

First published in Great Britain 2000 by
MACMILLAN PRESS LTD
Houndmills, Basingstoke, Hampshire RG21 6XS and London
Companies and representatives throughout the world

A catalogue record for this book is available from the British Library.

ISBN 0–333–76490–0 hardcover
ISBN 0–333–76493–5 paperback

First published in the United States of America 2000 by
ST. MARTIN'S PRESS, LLC,
Scholarly and Reference Division,
175 Fifth Avenue, New York, N.Y. 10010

ISBN 0–312–23236–5

Library of Congress Cataloging-in-Publication Data
Risk, trust and welfare / edited by Peter Taylor-Gooby.
p. cm.
Includes bibliographical references and index.
ISBN 0–312–23236–5 (cloth)
1. Risk management. 2. Risk—Social aspects. 3. Social policy. I. Taylor-Gooby,
Peter.

HD61 .R575   2000
658.15'5—dc21

00–020048

This book is printed on paper suitable for recycling and made from fully managed and sustained
forest sources.

Transferred to digital printing 2001

Printed and bound by Antony Rowe Ltd, Eastbourne

Contents

List of Tables

List of Figures

Preface

This book is a companion to *Choice and Public Policy*, published by Macmillan in 1998. Both books arose from the *Economic Beliefs and Behaviour* research programme in which the UK government's Economic and Social Research Council invested £1.6 million between 1994 and 1999. The 14 projects included in the programme range from studies of economic choice in everyday life, for example in the decisions people make in planning to finance their social care in old age, in the process of buying and selling owner-occupied housing and in ethical investment as against investment driven by the traditional balance of return and security, to carefully controlled laboratory experiments concerned with the factors that influence the perception of risk and how it influences choice and the question of what makes a particular alternative salient, and to theoretical work on the parallels between the development and sustenance of social norms and genetic evolution. A full list of projects and publications is given in the Appendix.

The earlier book examined the implications of the programme's work for the understanding of choice. It reviewed findings from projects on the way people arrived at their decisions in everyday life contexts ranging from care insurance to wage determination, from entrepreneurship to investment, and concluded that:

> at the theoretical level, economic behaviour cannot be understood as simply deliberative, rational and instrumental. In affecting how people choose, cultural values matter, social context matters and experience matters. At the practical level, any approach to policy-making that assumes that individuals will behave as active consumers or as service entrepreneurs in a welfare market runs the risk of disappointment. The new directions in public policy that stress privatisation and the role of markets are based on a flawed approach to behaviour.

The current book takes the argument further by examining the themes of risk and trust. It shows that any analysis of the way people understand and respond to risk, choice and opportunity must take into account the fact that choices are made within and shaped by a social context. Such contexts include assumptions about the appropriate agency to take responsibility for dealing with a particular risk – the state, the family or the individual themselves. They include the expectations of neighbours and other members of the community which are powerful factors in influencing how people negotiate moral choices in relation to parenting, partnerships and other aspects of family life. The crude imposition of market-driven polices, resting on the belief that people function as self-interested individualistic rational actors, whose response to incentives is entirely predictable, risks damaging cohesive social institutions at a cost to both efficiency and civility.

The book draws on the work of researchers funded by the programme and of others who attended conferences or networking meetings or were otherwise involved in programme activities. Like the former volume, it is firmly grounded in empirical research. Both books seek to engage critically with the dominant theoretical approaches in the field – 'rational choice' theory, derived from economics, and 'risk society' theories, currently influential in sociology – and are strongly concerned with the policy relevance of the work.

The new public policy opens up the way to a radical restructuring of the balance of state, individual and family responsibility. The work of the programme indicates that an understanding of the impact of the new policies cannot be derived *a priori* from the axioms of rational choice theory, but requires an analysis that takes seriously the point that economic choice is a social process, and involves examination of the operation of policies in concrete situations. It shows how the discriminating scepticism of active and reflexive citizens in response to perceptions of risk functions in a more complex and sophisticated way than much theoretical work allows.

Recent developments in social science call into question the traditional model of economic behaviour which understands choice as governed by the rational assessment of alternative means to achieve an individual's goals. A growing body of work in psychology, sociology, social anthropology and economics demonstrates that pressure from social groups, cultural values, changing perceptions of individual interests, messages received from the media and many other factors affect the choices people make in the real world.

At the practical level, the research programme has examined how people's beliefs, values, moral principles and cultural attitudes relate to their actions as employers, managers and workers, their choices as consumers, tax-payers and investors and the decisions they take in managing their family lives as parents and as carers. Many factors have contributed to the current interest of policy-makers in perceptions of risk, market behaviour and market choice. These include: the growing flexibility of labour markets, the expansion of world markets and the increased awareness of international competition, the shift towards the privatisation of state services and the fact that many people have more money to spend and more choices to make, while some do not.

Choices are at once more complex and more decisive in their impact, both at the individual level and the level of the firm or the nation. Policy is increasingly about modifying behaviour rather than providing services to deal with the outcome of people's actions. The assumptions that individuals are increasingly active and discriminating as citizens and consumers and that incentives will direct behaviour in desired directions without problems lead to policies which favour state retrenchment and market solutions. Provided the framework of costs and advantages is right people can be relied on to act in ways that meet their own needs as they understand them. Policy goals can similarly be attained, it is supposed, through the predictable response to incentives.

The central theme in our research is that people understand the opportunities open to them and the risks that confront them as a social process, not the outcome of a rational and individual calculus comparing the costs and benefits of alternatives. Choices are not made in terms of the relative utilities of a particular range of options, but are influenced by cultural expectations and preconceptions, by the norms prevalent in society, by the moral considerations that govern duty and obligation and by experience and learning from the experience of others. This book is intended to contribute to the growing body of empirically-grounded work in this field and to challenge the assumption that a simplistic approach derived from a single discipline can give an adequate account of the way people actually behave in everyday life.

University of Kent   PETER TAYLOR-GOOBY

Acknowledgements

Preparation of this book has involved contributions and influences too numerous to acknowledge adequately. Mention must be made of the encouragement of the Steering Committee – Ruth Byrne, Bill Callaghan, Chris Downes, John Hey (who attended the meetings of the book's contributors), Anthea Tinker, Bob Tyrell, Jeannette Weir and the chair, George Wright, of the ESRC staff involved with the programme, particularly our programme officers, Lindsey Fidler, Andrew Lester, Alex Monckton, Mohammed Quraishi, Phil Sooben, Ed Weir and of course the 76 academic investigators, co-applicants, research fellows, officers and assistants, and their technicians and support staff who carried out the work in 26 university departments and research institutes. Ms Patricia Smith, the administrator, ensured the smooth running of the programme. We owe a special debt to the respondents to our seemingly irrelevant, perplexing and sometimes, we hope, intriguing investigations, who number, taken together, in excess of 7200 people in Britain and the US. We also gratefully acknowledge the support of the ESRC for the programme research under grants L122521001-14.

Notes on the Contributors

Anne Barlow is a Lecturer in Law at the University of Wales, Aberystwyth. She has a particular interest in Family Law, especially the law relating to cohabitants. Recent publications include 'Family Redefinition under Part III of the Family Law Bill 1996' (with Craig Lind), *Web Journal of Current Legal Issues*, 1996, 'The Housing Implications of Part IV, Family Law Act 1996', *Journal of Housing Law*, 1998, *Cohabitants and the Law* and *Advising Gay and Lesbian Clients: A Guide for Lawyers* (with M. Bowley QC). She is currently undertaking comparative research into the varying legal responses to the phenomenon of cohabitation within Europe.

Paul Bissell is a Research Associate in the Drug Usage and Pharmacy Practice Group, School of Pharmacy and Pharmaceutical Sciences at the University of Manchester. He is a social scientist with an interest in lay people's use of medicines and medical technology. He is currently completing a PhD exploring compliance with diabetes therapy in ethnic minority groups.

Justine Blundell is a Research Fellow in the psychology department at University College London. She is working on an ESRC funded project on 'Risk and Household Saving' and researching the psychological dimensions of living and working as an actor.

Hartley Dean is Professor of Social Policy at the University of Luton. He is a former welfare rights workers and his research interests lie in the fields of poverty, inequality and citizenship. His key publications are: *Social Security and Social Control*, *Dependency Culture: The Explosion of a Myth* (with Peter Taylor-Gooby), *Welfare Law and Citizenship* and *Poverty, Riches and Social Citizenship* (with Margaret Melrose).

Simon Duncan is Reader in Comparative Social Policy at the University of Bradford. He has particular interests in the comparative analysis of gender inequality, parenting and work, the local state and housing provision. Recent publications include *Success and Failure in Housing Provision: European Systems Compared* (with J. Barlow), *Lone Mothers, Paid Work and Gendered Moral Rationalities* (with R. Edwards) and *Gender, Economy and Culture on the EU* (edited with B. Pfau-Effinger). He is currently working on socio-spatial differences in the moral rationalities of parenting and the implications for economic decision-making, partly as a member of the ESRC Research Group on *Care, Values and the Future of Social Policy*.

Rosalind Edwards is Reader in Social Policy at South Bank University. She has particular interests in motherhood and families, especially lone mothers and step-families, as well as feminist methodologies. Recent publications include *Feminist Dilemmas in Qualitative Research: Public Knowledge and Private Lives* (with J. Ribbens) and *Lone Mothers, Paid Work and Gendered Moral Rationalities* (with S. Duncan). She is co-editor of the *International Journal of Social Research Methodology, Theory and Practice*. She is currently researching children's understandings of parental involvement in education.

Janet Ford is Joseph Rowntree Professor of Housing Policy and Director of the Centre for Housing Policy at the University of York. Her key publications are: *Bridging the Gap? Safety Nets for Mortgage Borrowers* (with E. Kempson), 'The Costs of Unsustainable Home Ownership' (with R. Burrows), *Journal of Social Policy* (1997) and *Precarious Jobs? Precarious Homes?*

Bruno S. Frey is Professor of Economics at the University of Zurich. He was Visiting Professor at various European and American universities, among others, Visiting Professor at the Chicago University. He received an honorary doctorate in economics from the University of St Gallen (Switzerland, 1998) and the University of Goeteborg (Sweden, 1998). He is the author of many articles in professional journals as well as of twelve books, some of which have been translated into nine languages. The latest two books are *Not Just for the Money: An Economic Theory of Personal Motivation* and *FOCJ: Functional, Operating and Competing Jurisdictions – A New Federalism for Europe*.

Julian Le Grand is the Richard Titmuss Professor of Social Policy at the London School of Economics. He is the author, co-author or editor of twelve books and over seventy articles and book chapters on public policy and the welfare state, including *The Economics of Social Problems* (with Ray Robinson and Carol Propper) and *Quasi-Markets and Social Policy* (with Will Bartlett).

Peter Lunt is a social psychologist at University College London. His previous books include *Mass Consumption and Personal Identity* (with Sonia Livingstone) and *Economic Socialisation* (with Adrian Furnham). His current research interests are the social and psychological aspects of e-commerce, risk and household savings and the relationship between social psychology and social theory.

Moira Munro is Professor of Planning and Housing at Heriot Watt University. She is an economist with research interests in the operation of the housing market, housing finance and gender and the meaning of the home. She edits *Housing Studies* and is author of *Housing Finance* and a wide range of journal articles.

Peter Noyce is Boots Professor of Pharmacy Practice in the School of Pharmacy and Pharmaceutical Sciences at the University of Manchester. His interests are in consumer and clinician decision-making related to the choice and use of medicines.

Gillian Parker is Nuffield Professor of Community Care at the University of Leicester and Director of the Nuffield Community Care Studies Unit. Her publications include *With This Body: Caring and Disability in Marriage, Different Types of Care, Different Types of Carer* (with Dorothy Lawton), and *With Due Care and Attention: a Review of Research on Informal Care*. Her current research interests include informal care and disability, population forecasting for long-term care needs and finance for long-term care.

Peter Taylor-Gooby is Professor of Social Policy at the University of Kent. His main research interests lie in understanding the relationship between values, attitudes and choice and in European social policy. Among his recent publications are *European Welfare Futures* (with V. George and G. Bonoli), *European Welfare Policy* (with V. George) and *Social Change, Social Welfare and Social Science*.

Paul Ward is a Research Associate in the Drug Usage and Pharmacy Practice Group, School of Pharmacy and Pharmaceutical Sciences at the University of Manchester. He is a social scientist with a particular interest in the social aspects of medicines usage. He is currently undertaking a PhD which seeks to map and understand prescribing for specific therapeutics drug groups.

1
Risk and Welfare

Peter Taylor-Gooby

Responding to risk: new policies and academic perspectives

Those alive today enjoy the highest living standards ever achieved on a mass scale in this country. However, unprecedented mass affluence is conditioned by awareness of economic vulnerability. Apprehensions about future uncertainties, fuelled by fears of redundancy, of negative equity in the housing market, of not having a decent pension, of being unable to pay for care needs in old age, are becoming increasingly important, just at the time when some of the traditional mutual and state welfare mechanisms that helped people cope with such risks are undergoing critical review.

Public policy is our collective response to risk. New directions in policy reflect considerations derived from economic and social theory. On the one hand, the assumption that citizens behave simply as the rational incentive-driven actors of traditional economic theory is evident in areas ranging from Welfare to Work to performance-related pay in the public sector. This approach implies that the combination of 'risk society' and welfare retrenchment does not constitute a problem – people will adapt their behaviour and save or take out insurance to meet the risks they face, as they judge best. What they need is good information and a well-regulated market. Policy goals are to be achieved by the appropriate structure of incentives.

On the other hand, the notion that service-users are becoming more discriminating has tended to reinforce a new and critical approach to the role of government in welfare provision by academics. In particular, influential sociologists argue that state welfare systems are vulnerable to loss of authority in late- or post-modern society because the decisions made by professionals or administrators are open to challenge by increasingly well-informed and sceptical users, and because citizens simply will not pay the taxes necessary to maintain them. Economic rational choice theory and the sociology of reflexivity and risk society thus combine to drive policies based on the assumption that state welfare must contract because pro-active individuals will increasingly reject it.

This book is concerned with current policy developments and the social science (both rational actor economic models and risk society sociological models) on which it rests. It analyses recent empirical evidence on the way in which people respond to the risks they face in everyday life and the sources of support on which they call. It shows that the uncertainties that people perceive and the ways in which they deal with them can only be understood in terms of a perspective that takes cultural values and institutions into account. Different social groups may have different ideas about obligation and responsibility and differing levels of confidence in their ability to make successful choices. There is strong evidence of continuing trust in government as welfare-provider, and of mistrust of the available private alternatives. The social science that underlies welfare state retrenchment fails to capture the complexity of the way people perceive and manage risk. Policies designed on the assumption that social actors are primarily motivated by individualised and immediate self-interest ignore the various moral rationalities which govern many aspects of behaviour and may damage the benign motivations that inform welfare state citizenship.

Risk society and the retreat of state welfare

The half-century experiment of the British welfare state is everywhere in retreat. More importantly, politicians in the UK are not prepared to make the political commitment and the investment of resources necessary to restore it. The Beveridge settlement promised universal care, 'from the cradle to the grave' as the *Daily Mirror* headline put it in 1942 (Timmins, 1996, p. 178). Modern politicians are more modest and rely on market solutions wherever practical, offering 'work for those who can' and restricting security only 'to those who cannot' in an efficient system 'where costs are manageable' (Tony Blair, DSS, 1998c, pp. iii, v). Leading academics call for the welfare state to restrict itself to its 'core business' of health care, schooling and poverty (Glennerster, 1998, p. 11).

At the same time perceptions of risk have changed. This does not mean that the risks most people face are more severe or that the course of everyday life has somehow grown more uncertain, as some of the more enthusiastic proponents of the risk society thesis appear to claim (Adams, 1995, chapter 10; Madden, 1998). In point of fact, material levels of security in the western world are higher than ever before (Wildavsky, 1988). Most people eat more, live in warmer houses and spend more on luxuries. However, the sources of uncertainty and the mechanisms available to most people to deal with them have changed, leading to the paradox of timid prosperity – growing uncertainty amid rising mass affluence.

In part this change results from developments in the labour market and in the family, so that the possibilities of loss of income from employment or of restructuring of the pattern of dependency and support available through the family appear more pressing. Increased life expectancy extends the period of old age dependency. In part uncertainty results from the decay of the mechanisms that had previously dealt with risks. The retreat of the welfare state is part of this process. Many commentators have argued that it is compounded by a less obvious development. Official position or the claims to privileged knowledge by professionals duly accredited by established self-regulating bodies carry a certain authority. As education and access to alternative viewpoints and sources of information become more widespread the exercise of official authority and the claims of expertise are increasingly opened up to question and to critical examination. The disquiet surrounding the old centralist solutions reinforces the reluctance of politicians to propose a return to a welfare expansionism predicated on the assumption that government knows best.

These changes direct attention toward the uncertainties that people believe they face in everyday life and to the resources made available to meet them. The way in which social scientists understand risk and the response to it has also changed. Economists have become more aware of the social and psychological factors that influence perceptions of risk as evidence accumulates to highlight the shortcomings of models that constitute people as predominantly rational actors, choosing self-consciously between alternatives on the basis of a deliberative calculus of benefits and disadvantages (Loomes, 1998, p. 486; Hargreaves-Heap *et al.*, 1992, chapter 4; Adams, 1995, chapters 4 and 5). Psychologists have learnt to incorporate the methodological strengths of econometric approaches to the evaluation and comparison of risks (Lea *et al.*, 1985; Lewis *et al.*, 1995). An increasing body of sociological work uses the resources of large, longitudinal surveys to assess risks faced in everyday life, and has developed middle range theories such as the notion of a 'coping strategy' to analyse patterns of behaviour (Buck *et al.*, 1994;

Crow, 1989; Forrest and Kennett, 1996). The patterns of social values which affect the way particular social groups understand their needs and opportunities and the social institutions which form the context for their response exert an important influence on risk behaviour.

This book reviews recent work on risk and motivation in the context of current public policy. At an academic level, it demonstrates that an interdisciplinary approach which seeks to understand the link between apprehension of uncertainty and the social context of people's lives is essential to understand the way in which people behave in response to risk. The relevance of this point to practical policy-making is considerable. Any approach based on the traditional assumptions of economic consumer theory – in particular, the view that behaviour is the outcome of rational deliberation between alternatives and reveals overall and independent preferences – runs the risk of being seriously misleading. Many other factors also influence the choices people make in real-life contexts. Of particular significance is the evidence that choices are shaped by context, and context includes the policies designed in response to assumptions about the choices people will make. A welfare system which assumes that deliberative self-interest is the key motivation may create circumstances which diminish acceptance of the mutual obligations of welfare citizenship. The enthusiasm of policy-makers for private market alternatives to collective state provision requires re-assessment.

Approaches to policy which assume that a stronger sense of insecurity within a prosperous society coupled with a more discriminating scepticism on the part of welfare consumers will automatically lead to a rejection of state welfare solutions may also mislead. Awareness of the possible shortcomings of state welfare does not necessarily convince people that non-state solutions are superior. In this chapter I will first review the four main features of contemporary discussion of welfare and risk: people are more conscious of risk, despite rising real living standards; concern is pervasive although vulnerability is concentrated among the weakest groups in an increasingly unequal society; despite this concern, state policies to manage risk are constrained by retrenchment; and the professional expertise underlying official policy prescription is increasingly challenged. We will then go on to consider the recent development of state policy, dominated both by retrenchment and by a simplistic rational actor model of individual behaviour in a welfare state. We will conclude by reviewing the evidence to be presented in the book.

The paradox: risk amid affluence

In material terms, contemporary society is richer than ever before. GDP rose by very nearly one-fifth in the quarter century to 1997 with only brief interruptions to the pattern of continuing but uneven growth in 1974/75, 1980/81 and 1991/92 (ONS 1998, table 14.6). Real disposable incomes for households, calculated to take differences in household membership into account, rose by about two-fifths between 1972 and 1994 (CSO, 1995, table 5.1). Incomes have also grown markedly more unequal – the rise for the top 25 per cent was very close to 60 per cent and for the bottom 25 per cent about 30 per cent. However only those at the very bottom have experienced real falls in living standards in recent years – the incomes of the bottom 10 per cent actually fell by 12 per cent between 1979 and 1994, after housing costs had been taken into account (DSS, 1998d, table H3.01).

In 1972 about a third of households had central heating, two-fifths a telephone and two-thirds a washing machine. By 1996 the corresponding proportion was greater than nine out of ten (ONS, 1998, table 15.4; 1985, table 15.3). In 1972, 8 per cent of families took a holiday abroad. By the mid-1990s, some 37 per cent were doing so (CSO, 1995, table 13.1). Some groups (notably those without secure employment) have not shared in rising affluence, but most people are indisputably better off than ever before. Why then do social scientists talk about the uncertainties of a 'risk society', and why do voters question whether we can afford to continue the current level of welfare spending?

The social changes that contribute to a heightened awareness of threats to security are discussed in more detail in the companion volume, *Choice and Public Policy* (Taylor-Gooby, 1998) and elsewhere. Changes in the labour market (most importantly the introduction of new technology which particularly threatens unskilled jobs and also, in some sectors, a higher level of competition from overseas as a result of improved communications and the removal of tariff barriers, CEC, 1993, p. 11) create a situation in which employment for some becomes more insecure. Demographic shifts, especially the fact that more people live to a greater age than before, lead to a longer period of dependency in old age. The proportion of the population of pensionable age rose from 15 per cent in 1961 to 18 per cent in 1991 and is projected to rise further to 20 per cent by 2021 (ONS, 1998, table 2.2). Changes in the family, which have been especially marked in the UK, have led to the highest proportion of one-parent families in Europe (Hantrais, 1998, graph 18). This group typically has unsatisfactory access both to labour market incomes and to social security benefits (Evandrou and Falkingham, 1995). The *British Household Panel Survey* shows that very nearly half the women who separated from their partners between the 1991 and 1992 waves of the survey experienced a substantial fall in personal income, about a fifth falling at least four tenths of the way down the income distribution. Less than a fifth of men who had separated experienced income falls and only three per cent by four deciles (Buck *et al.*, 1994, p. 93). A higher incidence of divorce and re-partnering has generated a greater fluidity in family life, disrupting traditional mechanisms for transferring income inter-generationally to provide support for children and older people (Glennerster and Hills, 1998, pp. 245–6).

Other factors have reinforced the apprehension of risk in the welfare arena. The housing market recession of the early 1990s confronted mortgage-holders with the possibility of negative equity in a field of investment previously regarded as secure (see chapters six and nine). Concerns about social care in old age were promoted by the national endorsement of means-testing for care support in 1993. Pension policies from the late 1980s onwards have cut back state provision despite the weakness and scandalous mis-selling of private pensions in the early 1990s (Waine, 1995, pp. 326–7). NHS policies have imposed restrictions on the range of prescription drugs available and on the procedures that Health Authorities will fund (Le Grand and Vizard, 1998, pp. 84–5).

The social distribution of risk

These developments have led to an explosion of concern about risk, vulnerability and social need. In fact, the available evidence indicates that the incidence of the disasters people fear most has not risen proportionately. For example, unemployment tends to be concentrated among particular groups – young people, those without qualifications or skills, some ethnic minorities. The change in the 1990s is not so much that unemployment has risen dramatically since the oil crisis of the 1970s but that it is beginning to be felt among sectors of the labour market which had previously been insulated from its impact. In the mid-1970s unemployment stood at six per cent among semi- and unskilled workers but at one per cent among professionals, employers and managers. In the recession of 1993 the corresponding rates were 17 and five per cent. The rapid pace of industrial restructuring of the 1980s and 1990s, the changes in working practices consequent on de-nationalisation, the reorganisation of the state sector and the impact of cross-national competition affected the vulnerable lower-skilled groups most sharply. In addition and for the first time in the post-war period, the possibility of redundancy also become a reality for appreciable numbers in those groups whose position in the labour market had previously seemed secure. Survey data in 1995 showed that nearly one third of British employees had experienced a spell of unemployment lasting longer than a month during their working lives (ONS, 1997, table 4.27). The fear of unemployment has spread more rapidly than unemployment rates have risen.

In general, living standards continue to improve for the most people. The solution to the problem of understanding the paradox of insecurity amid affluence is the recognition that awareness of risk permeates society to a much greater extent than do the risks themselves, and that risks traditionally confined to lower social groups have become more prominent in the social world of the middle classes. The apprehension of risk is heightened by the decay of the traditional mechanisms that dealt with it.

The retreat of the welfare state

The shift from the confident expansion of state welfare in the quarter century after Beveridge to the retrenchment of the 1980s and 1990s has been so extensively chronicled that it is unnecessary to reiterate the main points here. Glennerster and Hills (1998, chapters 2 and 8) provide an excellent contemporary review and Timmins (1996, especially part VI) a longer term perspective. Esping-Andersen (1996, chapter 1) or Bonoli, George and Taylor-Gooby (2000, chapters 2 and 7) offer cross-national accounts. The main social services have been starved of resources. Nonetheless, standards in almost all areas have risen to some extent – one of the most striking efficiency gains of modern times and far out-stripping any achievements of the private sector (Glennerster and Hills, 1998, p. 325). However for a variety of reasons (most important being the fear of electoral punishment) politicians of all main parties refuse to make the substantial increases in taxation necessary to restore the levels of service to those that will meet the expectations of an increasingly affluent modern society.

The result is that modern welfare systems call on private sources of finance and provision (through fees, private-public partnerships, the regulation and sometimes the subsidy of private provision) in a wide range of areas, including higher education, sickness benefit, retirement pensions, dental and optical treatment, social housing, mortgage protection, the care of older and disabled people and capital programmes in schools, further and higher education and the NHS. Welfare state mechanisms for dealing with risk appear unsatisfactory to those who are used to the more substantial real advances made with the greater resources available in the private sector. Political debates across the main parties assume that retrenchment will continue. The apparent decline of one of the most important sources of support throughout the post-war period increases disquiet at the risks discussed above. We discuss the way state provision has altered in relation to the needs that people experience or anticipate in more detail in chapters 6, 9 and 10.

Reflexivity and the erosion of expert authority

Developments in relation to the incidence of risk and the under-funding of welfare state mechanisms to cope with it chime in tune with shifts in the climate of ideas. These issues have captured the attention of theoretical sociologists concerned with modern culture. Unfortunately much of the debate has taken place in an abstracted and technical language and with little interest in empirical evidence, so that while the conclusions have been influential, the details of the argument has received little attention from those working in other fields (see for example, Luhmann, 1993; Beck, 1992; Toulmin, 1990; Turner, 1992, and, most important in relation to UK policy debates, Giddens, 1990, 1991, 1994, 1998).

A core argument of this approach is that the kind of society in which we live is characterised by *reflexivity*. The central point is that, in contrast to previous *traditional* societies in which authority and the assumptions on which it was based proceeded from the top down and commanded a relatively uncritical acceptance, transitional late modern societies rely on critical attitudes to old approaches and on the increasingly broader (and more democratic) diffusion of knowledge. Knowledge-based society is thus distinguished from the traditional forms of factory-based industrialism, state-socialist or capitalist, as well as mercantile, feudal, slave or mandarin society. Not only do we know more about the material world, we know more – and are more confident in our knowledge – about the workings of our own society.

Material innovation is at the heart of competitive capitalism. Members of society increasingly face, and have to make, the choices that determine their own life-course, not only in democratic politics, but also in education, in careers, in personal relationships and in other aspects of life. This demands assessment and appraisal of what is available. At the same time, the level of knowledge and of awareness of alternative perspectives continually expands. People become more self-aware and more aware of their social context – 'a world of *clever people*', as Giddens (1994, p. 7) puts it. This takes place not only through the expansion of the formal schooling, college and university system, but also through the ready availability of communication from radio to Internet to printed word. The outcome is that people are less likely to take authority on trust, more inclined to call into question the pre-scriptions of groups which in the past could confidently rely on their social standing and on the fact that their claims to know best were based on professional status or accredited technical expertise.

Such challenges emerge, for example, in the proliferation of different approaches to medicine and health, not only in terms of 'alternative medicine' but also in terms of lifestyle change or self-prescription (Williams and Calnan, 1996, p. 1616 – see chapter 8); in the legal challenges mounted against authorities in areas like social work services, the professional decisions of surgeons or the resource priorities of the education system (Swanson, 1992); and in the diffusion of alternative and often oppositional expertise in environmental politics (Adams, 1995, pp. 38–40). One implication of the spread of knowledge is a wider diffusion of responsibility. Individuals have greater confidence in their own capacity to make choices, not only in the material arena commanded by rising living standards, but also in awareness of the alternatives that can inform their life-planning. The services which cater to meet uncertainty in areas like the ability to earn an income or provide care when it is needed for oneself or family members cannot assume with the same confidence as in the past that what they offer will automatically be accepted. Trust must be earned and, conversely, individuals have increasingly to make a more-or-less conscious choice about where they place their trust. This has particular implications for key professional services such as medicine, social care, education or mental health services which were once able to rely on the passive acceptance of their authority. Similar points apply to the private financial sector, especially as it assumes the dominant role in housing finance, pension provision and perhaps insurance against risks like the need for social care in old age, disability or inability to pay for housing through unemployment (see chapters 6, 7, 9 and 10).

The retreat of the welfare state is compounded by a new uncertainty about exactly who can be trusted to meet the needs that people may experience now or in the future. In this further sense 'risk society' is more than the response to the new perceptions of uncertainty about factors which affect peoples interests. To sum up: the new climate of risk includes four mutually reinforcing factors. First, the risks that people face in their everyday lives are perhaps somewhat more marked than in the period of secure growth that followed the war, but are heavily concentrated among certain social groups and set in the context of an enhanced overall affluence that does much to counteract the penalties that may be incurred. Secondly, many of the new risks are seen to derive from factors whose incidence is hard to predict but which may well be more socially pervasive, a perception strengthened by experience of social contact with others who have suffered damage from these sources. Thirdly, the retreat of state welfare in coverage and also in terms of the quality of provision is much publicised, leading to apprehension that one of the major mechanisms for managing insecurity is no longer available. Finally, changes in the way in which people tend to think about their social world, resulting from the broader diffusion of knowledge and of more critical attitudes to received wisdom and to professional expertise, tend to undermine trust in the capacity of both private and state services to handle the consequences of uncertainty, and this again increases the apprehension of risk.

Welfare markets: new directions in policy-making

Paralleling the shift from the confident and progressive climate of the 1950s and 1960s towards greater apprehension of uncertainty in welfare is a shift from direct state provision to the much greater use of market institutions in social policy-making (for details see Taylor-Gooby, 1998). The main factors are: first, rising real incomes, which permit individuals to pursue private services to meet the needs they identify or anticipate at a time of constraint in state provision; secondly, a shift in the dominant approach in policy-making away from the centralised administrative allocation of resources towards the decentralisation of management and of budgetary control in competitive internal markets; thirdly, active state policies, designed to encourage the development of private provision in a wide range of areas including pensions, social housing and social care, often through the development of partnerships between government and non-government services or subsidy of the private sector; and fourthly, the dominance of an understanding of individual action in line with the rational actor model of traditional economic theory, which implies that service users will be active and ingenious in finding ways to pursue their own interests rather than passive recipients who accept common services designed by others in the mass interest. Thus, for example, benefit systems may generate perverse incentives if claimers can find ways of getting incomes while avoiding the responsibility to seek employment or to maintain dependants. Similarly, comprehensive education policies designed to promote equal opportunities may be subverted by middle-class parents who move house to cluster in the catchment areas of desirable schools.

The first factor promotes a secular tendency to the expansion of private services, particularly marked where it is promoted by state subsidies. The second has resulted in the growth of competitive markets largely internal to state services in the health and personal social services and in schooling and further education. Market structures are being maintained in these areas and are expanding into higher education, despite a shift in official rhetoric on the change of government in 1997. The third has achieved a massive expansion in private pensions and owner-occupation and less marked privatisations elsewhere. The fourth has led to a strong emphasis on motive and behaviour in policy design in order to curb the assumed problem of perverse incentives and moral hazard 'scrounging' noted above, or limit the opportunities for middle-class people to use their superior social and financial resources to gain privileged access to universal services like health care or education (see chapters 2, 4 and 5).

The market approach assumes that behaviour typically does not conform to the ideals of the citizenship tradition of the welfare state. If choices are sometimes influenced by citizenship obligation, altruism, moral principle or commitment to an activity for its own sake as well as by rational deliberation and response to market incentives, policy that relies on such incentives may fail to achieve the anticipated outcome leading to inefficiency. A market-based policy may be damaging because it nourishes one among the various patterns of incentives that exist within particular institutions. In addition, it may undermine pre-existing and benign motivations (chapters 2, 3, 4 and 5). The intellectual dominance of market ideas – one of the few areas in which an approach whose rationale is based on professional expertise goes relatively unchallenged – may lead to policies which are damaging to human interests in tackling the uncertainties that citizens face.

The following chapters consider the way citizens and policy-makers have responded to the pressures on modern welfare states, examining the shortcomings of the dominant themes that direct policy and the evidence from large scale studies of the way in which people identify and seek to cope with economic uncertainties in their lives. I will now review the main points, to show how critique of the 'rational actor' theory of behaviour currently dominant in welfare policy-making and the evident complexity of responses to risk suggest that new approaches, based on a different understanding, may help to restore the elements of solidarity in welfare state citizenship. Such a development requires both a broader interdisciplinary approach to the understanding of welfare choice and greater attention to the way in which social values and institutions influence the way people deal with the risks they recognise in practical contexts.

Welfare choices: the structure of the book

Motives, policy and behaviour

The first section analyses some fundamental weaknesses of the new incentive-driven social policy. Le Grand (chapter 2) raises the possibility that motives are not always determined by preferences that are completely independent from the policy context. If context can influence motives and a particular policy can alter the way in which people respond to the incentives it contains, there is a real risk that proposals which are designed to harness fundamentally selfish motivations will shift unselfish motivations in that direction. For example, a payment system which treats hospital doctors or teachers as responsive only to cash rewards may lead those whose work is motivated partly by commitment to the NHS or education to feel that their altruism is devalued, so that their altruistic intention is undermined. While the findings of some studies supports this view, other work, notably that on the impact of payments on caring behaviour, indicates that cash incentives may reinforce rather than diminish altruistic motivations. Le Grand proposes a new theory of thresholds in motivation to reconcile the conflicting evidence.

In the next chapter, Bruno S. Frey pursues a more formal argument, distinguishing intrinsic motivation, driven by engagement with a particular course of action for its own sake, from extrinsic motivation, where the actor responds to some external reward. From a strictly economic perspective, the application of external incentives to fields where there is intrinsic motivation may prove inefficient: if people are doing something anyway, paying them for it will not necessarily make them work any harder. Such a policy may simply substitute the motivation of cash for the intrinsic motivation of enjoyment or commitment at the cost of wasted resources and possible erosion of one source of social solidarity. The chapter goes on to discuss possible factors which enhance intrinsic motivation such as employee participation or interest in the work and how these may be harnessed in social provision.

Hartley Dean (chapter 4) focuses on citizenship and social security. Recent UK policy has adopted an increasingly stringent system of withholding benefits and ensuring that any supplementation of basic payments is conditional on an approved response in order to direct the behaviour of claimers, particularly those whom it wishes to motivate towards work. The chapter argues that such an approach, which reduces citizenship duty to the status of a cash contract, may tend to undermine peoples' sense of broader social obligations and encourage the dependency it is designed to curb.

These three chapters all point to the risk that new directions in social policy may damage some of the mechanisms that have contributed to the past success of the welfare state. The UK welfare system manages to deliver a high standard of provision, despite the substantial financial constraints of recent years. An insensitive shift in the direction of market mechanisms may weaken altruism, stifle intrinsic motivations and exhaust citizenship with the result that public services decline in efficiency. Of particular importance is the fact that the first two of these chapters start out by applying new thinking to the assumptions of the traditional economic methodology that underlies the most significant new departure in welfare policy since the Beveridge settlement – the welfare cut-backs and the expansion of markets and private provision relying on individual economic incentives. These assumptions are shown to include a narrow approach to motivation which fails to explain much of the data from empirical studies. Chapter 4 uses qualitative sociological methods to arrive at a similar conclusion.

Responses to risk

The second section of the book is concerned to develop the argument by reviewing and discussing evidence on the ways in which individuals respond to the risks they perceive and the considerations – moral, habitual and rational – that underlie their behaviour. Much of the debate about the supposed transition to a 'risk society' and its implications rests on *a priori* argument. Empirical analysis is particularly important in this field. In chapter 5, Anne Barlow, Simon Duncan and Rosalind Edwards examine the assumptions about behaviour implicit in the family policies of the current government. The core ideology of New Labour values both participation in paid work and the importance of parenting to promote social cohesion and economic success. The outcome is a policy stance concerned to promote two-parent married families, on the grounds that they are better suited to combine paid employment and parenting, but refusing equivalent recognition to one-parent and other family forms. This approach is characterised in the way the *Supporting Families* Green Paper offers a detailed support framework for two parent families but has no more than workfare for lone parents.

These policies are pursued through rational actor approaches, which assume that parents will respond to the balance of advantage and penalty implicit in the incentives built into benefit and other policies. The research shows that many lone parents reject the basic assumptions of the 'New Deal for Lone Parents', because they value mothering as their central activity, and thus do not respond to policies which enhance work incentives and cut benefits. Similarly many cohabiting couples do not wish to marry because they do not see marriage as appropriate to their relationship, and thus are unlikely to respond to the incentive structure of 'Supporting Families'. This group is penalized by the failure of the government to consider a supportive and flexible legal framework for cohabitation alongside marriage as governments elsewhere in Europe are doing. This research shows clearly how the use of economic incentives based on a rational actor model is unsuccessful when individual choices in family life are driven more by moral assumptions and rationalities which conflict with those to which the policies are directed.

In the next chapter Janet Ford considers responses to the risk of unemployment and in particular the extent to which people seek to protect mortgage repayments through insurance. Using major longitudinal surveys and discursive interviews she shows that most people are not very successful in assessing the risks they face in an increasingly flexible labour market. Mortgage protection insurance is ineffective in reaching those in need of such cover – indeed those most at risk are least likely to be covered. There is widespread suspicion of the adequacy of cover provided by existing policies, partly founded on experience. She goes on to explore the complexity of the responses to perceived risk that individuals pursue, describing the range of different strategies that members of her sample adopt. This research again shows that simple models of economic rationality or of risk aversion are unable to do justice to the way people behave in the face of the contingencies they confront in everyday life.

Chapter 7, by Peter Lunt, uses evidence from focus group interviews to explore the implications of Bourdieu's theory of consumption and Giddens' theories of individual reflexivity for the marketing and regulation of financial services as the private commercial sector is increasingly substituted for state provision. Bourdieu's theoretical work emphasises the role of cultural capital in consumption, and particularly in discrimination, so that some social groups are better able than others to understand the risks of different financial products. Conversely, regulation faces different requirements in different social contexts.

Giddens' great insight is to link individual and institutional reflexivity in the modern world. Reflexive individuals are highly self-aware and responsive to the opportunities in their social environment and more inclined to live their lives as an active project oriented to goals of self-fulfilment rather than the common life-style of a mass society. This requires an individual tailoring of institutions (among them financial services) so that the demands on regulation are made more complex. The interviews show differences between different social class, age and gender groups in their access to the cultural capital necessary for financial competence. There is widespread scepticism of the claims of the financial services industry. It is also clear that very few couples discuss the financial commitments and pressures that changes in their circumstances resulting from the contingencies of modern life such as divorce, repartnering or death would imply. The research shows that the model of the active and discriminating consumer must take into account substantial differences in social reflexivity between different social groups.

Paul Ward and his colleagues (chapter 8) are also concerned to analyse consumer reflexivity in the context of the deregulation of proprietary medicines which accompanied the recent restrictions on NHS prescribing. The evidence shows the complexity of individual response to the risks associated with medication. In general people tend to accept the authority of accredited medical experts. If drugs are presented by professional pharmacists and endorsed by government as safe for over the counter sales, consumers confidently accept that judgement. However, when that authority is called into question on plausible grounds, they adopt more critical attitudes, challenging official expertise and actively seeking out information in order to make a decision as to whether to continue with the therapy. Both docile and critical approaches to authority co-exist, to be drawn on as appropriate. In this context, people handle professional authority in a more sophisticated way than either the traditional deference model or the 'risk society' approach, which implies that challenge is chronic and endemic, allow.

The next chapter, by Moira Munro, focuses on the way in which people handle the demands and pressures of the housing market, with its periodic instabilities, as the supports of mortgage interest tax relief, local authority social housing, mortgage protection through the social security system and the mutual building society movement are weakened. Market choices are influenced as much by particular situational and local factors as by the rational evaluation of national trends. In particular, it is life-events (partnering or repartnering, birth of a child, retirement, bereavement) that influence decisions, rather than the cumulative response to investment opportunities. Most people are aware that price fluctuations and the possibility that unemployment may make it impossible to meet mortgage repayments create real risks in the housing market. They are also aware of the financial advantages of owner-occupation. On balance they support the enhanced opportunities for private home ownership, but there is also clear endorsement of a stronger role for the state in providing social housing and support for mortgage repayments for those who lose their income to mitigate the risks.

In the final chapter, Gillian Parker examines the risks and uncertainties associated with the need for social care in old age. These issues have been the subject of intense debate in recent years as policy-makers anticipate a continuing increase in the numbers of frail older people while demographic and social trends reduce the availability of informal care. Parker's research shows that considerable uncertainty surrounds both the likelihood of needing care and the mechanisms to provide it. Few people feel they have sufficient financial resources to pay the full costs of the care they might need in old age themselves. A substantial majority believes the government should take responsibility for provision. They are strongly critical of the current policy of means-testing support and are particularly concerned about the requirement that people should use the equity value of the family home to finance care rather than pass it on to children.

The second part of the book continues the methodological arguments of the first section by demonstrating deficiencies in the assumptions underlying the traditional market economics that has been the dominant force in recent social policy thinking. It goes on to show that the way in which people perceive and respond to risks across a wide range of aspects of their lives cannot be understood without taking into account the fact that behaviour is embedded in a social context and that responses differ in different contexts. In addition, behaviour is often directed by moral considerations so that people do not necessarily respond to incentives as the balance of immediate cost and benefit might predict.

The theories of reflexivity and 'risk society' contributed by recent sociological thinking contain important insights into the relation between individual and institution. However, the practical operation of reflexivity is more complex than much discussion allows. Individuals may pursue a variety of strategies in responding to risks they perceive. The extent to which they offer a sceptical or a trusting face to authority is influenced by context and experience. Different social groups may have very different capacities to act as discriminating and proactive consumers. There is considerable uncertainty and ignorance about the incidence of some major risks. The risk society analysis must also recognise the importance of social embeddedness.

The assumption that individuals can be treated purely as market actors, solely responsive to a calculus of opportunity and penalty, may lead to unfortunate policies. The longer-term plans that individuals pursue may be disrupted or confused by sharp policy changes. This is compounded by the instability which results when abrupt redirections of policy by government are feared. Similarly, the assumption that individuals are always critical, active and deliberative in their response to state services and private alternatives is shown to require considerable modification.

Conclusion

The arguments and evidence presented in this book lead to three main conclusions: first, models which rely on incentives and the spur of egoism must be applied with caution in welfare policy, lest they drive out benign motives and damage the pattern of citizenship obligation that contributes both to efficiency and civility. Moral considerations are also important in behaviour and moral rationalities cannot be restructured simply by tinkering with cash incentives.

Secondly, currently influential academic approaches are inadequate to understand the way people perceive and respond to risk. The risk society approach with its emphasis on the rational consumer must take into account the limitations on consumer knowledge, the social factors that lead to differences in consumer behaviour and common enthusiasm for valued state services. The traditional rational actor model is not successful in explaining the evidence of an increasing number of studies of how people behave in real life contexts. Promising new lines of development focus on the notions that individual motivation is more complex than the incentive model allows, or alternatively that an individual approach to motivation is unable to do justice to the significance of social context and cultural factors in influencing choice.

These points reinforce the third conclusion: risk in everyday life must be understood as contextual. People are strongly influenced both by social values, established patterns of behaviour and moral rationalities, and by the structure of social institutions within which they lead their lives, as well as by apprehension of egoistic self-interest, in their response to the risks they perceive. In short, there is such a thing as society. Policies which do not recognise this will fail to do justice to their goals, their agents or their recipients.

Part I
Motives, Policy and Behaviour

2
From Knight to Knave? Public Policy and Market Incentives
Julian Le Grand

In the design of public policy, policy-makers have to consider how the people affected by those policies are motivated. In doing so, consciously or unconsciously, they tend to work with either of two crude assumptions about human motivation. One incorporates the belief that individuals are fundamentally motivated by their own self-interest – that is, in David Hume's term, they are 'knaves'.[1] Alternatively, they assume that individuals, especially those associated with the public sector, are motivated by a self-denying altruistic ethic that puts the interests of the people they are supposed to be serving above their own – that is, they are not knaves, but 'knights'.

I have argued elsewhere (Le Grand, 1997b) that recently we have seen a shift in policy-makers' beliefs about the motivation of those involved in the public sector in general and the welfare state in particular. There has been a gradual erosion of confidence in the reliability of the public service ethic as a motivational drive and a growing conviction that self-interest is the principal force motivating those involved in public services. Since the market is the quintessential mechanism for corralling self-interest to serve the public good, this in turn has led policy-makers to develop the use of market or quasi-market mechanisms in the delivery of public services: mechanisms that may rely on taxation or other revenues to finance the service concerned but that use market incentives to ensure that the service is provided in the most efficient and responsive manner possible.

The extent to which these changes in belief were well grounded, and, more generally, whether the market-oriented policy changes to which they gave rise have had the desired outcomes, have been extensively discussed elsewhere,[2] and I shall not dwell on that here. Instead, I want to concentrate on a slightly different issue – the fact that both sets of beliefs actually incorporate another assumption, one common to them both. This is that the balance of motivation – the extent to which individuals are motivated to behave as knights or knaves – is independent of the policy structures themselves. As has been pointed out by Philip Jones and colleagues, economists and other policy analysts, as well as policy-makers themselves, often take as given the proposition that individuals have a certain basic structure of motivation; and that the task of policy-makers is to accept that structure and to adapt their policies accordingly (see Jones, Cullis and Lewis (1998) and Jones and Cullis (forthcoming)). However, what if this assumption – the assumption that motivation is exogenous to policy change – is incorrect? What if policy changes do affect motivation itself? In particular, what if the shift towards the use of market incentives in public services, based on the assumption that people are primarily knaves, actually changes the balance of motivation in a more knavish direction? It is to these questions that this chapter is addressed.

I begin with a discussion of some of the research that suggests that the assumption that motivation is independent of policy change may be incorrect, especially with respect to the introduction of market incentives into areas where they did not exist before. Interestingly, this work does not all point in the same direction, with some parts suggesting that the introduction of the market 'devalues' knightly activity, leading to a reduction in that activity, while other parts suggest the opposite: that market payments 'revalue' or validate the activity concerned. I then try to reconcile some of these differences and briefly consider some of the implications of the proposed reconciliation for policy design.

Does the market devalue or revalue?

Perhaps the most prominent among the advocates of the view that the introduction of the market 'devalues' knightly activity – that is, it turns knights into knaves – was the distinguished social thinker Richard Titmuss. His key work in this area was the celebrated study of the supply of blood in Britain and the United States *The Gift Relationship* (Titmuss, 1971; Oakley and Ashton, 1997). Two economists had argued in a publication for the Institute of Economic Affairs that the solution to Britain's chronic problem of a shortage of blood for transfusion purposes was to follow the lead of certain parts of the United States and to begin paying blood donors (Cooper and Culyer, 1968). *The Gift Relationship* was Titmuss's response. There he argued that the introduction of cash payments into a system for supplying blood that previously relied upon voluntary donation, so far from leading to an increase in blood supply as the economists predicted, would lead to a diminution of altruistic motivation and in consequence to a reduction in both the quantity and quality of the blood supplied.

More specifically, Titmuss had four basic arguments. First, a market in blood products was what economists would call allocatively inefficient. It was highly wasteful; it created shortages and surpluses. More significantly, it led to the production of contaminated blood; that is, it damaged the quality of the product, with potentially disastrous consequences. This was because the suppliers of blood in a market, in contrast to a situation where blood is freely given, have an incentive to conceal any aspects of their previous health history that might have led to their blood being unsuitable for transfusion purposes (for example, contamination by hepatitis B or, currently, HIV); for otherwise they would not be able to get their payment.

Second, this market also suffered from inefficiency in production. It was bureaucratic in operation and administratively costly. In consequence it provided blood at a much greater expense than a voluntary system would. Third, the market was redistributive, but in the wrong direction. It distributed blood and blood products from poor to rich, from the disadvantaged and exploited to the privileged and powerful.

Finally, and of most relevance for our purposes, a market in blood was ultimately degrading for society as a whole. It drove out altruistic motivations for blood donation, replacing them with the cruder calculus of self-interest. Titmuss extended this argument to a broader critique of market incentives, arguing that 'the private market in blood, in profit-making hospitals, operating theatres, laboratories and in other sectors of social life limits the answers and narrows the choices for all men'. In direct opposition to the view that the government should introduce market incentives where possible he went on: 'It is the responsibility of the state ... to reduce or eliminate or control the forces of market coercions which place men in situations in which they have less freedom or little freedom to make moral choices and to behave altruistically if they so will' (1971/1977, pp. 310–11).

The Gift Relationship is now nearly thirty years old and, as I have noted elsewhere (Le Grand, 1997a), some of these arguments have not weathered the passage of time. For instance, the argument that markets in blood are always wasteful and necessarily create shortages and surpluses – and its corollary, that the voluntary system always does better – has not been borne out by experience either in Britain or in the United

States (Berridge, 1997). This part of the argument was always a little suspect in any case because of its lack of a theoretical base; Titmuss offers no theoretical explanation as to exactly why a voluntary system would closely match supply and demand, nor indeed why a market system would fail to do so. The excessive bureaucracy argument has also lost its power. Later analyses suggested that the British blood service was almost certainly heavily *under*managed at the time of Titmuss' investigations, with damaging consequences that became apparent a few years later (see Jones, Cullis and Lewis, 1998; and Jones and Cullis, forthcoming). Hence more resources devoted to management would probably have been desirable and would have contributed to greater efficiency rather than detracted from it.

However, the arguments concerning the impact of introducing market incentives on motivation seem to be more robust. Titmuss relied on international comparisons of the performance of existing systems of blood supply (especially between the market systems of the US and the voluntary system in the UK) to provide indirect support for his proposition that the introduction of cash payments into a voluntary system would reduce both the quantity and quality of blood supplied. More direct empirical support comes from a study that interviewed a sample of the (American) public to discover their attitudes towards blood donation (see Lepper and Green, 1978, p. 72). Part of the sample was then offered a cash inducement to participate in a blood donation programme and part was not. Of those who indicated they were interested in donating blood, those in the group offered cash compensation were less likely actually to supply it than those in the group that was not. For those who were not interested, the offer of cash compensation made little difference.

Titmuss did not draw on it, but his proposition is buttressed by the findings of a large psychological literature. (Lepper and Greene, 1978; Deci and Ryan, 1985; Lane, 1991, pp. 371–4). This illustrates the ways in which so-called 'extrinsic' motivation can drive out 'intrinsic' motivation: that is, motivations activated by external factors, such as monetary incentives, can crowd out motivations that are internal to the individual, such as more altruistic concerns. In consequence, if an individual is motivated for intrinsic reasons to undertake a certain activity, such as blood donation, then that motivation may be damaged by the introduction of external motivating factors and the individual may reduce his or her level of the activity concerned – such as supplying blood.

On reviewing this literature, it is tempting to read directly across from 'extrinsic' and 'intrinsic' motivations to 'knavish' and 'knightly' ones respectively. However this would not be quite correct. In that literature, 'extrinsic' motivational factors do seem to be largely confined to what we consider to be the knavish ones of cash payments. On the other hand, 'intrinsic' motivation seems to include essentially self-interested factors such as enjoyment of the task itself, satisfying one's curiosity etc, as well as the gratification received from performing knightly acts. Moreover, it is not always possible to easily distinguish between 'intrinsic' and 'extrinsic' (see Lane, 1991, pp. 367–9, for a discussion of some of the difficulties involved).

However, for our purposes we are only interested in the potential clash between extrinsic or egoistical motivation and those elements of intrinsic motivation that are altruistic. Here there are some interesting recent findings by Bruno Frey (Frey and Oberholzer-Gee, 1997; see also Frey, 1997). He has drawn on the social psychological work to test the proposition that extrinsic motivation can drive out altruistic elements of intrinsic motivation in the context of using monetary compensation to persuade residents of certain communities in Switzerland to accept a nuclear waste depository located in their community. A survey of more than 300 residents found that more than half (51 per cent) supported the siting of the facility in their community, despite a widespread knowledge of the risks involved. The question was then repeated with the additional comment that the government had decided to compensate all residents of the host community. Varying amounts of compensation were offered to different groups of respondents, some quite substantial (equivalent to 12 per cent of Swiss median income in the relevant year). Despite its magnitude, the offer of monetary compensation actually *reduced* the level of public support for the facility by more than half (to 25 per cent).

It would seem that there is some empirical basis for the view that the introduction of market incentives does affect the balance of motivation and, moreover, that it does so in a way that turns the knight into the knave. However, other research suggests that things may not be quite that straightforward. In particular, there is a strand of literature in the area of informal care and voluntary work that points in a rather different direction. That literature discusses among other things, the merits or otherwise of paying carers or paying 'volunteers' to care for people in need of such care (see, for instance, Evers, Pijl and Ungerson, 1994). Now some of this makes the Titmuss/Frey argument, claiming that such payments erode the spirit of altruism (for instance, Evers, 1994, p. 30). But there is also some evidence to suggest that, in these situations, market incentives can 'revalue' or validate knightly behaviour.[3]

For instance, Diana Leat (1990) interviewed 87 people (mostly women) engaged in caring activities of various kinds. These included child minders, foster parents, adult family placement carers (carers who took mostly elderly people in need of care into their – the carers' – own home), and agency carers (carers who provided day care for elderly people in their – the elderly person's – own home). She found that the carers did not provide care for strangers solely for the money, but also that few would have done it without payment; they regarded it as something that should not be expected without payment. However, the fact of being paid was more important to them than the level of pay for the job. Moreover, carers did not necessarily expect the market rate for the job; and sometimes they preferred their payments to be labelled 'expenses'. Further, as caring continued, carers did what they felt a client needed, not what they originally said they would or would not do – and they did not demand extra payment for it.

So payment here seems to encourage the supply of the service concerned, not discourage it. Further support for this comes from an earlier piece of work in which Diana Leat was also involved. Leat and Gay (1987) investigated attitudes in ten local authorities towards paying volunteers for care, where the paid individual was an 'ordinary person': something between a completely unpaid volunteer and a salaried social worker or waged home help. In all cases the payment was low and could not be thought of as in any sense a wage for the job; indeed, sometimes it was described as expenses. Some of the officials interviewed were aware of the possible discouragement effect on unpaid family care of introducing paid volunteers. So, for instance, one said that 'families may feel a bit resentful – we pay other people to care and not them. Payment may devalue altruism and duty' (p. 51). However, there was no mention of any negative impact on the care supplied by the volunteers themselves. Indeed the majority of those interviewed were very enthusiastic about the scheme, clearly feeling that, even if there were problems with respect to unpaid family care, they were more than offset by the increase in care supplied by the 'volunteers'. In such cases, Leat and Gay argue, carers know what they are doing is worthwhile – and that they would not do it for the money alone. 'Money may not buy love and care, but it may not kill it either' (Qureshi and Abrams, cited in Leat and Gay, p. 66).

One set of research results suggests that market incentives devalue altruistic activities, another set that they revalue them. Is there any way in which these conflicting results can be reconciled? One possible explanation lies in the gendered nature of the caring activities researched.

The vast majority of the individuals concerned in the carers' research were women; as Janet Finch observes: 'Altruistic qualities, especially in family relationships, are more frequently associated with women than with men, and therefore altruism is a concept which legitimizes the many self-sacrifices women make for other members of their family' (1989, p. 223). More specifically, women's caring activities could be viewed as examples of 'compulsory altruism' (Land and Rose, 1985).[4] In some cases of family caring, especially where violent men are concerned, women may be physically coerced into caring activities; in other cases they may be pressured by family, friends or an overriding internal sense of responsibility, and a feeling that no-one else will do it for them. In other words, the individuals concerned do not feel they really have a choice between altruistic and self-interested behaviour that they can exercise. In that case their behaviour will not change whatever happens; however, if a payment for their caring activities were offered, then it would still be viewed favourably, either because it offered some kind of symbolic recognition of the work they are doing, or because it provided some (doubtless inadequate) compensation for that work. The payment is not viewed as a kind of bribe, and therefore morally devaluing, as it might have been if it could have changed their behaviour.

However, this does not quite capture the situations investigated in the research concerned. In most of those cases – child-minding, caring for unrelated elderly people – the women voluntarily chose the caring activity. Hence they do not seem to be examples of compulsory altruism in the sense that they faced a total absence of choice. So at least in these cases we have to look elsewhere for a reconciliation.

A second possible explanation concerns the differences in the magnitudes of the situations being investigated. Blood donation has some costs associated with it; it takes an hour or two, there is a certain amount of physical discomfort associated with the actual process and some people experience a temporary feeling of lassitude after it. However, these costs pale into insignificance when compared to the costs associated with foster-parenting or looking after elderly people on a long-term basis. Hence it would not be surprising if, although people are willing to undergo the minor degree of self-sacrifice required in giving blood without compensation, they are not prepared to do so for the much larger sacrifices required by caring. In short there might be a 'threshold effect', whereby people are prepared to make sacrifices for the sake of others up to a certain level of sacrifice, but beyond that point they require some compensation.

There is surely something to this argument. It was always a weakness of Titmuss's claims concerning the essential benevolence of human nature that they were based on an example of relatively limited self-sacrifice; and one should be careful before generalising from this to cases involving much greater sacrifices. However, again the argument does not wholly resolve the paradox. There remains the Frey case where, for the sake of the community, people did seem prepared to accept rather larger sacrifices (such as an increase in environmental hazards and the devaluation of property) than in the case of blood donation; although the costs in this situation are perhaps still not as great as those involved in caring situations, they are not offset by any benefits in terms of feelings of tenderness or gratitude that might accompany caring. Moreover, the level of support actually dropped when compensation was offered which is precisely the opposite of the effect that the threshold argument would predict. Also, there are features of the caring situation that remain unexplained by the cost argument; for instance, the fact that some people did not expect to receive a market wage for their activities and indeed preferred payments to be labelled as compensation or expenses rather than as wages.

I think it is here that the explanation lies for the resolution of the apparent paradox. In cases of knightly activity that involve large sacrifices, people do value some form of payment both as a form of recognition and as partial compensation for the costs involved. However, that payment should not be so great so as to compensate fully for the sacrifice, for, if it did, there would be no satisfaction from making the sacrifice in the first place. In fact if they were paid an amount that fully compensated them – or more than fully compensated them – the effect might be perverse, reducing rather than increasing the supply of the activity concerned.

We can illustrate the argument with a formal example. Suppose an individual engages in an altruistic action from which he or she derives some benefit (B), and which also involves some cost (C). Presumably the benefits are greater than the costs ($B-C$ is greater than zero); otherwise the individual would not engage in the activity. Now suppose further that the benefit to the individual of this activity derives from the fact that there *is* a cost. He or she feels good about doing good, because there is some sacrifice involved.[5] This seems a reasonable psychological assumption to make; an activity that does good for others but that involves no sacrifice on the part of the doer is probably going to be quite unsatisfying, even to the most committed altruist.

Now suppose some compensation payment (D) is offered for the costs involved. This payment has the effect of reducing the net cost to the individual of the activity; this cost then becomes the difference between the gross costs of the activity and the compensation offered (C − D). If the individual feels that the compensation is only partial and that some costs remain (C − D is greater than zero), then the benefit he or she derives from the activity will remain at its previous level and he or she will not change his or her behaviour. Indeed, since the net benefit (B − C + D) will have risen, he or she may actually do more of it. If on the other hand, the compensation is sufficient to compensate him or her for the cost (C − D equals zero), then the benefit to the individual of the altruistic activity will also fall to zero. Hence his or her altruistic motivation will be completely eroded and he or she will cease from the activity.

This example contains some simplistic psychological assumptions and is obviously quite stylised as a description of human behaviour. However, it can offer some insights into the apparent contradictions in the research results that we have been discussing above. The carers who welcome compensation and do not change their activity when offered it (or even do more) may be in the situation where the net costs of the activity have not fallen to zero; hence some sacrifice is still involved and in consequence they continue to 'value' the activity. Indeed the compensation, through indicating a measure of social approval for the activity, may have actually increased the benefit they derive from it. The paid blood donors and those offered compensation for the nuclear waste disposal facility, on the other hand, may be in the situation where the compensation is adequate or more than adequate to compensate them for their perceived sacrifice: hence there is no net sacrifice, no altruistic satisfaction from the activity concerned and supply is reduced.

Conclusion

If the analysis of the previous section is broadly correct, what are its implications of this for the use of market payments in the delivery of public services? It is that these need to be employed with care. If they are small then, they could well have no crowding out effect on altruistic motivation; indeed they might even complement it. If, on the other hand, they are too great, they may well erode people's sense of sacrifice and thereby reduce their intrinsic motivation to perform the activities concerned. Of course, as market payments increase, they will increase extrinsic motivation: that is to say, they will appeal to individuals' self-interest, and hence induce further supply of that activity that way. However, as the contaminated blood supply example illustrates, there may be costs in relying on knavish incentives in welfare areas. Moreover, the destruction of altruistic motivations may be viewed as undesirable in and of itself; a world populated by knights, or at least by people with knightly impulses, is likely to be a more attractive and more agreeable place in which to live than one inhabited solely by knaves.

More generally, whatever the detail of the results, it is clear that policy structures can influence the balance of knightly and knavish motivations in the individuals concerned. This is a truth that policy-makers must learn to recognise; for, if they do not, their policies are likely to fail, with unfortunate consequences both for those who implement the policies and for those who are intended to benefit from them.

Notes

1 'In contriving any system of government, and fixing the several checks and controls of the constitution, every man ought to be supposed a knave and to have no other end, in all his actions, than private interest. By this interest, we must govern him and, by means of it, notwithstanding his insatiable avarice and ambition, co-operate to the public good'. Hume (1875, pp. 117–18).

2 See, among many others, Le Grand and Bartlett (1993); Bartlett, Le Grand and Roberts (1998); Le Grand, Mays and Mulligan (1998); and Taylor-Gooby (1999).

3 I am indebted to Clare Ungerson for this point and for drawing my attention to the relevant literature.

4 See also Leat and Gay's comment that women do not 'choose' to care (1987, p. 59).

5 In fact B may vary directly with C; that is, the greater the sacrifice the greater the perceived benefit. That assumption is not necessary for what follows, however; all that is required is for B to be positive when C is positive.

3
Motivation and Human Behaviour
Bruno S. Frey

Economic incentives and other motivations

Economics has a straightforward and well worked out theory of human behaviour. Individuals are taken to be influenced by both preferences (normally represented by an egoistic utility function) and constraints (most importantly the budget and time). As economists find preferences to be rather elusive and hard to measure independent of the behaviour in question, they assume preferences to be constant, and thus take changes in constraints systematically to determine behaviour[1] (Becker, 1976; Frey, 1992).

This model of human behaviour can be used immediately for policy purposes. Individuals act differently when the constraints are manipulated. An individual is confronted with changed relative prices for the opportunities available and quickly adjusts to them. If, for instance, the compensation for an activity is raised *ceteris paribus*, the person in question is given an incentive to switch his or her use of time in its favour. Similarly, when an activity becomes more time-consuming (for example a mode of traffic), there is an incentive to switch to a less time-consuming activity. This straightforward incentive theory has been used to derive optimal incentive schemes. In particular, principal-agent theory relies on wages to be aligned as closely as possible to the desired output (taking into account transaction costs). On this basis, pay-for-performance is the ideal compensation system.

This 'economic approach to human behaviour' has had considerable success and has been introduced into other disciplines, most notably into political science (where it is called 'Public Choice'), sociology (where it is called the 'Rational Choice Approach'), or law (where it is called 'Law and Economics'). Thus economic analysis has far transgressed the boundaries of the economy and has been used with considerable success to study aspects of the family, crime, sports, religion and art. Some scholars therefore consider economics to be the 'Queen of the Social Sciences' while others speak of 'economic imperialism' (Stigler, 1984; Hirshleifer, 1985).

Traditional social sciences, in particular sociology, political science, but also law and psychology, acknowledge the incentive effects of material (economic) incentives. They hasten, however, to add non-material incentives such as power, fame, recognition or love. Economists do not, in principle, object to add these motivating forces (they can subsume them under a particular type of 'price') but deep down in their hearts they are convinced of the power of material incentives.[2]

But the traditional social sciences go further. They posit quite a different kind of force shaping behaviour, *intrinsic motivation*. It designates those activities which are undertaken 'for their own sake' (Deci, 1971). The reward thus lies in the activity itself and does not come from outside as is the case with extrinsic motivation. But again, economists are not shaken; they subsume it as an additional, and independent, part of total incentives influencing human behaviour. Consider the supply of an activity by an individual as shown in Figure 3.1.

Intrinsic motivation simply means that this individual is prepared to offer the amount q^{IM} of the activity without payment. Supply can be further increased by raising price (say from 0 to p_1) which leads to a

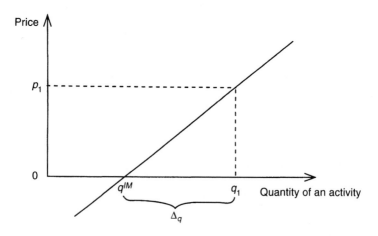

Figure 3.1 Conventional supply theory

total supply q_1. This reasoning is totally accepted in economics, so far so that economists are unable to even see an alternative. This has, for instance, been evidenced in the discussion about the supply of blood where two famous economists (Arrow, 1972, and Solow, 1971, who both received the Nobel Prize) were incapable or at least unwilling to question this approach. They could not even imagine why to pay people for giving blood should not increase the total quantity of blood supplied.

Yet the crucial aspect of differentiating intrinsic and extrinsic motivation consists in their *dynamic interaction*. The *Crowding-Out Effect* leads to a decrease in intrinsic motivation when an extrinsic reward is applied. Figure 3.2 shows that the Crowding-Out Effect leads to a shift of the supply curve to the left, from S to S′ and S″.

A rise in price reduces supply from q^{IM} to points C and D. Only when intrinsic motivation has been completely crowded out (indicated by point D), a rise in price leads again to a rise in supply along the (now stable) supply curve S″.

It is important to see that there are two effects at work simultaneously: the Relative Price Effect gives an incentive to supply more of the activity along the supply curves, and the Crowding-Out Effect which undermines the existing intrinsic motivation and reduces the supply. The net outcome depends on the relative size of the two effects. The conventional economic theory of behaviour is correct if the Crowding-Out

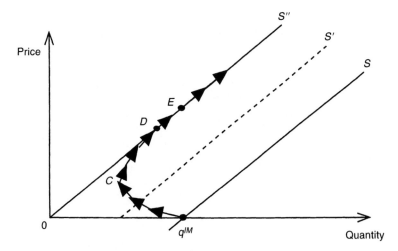

Figure 3.2   Supply including crowding-out effect

Effect is comparatively small or non-existent, but it is mistaken if the Crowding-Out Effect dominates the Relative Price Effect.

This dynamic interaction between intrinsic and extrinsic motivation can be generalized in two dimensions:

1 The external intervention affecting intrinsic motivation may not only consist in monetary or other material rewards but also in *regulatory interventions* such as commands. What matters is whether the individuals perceive the outside intervention to be *controlling*, i.e. reducing their sphere of self-determination and self-esteem.
2 An external intervention *crowds-out* intrinsic motivation when it is felt to be controlling but *crowds-in* intrinsic motivation when it is perceived to be *supporting* self-determination and self-esteem.

The conditions under which an intervention is perceived to be controlling or supporting have been carefully studied in controlled experiments by psychologists. The Crowding-Out Effect has been found to be the stronger (Deci and Ryan, 1987, pp. 1026-7):

• the more the rewards are expected. Unexpected rewards have a weaker or no negative effect on intrinsic motivation;
• the more salient the reward is;
• the more contingent the reward is on the task or on performance;
• the more deadlines and threats are used;
• the more intensive the surveillance is.

These psychological conditions have been placed in the context of identifiable (institutional) conditions (Frey, 1997a). It is thus possible to state under which empirical circumstances an external intervention crowds-out or crowds-in intrinsic motivation. Obviously, the Crowding-Out Effect is only relevant if the persons concerned have some amount of intrinsic motivation (see, for example, Brockner, Tyler and Cooper-Schneider, 1992). For economics, the undermining version of the Effect is of great importance because it puts into doubt the conventional, and so far undisputed, Relative Price Effect. Indeed, it is the only effect which systematically works in the *opposite* direction to the Relative Price Effect on which modern economics, and its policy advice, is based[3].

This paper deals with the consequences for economic policy of intrinsic motivation and the Crowding Effects. Section II discusses the extensive experimental evidence available from social psychological research. The following section considers the Crowding Effects at the constitutional level of policy making where the fundamental rules governing the economy and society are determined. Section IV looks at

Crowding Effects in the current politico-economic process (within the rules of the game). The last section offers concluding remarks.

Crowding-out and crowding-in intrinsic motivation

The crowding-out effect

This relationship posits a systematic and a theoretically and empirically well-established negative relationship between intrinsic and extrinsic motivation. Under identifiable conditions, employees' work ethic (as a specific form of intrinsic motivation in the firm) is undermined when they are subjected to an external intervention, be it rewards or commands. In particular, employees' work ethic may be reduced when they receive monetary incentives that are contingent on their performance.

Rewards thus crowd out intrinsic motivation under particular conditions. This effect is known in psychology as 'hidden costs of reward' (Lepper and Greene, 1978) or 'the corruption effect of extrinsic motivation' (Deci, 1975).

The fact that rewards could, under non-trivial conditions, undermine intrinsic motivation fits well with modern cognitively-oriented theories in psychology. Examples are goal orientations (Ames, 1984), reactance (Brehm, 1966), activity engagement (Higgins and Trope, 1990), personal causation (deCharms, 1968) or action identification (Vallacher and Wegner, 1987). Crowding-Out Theory has been the subject of such a large number of laboratory experiments that it is impossible to summarize their results here. Fortunately, there have already been not less than five formal meta-analytical studies of crowding theory.

Rummel and Feinberg (1988) used 45 experimental studies covering the period 1971–85; Wiersma (1992) 20 studies covering 1971–90; and Tang and Hall (1995) 50 studies from 1972–92. These meta-analyses essentially support the cognitive evaluation theory developed by Deci and his co-workers according to which intrinsic motivation is undermined if the externally applied rewards are perceived to be controlling by the recipients. This by now 'conventional' view was challenged by Cameron and Pierce (1994) and Eisenberger and Cameron (1996) who on the basis of their own meta-analysis covering studies published in the period 1971–1991 (the two studies are based on a virtually identical set of studies) concluded that the undermining effect is largely 'a myth' and that cognitive evaluation theory should therefore be abandoned. These studies attracted a great deal of attention, and many scholars on that basis seem to have concluded that no such thing as a Crowding-Out

Effect exists. Deci, Koestner and Ryan (1998) in a very extensive study were able to show that these conclusions are unwarranted and that the Crowding-Out Effect is a robust phenomenon of significant size under the conditions identified. This most recent meta-analysis includes all the studies considered by Cameron, Pierce and Eisenberger as well as several studies which have appeared since then. The 68 experiments reported in 59 articles span the period 1971–97, and refer to 97 experimental effects. It turns out that tangible rewards undermine intrinsic motivation for interesting tasks (i.e. tasks for which the experimental subjects show an intrinsic interest) in a highly significant and very reliable way, and that the effect is moderately large. Tangible rewards, in particular monetary compensations, are obviously perceived to be controlling by the experimental subjects and therefore tend to crowd out intrinsic motivation[4]. It is important to see that the experimental studies look at the net effect of a reward while we argue that the conventional Relative Price Effect should be separated from the Crowding-Out Effect, and that it is important to consider their relative size under various conditions.

The Crowding-Out Theory has also received strong support in field studies. A case study refers, for example, to the so-called 'token economies' where people living in old-age asylums were induced to undertake certain tasks (such as making their bed) in exchange for vouchers. As a consequence, after some time, these people were only willing to do anything at all if they received a compensation. The intended activation of the aged proved to be a failure (Kazdin, 1982). Crowding-out has also been the subject of econometric studies. For example, in an econometric study of 116 managers in medium-sized Dutch firms, Barkema (1995) found that the number of hours worked in the company decreased with the intensity of personal control effected by the superiors.

The Crowding-Out Effect may be attributed to two major psychological processes.

1. Self-determination is reduced

When people perceive an external intervention as a restriction to act autonomously, intrinsic motivation is substituted by these external interventions. The locus of control shifts from inside to outside the person (Rotter, 1966). The person in question no longer feels responsible but makes the outside intervention responsible instead. However, this shift in the locus of control only takes place when the intervention is considered to be controlling. In contrast, when the intervention is perceived to be informing about one's competence, internal control is strengthened. Intrinsic or extrinsic motivation is raised depending on which aspect is more prominent.

Self-determination is reduced mainly by the following two conditions:

• Pay-for-performance and bonus rewards that are contingent on individual output crowd out intrinsic motivation when the perceived controlling effect of rewards is stronger than the perceived informing effect. In such a situation, employees feel that their self-determination is curtailed. The crowding-out effect thus provides a possible explanation for the overwhelming empirical evidence that there is no significant connection between pay and performance (Lawler, 1990, p. 58). This also applies to managerial compensation (for example Güth, 1995; Jensen and Murphy, 1990).

• Commands restrict the perceived self-determination of the affected persons more strongly than the price system in the form of pay-for-performance or bonuses. Commands tend to disregard the motives of the recipients. In contrast, the price system provides more flexibility to the persons concerned as one has the option to reject a monetary incentive.

2. Reciprocity is violated

The implicit contract based on mutual acknowledgement of one's engagement is violated when a task undertaken by intrinsic motivation is rewarded extrinsically (Gouldner, 1960; Rousseau, 1995). Conversely, maintaining norms of reciprocity causes a higher willingness to perform and reduces shirking of work.

The crowding-in effect

This effect is also well supported by experimental (see again Deci, Koestner and Ryan, 1998) as well as field evidence. For example, an econometric analysis documents the positive effect of political participation possibilities on intrinsic motivation in the form of civic virtue (Frey, 1997b): Keeping all other influences constant, the citizens in those cantons of Switzerland with more developed institutions of direct democracy have a higher level of civic virtue resulting in a lower level of tax-cheating.

Intrinsic motivation is bolstered by the following factors:

1. Personal relationships foster intrinsic motivation

Mutual acknowledgement of one's obligations and responsibilities is appreciated among friends, colleagues and family members. Thus, team-based structures provide motivational benefits (Grant, 1996, p. 118).

2. Principals and agents communicate with each other

Communication is a precondition for reciprocity via learning about, and acknowledging the duties and responsibilities of other people. Experiments show that communication systematically raises the intrinsic motivation to cooperate (for example, Dawes, van de Kragt and Orbell, 1988; Frey and Bohnet, 1995).

3. Employees participate in decision-making

The greater the possibility to co-determine, the more the employees would adopt them as their own. Participation thus raises self-determination and is a precondition for reciprocity.

4. The work content is interesting on its own

Self-determination is supported when employees are aware of the results of their input, when they are responsible for the outcome, and when they consider their work to be meaningful (Hackman and Oldham, 1980).

Consequences for policy at the constitutional level

Market versus command

The market

The basic principle of the price system is that output and compensation correspond to each other. In a perfectly competitive economy, the wage rate is exactly equal to the marginal product. Thus, an extreme form of 'pay-for-performance' is realised.

Such compensation may, however, provoke a substitution of intrinsic by extrinsic motivation: If individuals who (at least partly) enjoy doing their work because they are interested in it are paid in exact correspondence to how they perform, their intrinsic motivation becomes superfluous. Maintaining their intrinsic motivation in this circumstance would mean that they are over-motivated for the particular task. It can therefore be expected that their intrinsic motivation is reduced. Their overall performance is thereby not necessarily reduced. Whether the employees affected work more or less depends on the relative size of the Relative Price and of the Crowding-Out Effect.

The extent to which work is performed by intrinsic or extrinsic motivation, however, affects the value of the work to the recipient as well as how it is performed. It often makes a difference, for example, if one receives a service from people who do a particular work for intrinsic reasons such as out of love rather than because they are paid. Most people would agree that this holds for sexual services but it is also true for a much wider range of services and even for some goods. The mixture of motivations also affects innovative activity. While monetary incentives are crucial for what might be called 'institutional' creativity, intrinsic motivation is of great importance when it comes to 'personal' creativity.[5] This is particularly true for the transfer of tacit (i.e. non-codable) knowledge within organizations (Osterloh and Frey, 1998). Principal-agent theory has extensively worked out that monetary payments are not efficient when either the necessary measurement and monitoring is costly, or when such activity differs between the various components of output. In the latter case, employees shift their work effort away from those tasks which cannot be adequately measured and compensated. This is another case in which intrinsic work motivation may be superior to monetary incentives.

Command

When individuals are forced to work by threat of punishment, intrinsic motivation is also crowded out. If they like to do the job for its own sake, a command leads to over-motivation. Indeed, commands undermine work morale more strongly than pay because the addressees are left with fewer choices. The total effect on work effort again depends on the comparative size of the Relative Price Effect (based on the cost of not obeying the command) and the Crowding-Out Effect. But as the latter effect tends to be systematically larger than with the price system, it can be expected that the application of commands in an economy often produces low work morale and initiative. More generally, citizens' civic virtue will be low and a cynical attitude towards the state and society will be widespread. These predictions are well borne out by the practical experiences of Soviet-type command economies. Thus, Lane (1986, p. 105) reports that the 'centralised Soviet economic system makes people lazy and immoral... Labour is... prone to a combination of cynicism, apathy and largency'. There was a pervasive 'middle class pessimism and cynicism' (Bushnell, 1979, p. 9). Another scholar states 'The observation that workers' efforts and morale tend to be poor in the USSR today is familiar enough. So is the perception that the economic system itself fosters shoddy work, idleness and dishonesty' (Hanson, 1984, p. 85).

According to this analysis, the virtual breakdown of the Soviet political and economic system is not only due to the lack of institutions (an aspect now fully appreciated by economists, see for example Shleifer, 1997), nor to the lack of monetary incentives (which was treated extensively by economists; see for example Murrell, 1991; Sachs and Woo, 1994; Blanchard, 1996), but also to the destruction of intrinsic motivation in the form of low work morale, civic virtue, social capital and trust.[6]

Table 3.1 lists social capital measured as trust ('Generally speaking, would you say that most people can be trusted, or that you cannot be too careful in dealing with people?') or as intensity of participation in a variety of civic activities such as social services for the elderly and deprived; education, art and cultural activities, local community affairs; activities related to conservation, environment and ecology; and work with youth. The data reported for various groups of countries were collected by the *World Values Survey* of 1000 people in each of the 40 countries from 1991–3 (World Values Study Group, 1991).

Group 1

Group 1 comprises Sweden, Norway, Finland, Denmark, Netherlands, Canada, United States, Ireland, United Kingdom, Iceland, Switzerland, Japan, Germany, Italy, Spain, Belgium, Austria, France and Portugal.

Group 2(a)

Group 2(a) is formed by Poland, Czeck Republic and Belorussia. 2(b) includes Russia, Lithuania, Bulgaria, Estonia, Hungary, Latvia, and Slovak Republic. In 2(c) China is included as well.

Group 3(a)

Group 3(a) consists of Mexico, Argentina, Chile and Brazil. Group 3(b) includes India, South Korea and Turkey. 3(c) includes South Africa and Nigeria.

Table 3.1 compares social capital for three groups of countries. Both indicators for social capital are much lower in Post-Soviet Transition Economies than in Developed Economies: the index for trust is 29.3 in the Post-Soviet countries compared to 44.5 in the developed ones; the index for the intensity of civic participation is 3.4 compared to 11.4. While trust in the Post-Soviet countries is slightly higher than in Developing Countries (29.3 compared to 24.2), the rate of participation – arguably a more suitable indicator of civic virtue – is much lower (3.4 compared to 5.9, i.e. only somewhat more than half as large).

Table 3.1 Social capital according to the World Values Survey (%: averages 1990–3)

Country groups	Trust	Participation
Group 1: Developed economies	44.5	11.4
Group 2: Post-Soviet transition economies	29.3	3.4
a) where participation not stated	29.3	n.a.
b) including countries with information about participation	26.5	3.4
c) including also China	29.3	3.4
Group 3: Developing countries	24.2	5.9
a) South America	21.5	4.9
b) Asia (including Turkey)	26.5	10.6[7]
c) Africa	26.1	n.a.
Mean	**35.3**	**6.9**

Source: *World Values Survey* (1991), own calculations.

This evidence is consistent with the proposition that the Soviet command system resulted in a crowding out of intrinsic motivation which still exists under present conditions as reflected in high crime and Mafia activities. Frye and Shleifer (1997) found in a survey undertaken in March and April 1996 that 39 per cent of 55 shop managers in Moscow were 'contacted by rackets in the last six months'. As a result, the transactions cost of doing business is high. Seventy-six per cent of the shop managers said that 'one needs a roof (i.e. a paid private security agency) to operate'. The situation may be better in some of the other post-Soviet economies (Shleifer, 1997, pp. 392–3) which may reflect the less stringent command systems (for example in Hungary).

We can observe a basic asymmetry. The price system can be, and has been, introduced by a 'sudden jump' (Sachs, 1993; Goldman, 1994) which individuals quickly adjust to. In contrast, the civic virtue crowded out by the preceding command system is difficult to build up again. As a consequence, the price system does not work better due to the high transaction costs entailed.

National planning and commands which were undertaken in Soviet economies were far from fulfilling a supportive function and thus did not crowd-in intrinsic motivation. Efforts to establish all sorts of non-monetary rewards such as orders ('hero of the Soviet Union', etc.) and rankings ('Most productive worker of the province', etc.) were unable to compensate for the undermining effects on work morale of rigid planning.

Our analysis suggests that a command economy is at a clear disadvantage relative to the market as the guiding decision-making system.

Command economies are not only less efficient but also more damaging to work morale and civic virtue than the price system. The same type of analysis undertaken here for the market and for commands could be done for other social decision making systems such as decisions by bargaining, tradition, or random mechanisms (lotteries). In all these cases, one would have to consider intrinsic motivation as an endogenous and dynamic factor in addition to the traditional efficiency aspects.

Discipline versus trust

Discipline

Constitutional rules serve to prevent 'knaves' from exploiting the other members of society. They should be strict enough to deter rational and egoistic individuals from acting as free riders or to take advantage of co-citizens. Individuals are generally assumed to act in an opportunistic way 'seeking their self-interest with guile' (as Williamson, 1985; 1993 puts it). This assumption is not claimed to be realistic but serves to construct institutions which are able to restrain the activities of the worst members of society.

This concept has been the foundation of constitutional economics beginning with Hume (1742) and John Stuart Mill (1861), to the modern formulations in Buchanan (1987), Brennan and Buchanan (1985), or Mueller (1995). It has become part of the theory of economic policy and need not be spelled out further here.

Trust

A different approach to constitutional economics puts faith in the citizens. They are not only assumed to be capable of making reasonable decisions. More importantly, citizens are assumed to have in principle good will. While they dislike being exploited by others, they are considered to have a good measure of civic virtue.

This view of human nature has been championed by scholars such as Cooter (1984), Kelman (1987), Dryzek (1992) or Mansbridge (1994). It has been concluded that in order to support the existing civic virtue, and to help to raise it further, the constitution should be benevolent towards the citizens. The constitution should put trust in the citizens (this is a different type of trust from that discussed above which was the trust citizens had towards government and society). This trust is reflected by giving individuals many direct participation rights. Citizens should not only be given the right to elect their representatives but also to participate directly by voting on issues (Frey, 1997b).

There exists considerable empirical evidence that this view of human nature is realistic and not overly optimistic. Individuals do not always seize any opportunity to take advantage of others as a large number of experiments indicate (see Bohnet, 1997, and Bohnet and Frey, 1997 for surveys, Frey and Bohnet, 1995 for specific experiments). Econometric studies for Swiss cantons and cities reveal that the more developed the institutions and the higher the participation possibilities for the citizens are, the lower is tax evasion and the greater is fiscal responsibility (i.e. the less likely is the budget to be in deficit), and the higher is *per capita* income, all *ceteris paribus* (see the survey by Feld and Kirchgässner, 1997, and the specific study by Feld and Savioz, 1997). The assumption that a significant amount of civic virtue exists among citizens, and that it is crowded-in by a constitution that puts faith in its citizens is thus warranted.

This does not mean that constitutions should only consider participation rights. As experimental evidence (Public Good and Prisoner's Dilemma experiments are especially relevant here, see for example Hey, 1991, chapter 11; Kagel and Roth, 1995, chapter III(A); Fehr and Gächter, 1998; see also experiments in the Ultimatum Game setting, for example Güth *et al.*, 1982) as well as everyday observations clearly indicate it is important to prevent individuals from being perceived to be systematically exploited by others. If they have this feeling, they would quickly start behaving in an egoistic way in an attempt to guard their position. A good constitution balances these two considerations.

Consequences for policy in the current process

Moral suasion and direct intervention

Moral suasion

On the basis of Crowding Theory, the role of moral suasion as an economic policy device must be reconsidered. The major function of psychological appeals is to support the intrinsic motivation of those persons who act according to the principles of civic virtue. This point has eluded economists who only deal with extrinsic incentives. It was appreciated long ago by legal scholars who argued that laws may be valuable even if they cannot be monitored and obeyed because they still indicate what is 'right'. Once a wider perspective on human motivation is adopted, moral suasion has a role to play in economic policy. Obviously, this instrument must be used with care and is no substitute for other policy actions. In particular, moral appeals lose their motivating force if they are used too often or under circumstances where following them would mean risking one's position. But moral suasion has been empirically shown to affect people's behaviour in a significant way in times of crisis (see for example Baumol and Oates, 1979).

Direct intervention

One of the insights gained by Crowding Theory is that government interventions are less effective than expected following the Relative Price Effects when intrinsic motivation is thereby induced to fall. This effect is particularly relevant in two policy areas.

Environmental policy

Direct interventions are still the most prominent instrument used to influence the quality of the natural environment (Hahn, 1989; OECD, 1994). Empirical evidence confirms that individuals display a measure of environmental responsibility especially if the corresponding costs are not high (for example Diekmann, 1995). The use of commands then risks crowding-out that intrinsic motivation if the persons concerned perceive that their own efforts to safeguard the environment are not appreciated by the policy makers. In that case, the same effect must be expected if market instruments such as environmental taxes, incentives and tradable licenses are used. But for the reasons given above the Crowding-Out Effect is likely to be less pronounced.

The Crowding-Out Effect may help to explain why environmental policy is often less effective than economists expect on the basis of the relative price effect and at the same time that the environment sometimes improves without much government intervention.

Regulatory policy

Government interventions via regulations can be seen as a generalization of most environmental policies. It can be applied to a very large range of areas, for instance, with respect to work conditions.

The economic approach evaluates the extent to which regulations are followed by using the model of expected utility maximization. In the economics of crime (Becker, 1968), individuals are assumed to be rational egoists and to observe regulations to the extent only that it is to their own benefit. Careful empirical work has established, however, that this approach is unable to explain the *level* of the disregard for the law in a satisfactory way. The level of tax evasion, for example, cannot be accounted for by the expected utility approach (as championed by Allingham and Sandmo, 1972; for surveys see Pommerehne, 1985; Roth, Scholz and Witte, 1989; Cuccia, 1994): the size of the expected punishment is simply too low even if individuals are quite risk averse.[8] After an extensive and careful analysis of the American IRS Taxpayer Compliance Measurement Program, Graetz and Wilde (1985, p. 358) were forced to conclude that 'the high compliance rate can only be explained either by taxpayers'... commitment to the responsibilities of citizenship and respect for the law or lack of opportunity for tax evasion'. The same authors (with Reinganum and Wilde, 1986) do attribute the observed falling tax compliance to the erosion of tax morale (see also Reckers, Sanders and Roark, 1994; Kaplan, Newberry and Reckers, 1997).

The expected utility model neither fares all too well with respect to explaining *marginal* effects on tax evasion. A large number of econometric studies has found that the partial coefficients of the probability of detection and the penalty rate while often having the expected negative sign are not statistically different from zero (see for example Pommerehne and Weck-Hannemann, 1996, for Switzerland and the references on p. 164 to other countries and time periods).

The discussion suggests that intrinsic motivation in the form of civic virtue has an important systematic effect on how government regulations work. Moreover, the corresponding state interventions may crowd-out, and sometimes crowd-in, this motivation depending on whether the addressees perceive them to be controlling (which is normally the case) or supporting. Empirical research in the area of work, environmental and health regulations (see for example Bardach and Kagan, 1982) are consistent with these conclusions.

Subsidies, volunteering and infrastructure

Agricultural subsidies

The support of farmers via guaranteed high food prices undertaken in many countries has led to huge distortions. A large oversupply of agricultural goods was produced but the hard work on the farms nevertheless induced many peasants to move to more suitable occupations often located in cities. The policy thus resulted in a considerable waste of human resources (as well as in negative effects on the environment through the pollution of the soil by chemical products) and did not reach the officially proclaimed goal of maintaining the traditional rural way of life.

In view of this failure, and based on efficiency theory, economists have long argued that price support should be substituted by direct income support of farmers. Some countries such as Switzerland have heeded this advice and now hand out direct income transfers to their farmers.

There can be little doubt that this policy prevents the production of excess supply because price distortions are reduced and, at least ideally, completely removed. From the point of view of Crowding Theory the policy looks less favourable. The transfer of money just for being a farmer may well undermine the extrinsic motivation of being a farmer. The subsidy for 'being like a farmer' is likely to affect their self-perception negatively: they now behave like farmers because they are paid for that. Many people will argue that this removes the essential reason for supporting people working in this sector. At the same time, keeping individuals and families on the farms will become more and more expensive in tandem with the speed with which the farmers lose their former intrinsic motivation. They now expect a compensation according to the inconveniences of the 'job' (for example having to work long hours during the day and night). Over the long run, voters and politicians will realise that this policy tends to destroy what it originally claims to support. Together with the large cost increases this may well lead to such strong political resistance that the direct support programme has to be scrapped. This analysis helps us to explain why the agricultural lobbies tend to oppose the switch from price to income supports. They possibly sense that such a development might take place and try to prevent it because it also undermines their own position as an interest group.

Volunteering

Psychological aspects such as Crowding Effects are of particular importance in the social area where intrinsic motivation can be expected to play a larger role than in many other sectors of the economy. For the sake of concreteness, I will consider only a specific activity, *volunteering*, which is responsible for about 40 percent of total work offered in the social service non-profit economy (Weisbrod, 1988, p. 131). Volunteering for charitable non-profit institutions has grown more rapidly than employment elsewhere (ibid., p. 132) so that it is becoming an increasingly important activity.

Neo-classical economics based on the Relative Price Effect is able to make a number of sharp predictions (Menchik and Weisbrod, 1987; Weisbrod, 1988). With respect to the supply side, it hypothesizes that (i) the higher the wage rate or income, the less voluntary work is offered due to the higher opportunity cost; (ii) individuals either volunteer or donate money but not both. For people who are more productive on the market and are willing to help others, they should work more and donate the money to a charitable or non-profit institution;

(iii) a complete substitution is also expected to take place between husband and wife, i.e. either he or she, but not both, offer voluntary work. On the other side of the market, economists normally assume a perfectly elastic demand for volunteers by the respective institutions (hypothesis iv).

Menchik and Weisbrod (1987) find that these hypotheses are supported by the data for the United States. A very careful and recent study by Freeman (1997) with new data for the US, however, finds that they are clearly refuted. He generally concludes that the standard labour supply theory explains only a minor share of empirical reality. In particular, volunteers have a significantly higher personal and family income than non-volunteers, thereby contradicting hypothesis (i) (see also Vaillancourt, 1994 for Canada). Hypotheses (ii) is also rejected because a volunteer worker normally donates money at the same time. Neither is there substitution between husband and wife as hypothesis (iii) claims but both typically work as volunteers.

This does not mean that Relative Price Effects have no explanatory power but do so only at a secondary level. While a higher wage rate is associated with more volunteering such people put in fewer hours than those earning less on the market. Also, because there is no substitution between volunteering and donating, higher income families contribute relatively fewer hours and give relatively more in cash[9].

These results (which have been gained using the state of the art theory and econometrics) strongly suggest that traditional economic theory misses something important. A good candidate for filling this gap is the concept of intrinsic motivation and its dynamization by Crowding Theory. The positive association between income and volunteering may be attributed to the fact that poorer people cannot afford to pursue their intrinsic motivation as easily as richer ones. This is exactly Bertolt Brecht's statement in the *Dreigroschenoper: 'zuerst kommt das Fressen, dann die Moral'* ('Food first, morals second'), which is supported by sound empirical evidence (for example Lane, 1991, part V). The positive association between volunteering and donating holds because the major underlying motivation for both actions is intrinsic motivation thereby rejecting any substitutive relationship. Rather, people who are intrinsically motivated to help others have an urge to help by all means. Actually, only economists and probably a few other people would even consider the relationship between volunteering and donating to be substitutive. Finally, the positive association of voluntary work by husband and wife can be explained by positive sorting with respect to intrinsic motivation and also by the person doing voluntary work, educating and motivating the others to do likewise. Freeman (1997, pp. 159–65) offers a narrower explanation, namely, 'the importance of being asked' to volunteer. This explanation is not inconsistent with an explanation in terms of intrinsic motivation. It has been emphasised throughout this paper that intrinsic motivation is not exogenously given but can for example be triggered by being asked to act according to this motivation. On the other hand, Freeman is careful to admit that people do not simply volunteer when they are asked but only if they consider it a worthy cause, and if the demand comes from trustworthy people. Thus, being asked is perhaps a necessary but not sufficient factor to explain volunteering.

Empirical research on the demand side also suggests the importance of intrinsic motivation (see Duncombe and Brudney, 1995). There are considerable costs involved for organizations using volunteers and therefore do not exhibit a perfectly elastic demand as claimed by hypothesis (iv). The costs actually go far beyond recruiting and training; volunteers are different from paid workers because they are more difficult to steer according to the wishes of the management. The concept of intrinsic motivation is again helpful in explaining this phenomenon. As volunteers are (mainly or exclusively) motivated by *their own* concept of what has to be done, they are less willing to conform to the demands of management compared to paid staff. From the managers' point of view 'paid staff ... may be more productive and provide higher quality service' (Duncombe and Brudney, 1995, pp. 359–60). Consequently, the managers make an effort to have a suitable balance between paid workers and volunteers which is reflected in a statistically significant negative elasticity of demand for volunteers (ibid., pp. 371; also Steinberg, 1990).

Infrastructural policy

Everyone considers a good infrastructure to be an important prerequisite for economic development. However, the earthworks and buildings necessary for roads, railway tracks, airports, etc. as well as the risks involved with projects such as nuclear power plants and depositories and prisons normally meet with heavy resistance by the local communities affected. Such undertakings meet the criteria of NIMBY phenomena, i.e. the desire to have those projects 'Not In My Back Yard' (for example, Easterling and Kunreuther, 1995). Economists have a handy tool to solve this problem, namely to compensate those communities that are prepared to host such an infrastructural project (for example, O'Hare, 1977; Portney, 1991). The best way to determine the required compensation efficiently is by auction (Kunreuther and Kleindorfer, 1986). Such a move is made possible because the projects by definition produce positive net benefits for society as a whole so that the winners can compensate the losers. Empirical evidence, however, shows convincingly that the compensation strategy does not work (for the United States, see Easterling and Kunreuther, 1995; Carnes *et al.*, 1983; for Switzerland, Oberholzer-Gee, 1998). Indeed, it has been found that the willingness to accept a nuclear waste repository in Switzerland *fell* from 50.8 to 24.6 percent of the population when a sizeable compensation was offered. This reaction which contradicts the relative price effect was attributed to the Crowding-Out Effect (Frey and Oberholzer-Gee, 1997).

The siting of infrastructural projects is another important instance where economic policies solely based on the relative price effect does not work, and may even worsen the situation. Rather, psychological elements such as the Crowding Effects have to be taken into account.

Concluding remarks

The intention of this paper is not to criticise existing economic theory and policy without presenting an alternative approach. What is proposed here is an extension of economic theory while completely accepting the crucial importance of the Relative Price Effect. An economic policy which takes the possibility of Crowding Effects seriously is less interventionist than present economics because it takes into account that adverse effects on intrinsic motivation occur under identifiable conditions. What is suggested here as a general policy rule is that individuals are reasonable human beings whose intrinsic motivation can be put to good effect and which should therefore be taken care of.

It would be a misunderstanding to assume that intrinsic motivation is always welcome. It is neither generally good nor bad. While intrinsic motivation in the form of work or environmental morale, solidarity in the private and civic virtue in the public domain are often most desirable, these same features are undesirable if they are put to bad use such as when working for a fraudulent firm, exerting nepotism or supporting a criminal political regime. It is crucial to face the issue *where* we need *what* motivation. So far, we have only limited knowledge in this regard. Hopefully what has been established here is that to disregard intrinsic motivation and Crowding Effects may lead to costly policy errors. At the same time an alternative to present policy design based on faith in human nature has been suggested.

Notes

1   This approach has been refined by considering 'basic' preferences depending on 'commodities' which in turn are 'produced' by other goods and time. This reformulation (due to Stigler and Becker, 1977; Becker, 1996) allows us to account for what is normally called 'preference change' by keeping the basic preferences constant, and attributing changes in behaviour to changes in the enlarged set of constraints.

2   This raises the question whether people who study economics become more materialistic, or whether more materialistically-minded persons tend to study economics. See Frank, Gilovich and Regan (1996) and Frey, Pommerehne and Gygi (1993).

3   The income effect *may* work in the opposite direction to the Relative Price Effect (for example when the wage is raised people have an incentive to work more, but because they therewith become richer, they may decide to enjoy more leisure time and to work less). But this opposite effect is *not systematic*. The behavioural anomalies recently identified (see for example Dawes, 1988; Thaler, 1992) tend to weaken but not to counteract Relative Price Effects.

4   See also the critique by Lepper, Keavny and Drake (1996), Kohn (1996) and Ryan and Deci (1996) of Eisenberger and Cameron (1996) as well as Eisenberger and Cameron's (1997) reply.

5   For a formal treatment see Frey (1998). A behavioural rationale for the emergence of a Crowding-Out Effect in the case of the voluntary provision of a public good has been formally developed by van Dijk and van Winden (1997). They argue that the public provision of a public good under some conditions leads to a decrease in total provision because it impedes the development of social ties. In Frey (1997b) personal relationships have indeed been identified as a crucial condition for supporting intrinsic motivation.

6   Important contributions to the analysis of trust are Gambetta (1988), Coleman (1990), Putnam (1993), Fukuyama (1995), Kramer and Tyler (1996), Nye, Zelikow and King (1997).

7   Refers to South Korea only. No data are available for Turkey and India.

8   Following Alm, McKee and Beck (1990, p. 24) calculations for empirical magnitudes for the US show that taxpayers would have 'to exhibit risk aversion far in excess of anything ever observed for compliance predicted by expected utility theory to approximate actual compliance'.

9   A staunch supporter of traditional economics might argue that this shows that the theory is correct after all provided it is correctly applied. This is a typical ex post argument and essentially states that the traditional theory is flexible and coherent enough to be adjusted to the empirical evidence. This is certainly a useful exercise (it allows us to determine where the theory works well and badly) but it is of little use for predictive purposes.

4
Managing Risk by Controlling Behaviour: Social Security Administration and the Erosion of Welfare Citizenship

Hartley Dean

The implication of the arguments advanced by Beck (1992) and Giddens (1994) which have been reviewed in Chapter 1 is that 'we no longer live in a class society, but a risk society' (Offe 1996, p. 33). Whereas the proper function once ascribed to the post-war welfare state had been the amelioration of class (Marshall, 1950), its role now, it is claimed, should become the management of risk (Giddens, 1994). To such ends, how-ever, welfare states and particularly income maintenance systems have always sought to control human behaviour. The disciplinary capacity of social security administration has been recognised in the past by such widely respected commentators as Peter Townsend:

> the act of making up income without strings would come into open conflict with the other values upon which all societies are built – for example, that incomes are earned by work, that men living as hus-bands with women should support them, that children living with parents should be supported by them, and so on. For the sake of preserving its order and cohesion, society insists that these values are upheld ... The function of [social security] schemes is as much to control behaviour as to meet need (Townsend, 1979, p. 823)

Social guarantees of income maintenance are based on particular nor-mative assumptions about individuals' liabilities to maintain themselves through paid employment, to maintain each other within (characteristi-cally patriarchal) families, and to submit to the rule of law. It has been variously argued that the development of the welfare state has been necessary to the maintenance of the capitalist wage labour system (e.g. Offe, 1984), and that modernity itself is characterised by the rise of state administrative processes which individuate and discipline the subject (Foucault, 1977).

The emergence of modern social security systems had been associated with a transition from coercive to more discreet and sophisticated forms of discipline; the social rights of citizenship afforded by welfare capitalism were not wholly emancipatory but have remained insepara-ble – in sometimes quite subtle ways – from the enforcement of socially-constructed duties (Dean, 1991; 1996). However, taking the case of the social security system in the UK, this chapter will examine recent changes which suggest a reversion in social security administration towards more explicitly coercive behavioural controls. Such changes do not necessarily represent regression to the older and more inflexible forms of social control associated, for example, with the Poor Law, but may portend a transition to an entirely new kind of welfare regime. The certainties of capitalism's class-based order are increasingly super-seded by a society conforming to more hazardous principles. The dull repression of 'modernity' is being supplanted by the seductive but bru-tal consumerism of what some call 'post-modernity' (Bauman, 1988). At the same time, the monolithic forms of administration and provision associated with the 'Fordist' welfare state are being replaced in the age of 'Post-Fordism' by more diverse kinds of management, regulation and control (Burrows and Loader, 1994). The evidence presented in this chapter raises questions about the extent to which associated transi-tions in social security administration are both effective and sustainable.

I shall initially outline the relevant changes which have occurred in the UK since the 1980s, before drawing on three pieces of recent research which suggest that manipulating conditions of entitlement to social security benefits is, at best, unlikely to influence the behaviour of recipients (or the risks to which they are subject) and, at worst, may undermine people's commitment to the principles of social democratic citizenship (and their associated sense of ontological security). The first of these projects investigated the alleged 'dependency culture' which changes in the benefits regime were intended to stamp out. The second investigated the fraudulent behaviour and illegal economic activity to which the retrenchment of benefits regimes may lead. The third inves-tigated the underlying beliefs and discourses upon which popular percep-tions of rights to welfare and the obligations of citizenship are based.

The transition to a more repressive system

The UK social security system has always been a 'hybrid' system. Using the categories seminally defined by Esping-Andersen (1990), it has com-bined features of a social-democratic regime (because some benefits are universal), a conservative/corporatist regime (because some benefits are contributory) and a liberal/residualist regime (because some benefits are means-tested). However, since the 1980s, the UK regime has increasingly emphasised the features of a liberal/residualist regime: a transition which might broadly be characterised as the 'Americanization' of social security policy (see, for example, Leibfried, 1993), or as a transition from a Keynesian Welfare State to a Schumpeterian Workfare State (Jessop, 1994) in which an increasingly heterogeneous and unequal populace is controlled by an increasingly technocratic and remote elite.

Though the changes have been incremental, they have fallen into three broad phases: Thatcherite retrenchment; the new moral agenda; New Labour workfarism.

Thatcherite retrenchment (1979–90)

For all the radicalism of the Thatcher governments, the impact which they had upon the welfare state in general and the social security system in particular was in some ways surprisingly modest. None the less, the changes brought about in this period have had significant and lasting effects. Although the Thatcher governments did not succeed in curtailing the growth of expenditure on social security, in their attempts to do so they succeeded in cutting the real levels of benefits, most importantly by changing the basis on which most benefits and pensions are annually uprated so as to link this to price inflation rather than earnings growth (Glennerster and Hills, 1998, p. 317): this was a move that ensured a more punitive gap between those on benefits and those in stable full-time employment. The Fowler Reviews (DHSS, 1985) led to a major overhaul in which the emphasis of the social security system was switched firmly towards 'targeted' provision for the most needy: this involved a widening of the scope for means-testing and its associated surveillance mechanisms and, for the poorest citizens, a return to a discretionary system of relief in the shape of the social fund (Andrews and Jacobs, 1990). There were also concerted attempts to privatize aspects of social security through the introduction of employer-mandated benefits for sickness and maternity (which handed new disciplinary powers to employers) and through the promotion of private and occupational pension provision (which penalize people with poor employment records). Finally, there was a barrage of changes to the rules associated with benefits for unemployed people, most of which were intended to enhance work incentives (Atkinson and Micklewright, 1988).

The new moral agenda (1990–7)

John Major's premiership witnessed, on the one hand, a significant attempt to redefine the basis of welfare state citizenship, and on the other the fruition of radical Right-wing initiatives actually begun in the preceding era. John Major's 'Citizen's Charter' (Prime Minister's Office, 1991) signalled the displacement of the Fordist public service ethic with a new managerialist doctrine (see, for example, Gray and Jenkins, 1993). This approach sought to reconstitute the citizen as a consumer of services and state administration as a business accountable for the quality of services through the discipline of market-like processes rather than through democratic accountability. The consequence was an uncoupling of social security administration from political processes – reflected in the creation of a semi-autonomous executive Benefits Agency – and a new vulnerability for social security claimants who became in a practical and symbolic sense individually responsible as competent consumers for getting the best out of the system: the basis of their rights and obligations as citizens had been diluted or, at least, abridged.

In the same period, the government introduced the Child Support Act (CSA) and Job Seeker's Allowance (JSA). Each in its way introduced starker and more simplistic notions of rights and obligation. Supported both by neo-conservatives and the moral Right (for example, Murray, 1994) on the one hand, and by ethical socialists (for example, Dennis and Erdos, 1993) on the other, the purpose of the CSA was to enforce upon biological parents an inviolable duty to support their children financially. In the process, it was hoped, lone-parenthood would be discouraged and the 'traditional' family upheld, and the cost of maintaining lone parents (mainly mothers) would be transferred from the state to private individuals ('absent' fathers – see Garnham and Knights, 1994). JSA was introduced to replace existing benefits arrangements for unemployed people and, by its very name, the new scheme announced that social protection for unemployed people would henceforth be available only to those who were seeking employment. Not only did the new scheme reduce the rights which had previously been enjoyed by unemployed people, but it introduced new mechanisms by which to control the behaviour of unemployed people and to discipline those who are not sufficiently compliant (Finn, 1997).

New Labour workfarism (1997–)

Though the election of the Labour government under Tony Blair's premiership is still quite recent, it is possible tentatively to observe the direction in which social security policy in the UK may develop. The 'New' Labour Party which, after 18 years in opposition, has finally wrested power from the Conservatives is conspicuously different from the 'Old' Labour Party that had presided over the creation of the modern welfare state in the post-Second World War period and which had developed it during later terms of office in the 1960s and 1970s. In the Labour manifesto (Labour Party 1997), to which the electorate gave its endorsement, Blair pledges a 'bond of trust' with 'the broad majority of people who work hard, play by the rules [and] pay their dues'. The manifesto proposes to implement welfare reform 'based on rights and duties going together', including a 'welfare-to-work programme' for unemployed people and a 'proactive' Employment Service for lone-parents. Blair had previously argued that 'the most meaningful stake anyone can have in society is the ability to earn a living and support a family' (1996). The kind of 'stakeholder capitalism' envisaged by Blair is ambiguously conceived. It is a concept which vacates the ground conventionally occupied by social democrats by calling both upon elements of an essentially conservative communitarianism and upon more individualistic moral repertoires (see, for example, Driver and Martell, 1997).

The tendency already evident in Conservative policies of tying training and employment initiatives increasingly closely to social security and unemployment relief had been taken as evidence of a shift towards 'workfare' on the coercive United States model. Though it rejects the term 'workfare' in favour of the expression 'welfare to work', New Labour's policy is informed by the recommendations of the Commission on Social Justice (Borrie, 1994, pp. 172–82) and the example of the Australian Jobs, Education and Training (JET) scheme. It is as much a labour market strategy as a social security policy (see Deacon, 1997). It envisages, not a job guarantee or direct investment in employment creation, but 'active' re-employment services, training to improve 'employability', encouragement of self-employment, after-school childcare initiatives and selective short-term employer subsidies. The 'New Deal' that is being offered to unemployed people, lone parents and disabled people is designed to promote 'opportunity not dependence' and a 'new welfare contract between government and the people [which] will give our citizens the means to achieve their full potential' (DSS, 1998a, p. 21).

The objectives of workfare may have been positively reframed in New Labour rhetoric but, in essence, the space between citizen and state is being 'hollowed out' (Jessop, 1994, p. 24) as the balance shifts

in favour of global market imperatives. The old social democratic welfare state required a trade-off between collective expectations and the
correlative obligations which constrain the individual citizen – to pay
such taxes and contributions as may be due, and/or to observe certain
rules attaching to the receipt of state services or benefits. Now, however, expectations are subordinated to economic forces and what
remains of the social trade-off can indeed be defined – in Tony Blair's
terms – as an individualized 'stake'. It is a stake which centre-Left
governments may claim to underwrite, but which also constitutes a
wider set of strictly individual obligations that are ultimately enforceable by the government through the conditions which attach to the
receipt of state services and benefits.

Eliminating dependency?

The social security policies introduced during the period of 'Thatcherite
retrenchment' were intended or justified by their proponents as an
attack upon the so-called 'dependency culture' (McGlone, 1987) as a
means to move people 'away from dependence towards independence'
(Moore, 1987). They were therefore designed to reinforce work incentives, encourage dependency on liable relatives and/or the wider family,
and increase the scrutiny to which welfare claims and claimants were
subject. In 1990 the author was involved in a qualitative study that
entailed in-depth interviews with 85 working age welfare benefit recipients. The objective was to determine the extent to which a distinctive
dependency culture could be said to exist among such recipients and
to which policies to limit state dependency were or might be effective
(see Dean and Taylor-Gooby, 1992). It was found that, though some
respondents plainly felt they were 'trapped' on benefits (*cf.* Jordan
et al., 1992), this did not mean that they were part of an identifiable
sub-culture, or that they did not subscribe to the norms and values of
mainstream culture. What is more, many of the changes to the benefits
system were rubbing 'against the grain' of popular expectations and
aspirations and were potentially corrosive of labour discipline, family
values and responsible attitudes to the state.

Labour discipline

One unemployed respondent in the study spoke for the majority when
he said 'I don't need encouraging [to find work]'. Fully three quarters
of the sample were plainly anxious to work, including many of
the lone parents who were not immediately in a position to seek work

(*cf.* McLaughlin *et al.*, 1989; Gallie and Vogler, 1990). Motivation to work or to take up education or training opportunities was plainly not at issue for most and, even the minority that did not wish to work either intended to do so at some stage or, in various ways, felt guilty about not working. For most respondents it was difficult to see what beneficial effect additional incentives could have. What came across most clearly was that paid employment was valued primarily as a means to self-esteem or identity and only secondarily as a means to material reward. Where material rewards were valued, there was virtue or 'worth' associated with the effort involved or the pride taken in one's work. Though some respondents declared themselves willing to take even 'shit jobs', others spoke of the demoralization and the loss of self-motivation which accepting such an option would entail. To this extent, measures intended to price benefit recipients into low paid or uncongenial jobs could undermine the value which people place on having worthwhile employment. Manipulating the benefits system to increase work incentives may adversely affect labour discipline and commitment.

Family values

Several respondents in the study expressly voiced a sense in which they felt it was 'wrong' to depend for income on, for example, one's parents or adult offspring. They took 'pride' in managing independently of their families. Two-thirds of the sample expressed disapproval of the idea that they should be required to turn for help to family or friends. What came across was the sense in which the family (in its individual nuclear manifestation) is valued primarily for its affective relationships and emotional rewards and only secondarily as a means to reciprocal material security. To the extent that material security is valued, its importance is restricted to obligations which are seen to arise during very specific socially constructed stages of the life-cycle – especially, childhood. Respondents were resentful that the state should interfere in the privacy of family relationships, or that it might seek to disturb or undermine the established patterns of dependency within their own immediate families.

In spite of the rapid social and economic changes which have borne on the family as an institution (Utting, 1995), considerable value is still placed on 'satisfying' family relationships. In many ways the relative independence or dependability which benefits and pensions have given people have played a part in strengthening the affective basis of family ties, and history suggests that manipulating welfare arrangements to reverse or adapt patterns of family obligation is likely to fail

(Finch, 1989; Dean, 1995). Alternatively, it may devalue the very family relationships which are by popular consensus important.

Attitudes to the state

One respondent in the study spoke for many when she said of benefit administrators – 'these people make you feel they're trying to do you out of something'. Virtually all the benefit recipients interviewed for this study had experienced difficulties with their claims for benefits and two-thirds said that they found the system as a whole to be unfair. The mistrust and resentment fostered by their experiences of the social security system were hardly conducive to a sense of citizenship. The impression received was that the increasingly stringent, coercive and punitive nature of the system was strengthening claimants' inclination to view the state as adversary; that it may even undermine their willingness to co-operate with the state or to accept the obligations of citizenship. This was most clearly to be seen when respondents were asked whether (if they knew they could get away with it) they would be willing to 'fiddle' their benefit claims in order to get extra money. More than half replied that they would and this willingness in principle to defraud the social security system appeared to be directly related to resentment about their experiences of the system and/or to their perceptions that the system was unfair. Implied here was the possibility that eroding the substance of people's rights to welfare may undermine their sense of formal obligation as citizens of a welfare state.

Encouraging illegality?

These findings were one of the factors which informed a small-scale qualitative study of social security benefit fraud which was undertaken by the author in 1994–5. Social security benefit fraud in the UK had been a cause of moral panic in the 1980s (Golding and Middleton, 1982; Cook, 1989) and increasingly draconian counter-measures by government throughout the 1990s (Deacon and Fairfoot, 1994; Sainsbury, 1996; and see DSS, 1998b). The study in question entailed in-depth interviews with 35 individuals who were fraudulently claiming social security benefits (Dean and Melrose, 1996, and 1997). Most of the fraud committed by this sample related to undisclosed earnings from informal employment. The study focused first on the motivations of these claimants, and secondly on their attitudes to the rights and obligations of citizenship.

Economic insecurity

Associated with the global economic forces which constrain national governments has been a drive in certain western countries to de-regulate labour markets and to maximize the flexibility of labour supply. The effect at the periphery of the labour market is sustained levels of unemployment, underemployment and 'hypercasualisation' (Jordan and Redley, 1994), the proliferation of casual, temporary employment and intermittent self-employment and the promotion of informal and illegal forms of employment, much of it covertly subsidized through social security fraud. This process has coincided, as we have seen, with a shift away from universal state welfare towards more selective forms of social security provision and the emergence of a more parsimonious yet increasingly complex benefits system. The effect of low benefit levels and the perverse incentives associated with means-tested schemes is to increase participation in the informal economy (Evason and Woods, 1995).

The predominant reason given by respondents in the study for defrauding the benefit system was that of economic necessity, of not obtaining sufficient income from benefits. For most respondents, the vicissitudes of life on a very low income represented a bigger worry than the prospect of getting caught for benefit fraud, the risk of which is in any event perceived to be relatively low (*cf.* Rowlingson *et al.*, 1997). None the less, many of these claimants did live with considerable anxiety. The only thing which would have dissuaded virtually all of them from continuing to defraud the benefit system was a 'proper' job at an acceptable wage. Hardly any of the respondents were at all 'streetwise' about the benefit system: they were neither knowledgeable about their entitlements nor keen to maximize or prolong their claims on the state. The overwhelming impression was that most people who claim benefits and work illegally are not exercising a conscious lifestyle choice, so much as muddling through and waiting for something better to turn up. Few of them felt that what they were doing was fundamentally dishonest, but most experienced the process as uncomfortable and hazardous; as part and parcel of struggling to make ends meet.

A sense of betrayal

In practice, most respondents had somewhat vague or depleted concepts of citizenship and its obligations. None the less, their understanding of citizenship could be explored through the way they talked about 'rights' and 'fairness'. Most believed they had a right to claim social security benefits, but this was not a right they valued highly because of the discomfort or stigma associated with exercising it. Most respondents (25 of the 35) were observed to have engaged with discourses by which they would justify their own disobedience as citizens. At their simplest, such discourses translated economic necessity into justification and sought to blame inadequate benefit levels and the perversities of the benefit system. However, some respondents, because of the difficulties entailed in establishing their claims to benefit, were reacting to the way they had been 'messed about' or given 'a hard time' by the system. Such discourses often touched directly on issues of equity or justice. Feeling they had not received that to which they were entitled, respondents might justify their actions with reference to the taxes and contributions which they or their parents had paid in the past. Implicit here was the idea that the welfare state has betrayed them: that the new regime was unfair.

This is not to say that respondents were by and large supportive of the welfare state. On the contrary, a few were openly hostile to it. However, there was a sense in which, for some respondents, the very nature of citizenship had been impoverished. Sometimes, with evident scepticism or resentment, they equated citizenship status with consumption, lifestyle or wealth. These respondents not only felt excluded from citizenship but also sensed that they were experiencing a retreat from the values associated with the social democratic welfare state.

In suggesting that fraudulent benefit claimants may be reacting to the changed nature of the welfare state it is important to emphasise that fraudulent claimants as a group are extremely diverse. The study demonstrated that those involved differed from one another in terms of the degree of reflexivity which they brought to fraudulent claiming and in the degree of anxiety which they experienced. Though reflexivity and chronic anxiety may be endemic (Giddens, 1991), it cannot be assumed that they affect all subjects uniformly. Of the claimants who were not especially reflexive, the few who were not anxious tended to be the least principled of all the respondents, while those who were anxious were characteristically fatalistic about their situation: the former group was unlikely to be deterred from benefit fraud, but the latter would probably be less inclined to defraud the system if the system itself was more transparent and predictable. Of the claimants who were relatively reflexive, the few who were not anxious tended to be the most subversive of all the respondents, while those who were anxious were acting largely out of desperation: the former group would probably not commit fraud if it was persuaded that the system was just, while the latter – the largest in the sample – would almost certainly not commit fraud if the system afforded them greater security. Since this research was conducted, the New Labour government has identified fraud as one of the 'fundamental problems' of the existing social security system (DSS, 1998a; 1998b), but its proposals for yet further measures to improve detection, deterrence and prevention would seem less likely, in the light of our findings, to have an impact on the extent of individual fraud than measures which might stimulate legitimate labour markets and/or enhance the trust which claimants have in the welfare state.

Reducing mutual obligation?

This work in turn informed a further study which sought more generally to explore popular perceptions and discourses in relation to poverty, wealth and citizenship. This latest study entailed in-depth interviews with 76 working adults with very widely differing levels of income (Dean with Melrose, 1998). The objectives of the study were concerned, not with matters of social security administration, but with the wider context in which people's expectations of the welfare state are generated and sustained. The study demonstrates, first the extent to which people draw on a contradictory range of moral discourses in relation to the rights and obligations of citizenship and secondly, that this helps to account, not only for the ambiguity of public opinion towards the welfare state, but also for the deep and complex background against which any system of behavioural controls and incentives is pitted.

Contradictory moral discourses

By and large, the findings suggest, people at every income level are predisposed to free-market individualism and harbour a certain fascination for wealth, but they retain a pragmatic and self-interested commitment to elements of state collectivism and a deep fear of poverty: a fear which extends right up the income scale. However much people may come to mistrust the state, the abhorrence of poverty exceeds the desire for wealth. By implication, the preference is for a form of citizenship that protects against the risk of poverty before it secures the opportunity to achieve personal wealth.

As in Runciman's study thirty years before (1966), respondents were seldom able to locate themselves within the social distribution of incomes. Asked to place themselves on a scale between rich and poor, few were able to do so with any accuracy (though they were able, by and large, to locate themselves in terms of their social or occupational class). In particular, participants with middle to higher incomes tended grossly to underestimate their relative standing. To a degree, it would seem, individuals in an unequal society may in fact be subject to the same 'veil of ignorance' about their relative material standing as that which Rawls (1972) had sought to impose upon the imaginary participants in his famous thought experiment. Ontological insecurity might incline people to subscribe to certain principles of social justice just as much as calculative rationality.

Despite this, respondents in the study frequently appeared indifferent or even incoherent with regard to the concept of 'citizenship'. In response to explicit questions some adopted narrow, nationalistic notions of citizenship, though others engaged with broader conceptions. None the less, virtually all the respondents could be seen to be drawing on a diversity of often contradictory moral discourses or discursive 'repertoires' bearing upon the nature of their rights and responsibilities. From the data it was possible to construct a taxonomy (see Figure 4.1) involving distinctions which are rather more complex than that discussed in Chapter 2 between 'knights' and 'knaves', but which relate in a similar manner to the discursive strategies upon which people draw in negotiating the everyday realities of living in an unequal society. The taxonomy draws on two dimensions or axes:

- The moral and ideological substance of the explanations which people employ; whether they tend to be predominantly *risk-embracing*, individualistic or autonomistic on the one hand, or predominantly *risk-averse*, solidaristic or universalistic on the other.
- The 'voice' or forms of expression upon which people call; whether they tend to be *reflexive* or radical conventions on the one hand, or *traditionalist* (founded that is in received myths or established conventions) on the other.

So, for example, people who drew on risk-embracing modes of explanation would characteristically blame poverty on the poor themselves. Of these, those who drew on reflexive modes of expression were characteristically *entrepreneurial* – for them, the way to resist poverty is through individual merit and the seizing of opportunity; but those who drew on traditionalist modes of expression were characteristically *survivalist* – for them, resisting poverty is a matter of good luck and of keeping ahead of the competition. In contrast, people who drew on risk-averse modes of explanation would characteristically regard the poor as the victims of social circumstance. Of these, those who drew on reflexive modes of expression were characteristically *reformist* – for them, resisting poverty is a matter of social justice and is a policy

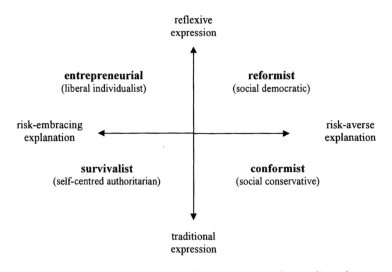

Figure 4.1 The moral repertoires underlying popular understanding of poverty, inequality and citizenship

question; but those who drew on traditionalist modes of expression were characteristically *conformist* – for them, though the poor might be deserving of help, poverty was an inevitable occurrence.

These categories are no more than heuristic devices which define not different kinds of people, but the various ways in which respondents in our study would at different moments attempt to 'make sense' of social inequality and the risks associated with it. It is possible for us to 'make sense' of the depleted or ambiguous conceptions of citizenship which people seem to exhibit when it is seen that popular discourse contains a complex mixture of explanations and voices, reflecting sometimes inconsistent expectations and traditions.

Support for state welfare

This goes some way towards explaining the ambiguous mixture of guarded altruism and pragmatic instrumentalism which characterises public opinion towards the welfare state in the UK (cf. Rentoul, 1989; Brook *et al.*, 1996). Expectations of the welfare state on the part of respondents in the study were found to be high, even when this was tempered by suspicion of it. As might be anticipated, respondents on very low incomes were more strongly in favour of redistributive state intervention than were respondents on very high incomes but, paradoxically, the poorest respondents were less inclined to indulge in solidaristic rhetoric than the richest ones: the former, perhaps have less occasion in the current climate to believe that the state is going to help them; the latter have more occasion to fear the potentially disruptive consequences of growing social inequality.

The analysis suggested a fundamental tension within popular discourse between:

- Concerns for social justice and the reformist impulse which stems largely from a pragmatic desire for the predictability and security that flow from greater equality. This is a discourse broadly consistent with social democratic political pretensions.
- Commitment to social cohesion and the essentially conformist impulse which is fuelled by an implicit conservatism and desire for certainty and stability. This is a discourse broadly consistent with social conservatism.
- Belief in meritocratic principles and the entrepreneurial impulse which would seize the potential for personal self advancement. This is a discourse broadly consistent with neo- or economic liberalism.
- A sense of fatalism and the survivalist impulse based on a presumption that inequality is to be contended with individually, as an inevitable hazard. This is a discourse consistent in some respects with a morally authoritarian political outlook and a desire to limit *other* people's freedoms.

In the event, none of these repertoires was ascendant. When account was taken of the full range of underlying moral discourses employed by the respondents in the study, it did appear that more individualistic, self-seeking repertoires dominated over more solidaristic, altruistic repertoires – but they by no means eclipsed them. There is no evidence to suggest that popular discourse unequivocally embraces the particular combination of political discourses which characterises New Labour workfarism, drawing as it does on economic liberalism, social conservatism and an element of moral authoritarianism. There is robustly surviving within popular discourse a paradigm which accepts a role for a social-democratic welfare state and a range of values which would support it. What is more, that paradigm and those values are not the evanescent vestiges of some bygone age, but reflections of contemporary fears and aspirations. Changing 'hearts and minds' requires more than changes in the nature of the prevailing welfare regime.

Conclusions: risk and welfare citizenship

Bringing together related threads from the different studies outlined above, it may be argued – first, that attempting to use the administrative rules of social security systems as a means to change or influence human behaviour is likely to be largely ineffectual; second, that attempting to use social security policy to curtail state dependency may lead on the one hand to an increase in fraud and illegal economic activity, and on the other to an erosion of people's sense of citizenship; third, that attempting to shift the underlying basis of a welfare regime cannot be undertaken without a clearer understanding of the complex ways in which the moral and practical significance of citizenship is socially constructed and popularly understood.

Risk and rationality

The effectiveness of incentives and penalties in the administration of social security provision will depend on the extent to which these accommodate the complex and sometimes irrational basis of popular beliefs and aspirations. It cannot be assumed that we are any of us model citizens. But neither is it helpful to base social security systems on the Hobbesian assumption that all subjects are venal, calculating and self-interested. It is both possible and, I would argue, necessary that social security rules should recognise and work with the grain of social expectations. In fairness, such an objective is partly implied in the New Labour government's Green Paper on welfare reform (DSS, 1998a), but the essential question is that of how to interpret the nature of popular aspirations. The Minister for Social Security Reform at the time of the Green Paper had argued elsewhere that 'self interest, not altruism is mankind's main driving force' (Field, 1996, p. 19). As a generalization this is quite simply wrong. The evidence outlined above indicates that people are capable of both selfishness *and* altruism, but what most aspire to above all is ontological security. If there is a lowest common denominator, it is that people seek a degree of material security that is not necessarily selfish and a degree of social security (based in belonging and reciprocity) that is not strictly altruistic. This is what the 'social dimension' of contemporary citizenship might reasonably be expected to provide.

Risk and responsibility

The insistence by Britain's New Labour government that rights are conditional on responsibilities is central to its attempt to recast the welfare state. In 1995, the constitution of the Labour Party was revised and, in place of an historic commitment to social equality on the basis of common ownership and popular administration, there was inserted a commitment to the creation of a community in which, *inter alia*, 'the rights we enjoy reflect the duties we owe' (Clause IV [4]), a refrain which the Labour Leader has promoted as a guiding axiom (for example, Blair, 1995). By common consensus, it is supposed, the 'golden age' of the Keynesian welfare state is past (Esping-Andersen, 1996) and, if the state can no longer protect its citizens from risk, it must manage its citizens to ensure they themselves take responsibility for the abatement of risk.

The evidence outlined above demonstrates that, by and large, people are by no means shy of responsibility: they wish to work, to provide for themselves and to care for other members of their families. However, it is not possible to reduce the relationship between rights and responsibilities to a mechanistic calculus. It is necessary to take into account the workings of social power (Taylor, 1996). More recent research, for example, has demonstrated how young people's willingness to undertake responsibilities in economically depressed local communities and in the labour market can be fatally undermined by experiences of systemic exclusion and exploitation: their desire for responsibility can be frustrated by the dominance of community elders and the failure of local employers to offer 'proper' (i.e. secure, well paying) jobs (France, 1998). Even within the intimacy of families the responsibilities that pertain between the generations are not susceptible to prescription, but have been shown to involve subtly balanced negotiation according to codes which are on the one hand highly gendered, but which on the other do not depend on crude reciprocity (Finch and Mason, 1993).

Our most basic rights as human beings, like our most basic needs, precede rather than follow from our responsibilities to contribute to human society. To demand otherwise is a recipe for greater tyranny. As Bill Jordan has pointed out, 'Big Brother – the fictional dictator of Orwell's communist totalitarianism – was strong on reciprocity, and had ways of making citizens do their bit' (1998, p. 59). Enforcing responsibilities upon people will not necessarily reduce the risks to which they are personally subject. Insisting, therefore, that rights should be conditional upon responsibilities may well increase the risk of resistance. We have seen that citizens who consider that their legitimate rights have been undermined may be less, not more willing to accept their responsibilities as citizens.

Entitlement and certainty

Perhaps the most persuasive and consistent finding from the three research projects outlined above is that people tend – by no means invariably, but primarily – to value ontological security, rather than risk and opportunity. To the extent that the protectionist welfare state of the Keynesian era represented a means to ensure social order, it succeeded because it provided a regime with which people felt inclined by and large to comply: the intrusive nature of a redistributive state was for the most part tolerable so long as it would guarantee a degree of material security. However, the thrust of welfare reform during the past 20 years has entailed a riskier approach to the distribution of resources in which, though the state has become no less intrusive, elements of welfare provision have become subject increasingly to the vagaries of market forces.

Social attitude data demonstrates the ambivalence of public opinion with regard to its support for state provision on the one hand and private provision on the other. While a substantial proportion of the population believe that people should be free to pay for better provision for health, education and pensions if they can afford to do so, they continue to favour increased spending on state services (Taylor-Gooby, 1991, chapter 5; 1994). It has been argued that, other things being equal, people would prefer to pay for private services and that their continuing support for the state sector arises because, being compelled to rely on the state for some services, they must hedge their bets (Saunders and Harris, 1989). However, the qualitative evidence outlined above suggests this is not so.

Drawing as they do on a range of contradictory discursive repertoires, people may be attracted to the freedom to buy private services (especially if they believe them to be of better quality than those which are publicly provided), but they also seek the certainty that an adequate level of provision is guaranteed. Recent social attitude data even suggests that people who have made themselves substantially independent of state welfare provision would support certain improvements in public services as being 'in the national interest' (Brook *et al.*, 1998). However, the moral repertoires which inform popular discourse are fluid. I have claimed that the repertoires which would sustain a level of security for all have not been extinguished, but more research will be required in order to assess the danger that shifts in social policy might in time reinforce not responsibility, but those moral repertoires which would tolerate security for some social groups at the expense of others' entitlements.

If it is accepted that people do by and large value paid employment, then the interface between income maintenance and labour market policies needs to reflect a rather different set of assumptions about human motivation. If it is accepted that family relationships are in themselves important, then social security and child support arrangements should not impair such relationships by enforcing involuntary dependency; or, where such relationships are dependent relationships, the dependability of parents or carers should be adequately underwritten. If it is accepted – regardless of wider ideological considerations – that citizenship is necessarily based on at least some measure of mutual security, then social security systems should genuinely enable claimants rather than manage them; they should lessen and not exacerbate the risks which claimants face; and they should prevent and not create social exclusion. In the process of meeting need, such systems will indeed affect behaviour, not least because they may serve to clarify, shape or sustain popular conceptions of citizenship.

Part II
Responses to Risk

5
The Rationality Mistake: New Labour's Communitarianism and 'Supporting Families'

Anne Barlow and Simon Duncan with Rosalind Edwards

Family law, social behaviour and government intervention

Following its landslide election victory in 1997, the 'New Labour' government in Britain has taken the express aim of changing social behaviour as part of its project of 'modernisation'. A major component in this drive is to use legislation to promote particular forms of partnership and parenting, and to discourage other, less favoured, forms. This is because, as Tony Blair put it, while 'family values' are the key to a 'decent society', there is a 'moral deficit' which leads to an 'indifference to the undermining of family life' (Blair, 1996a). Government should take action to inculcate appropriate values and so 'rebuild social order and stability' (Blair, 1996b). The New Labour version of what this means in policy terms has now been codified in its 1998 Green Paper *Supporting Families* (Home Office, 1998).

In this chapter we examine the validity of this enterprise in terms of its underlying assumptions about social behaviour and economic decision-making, and how this might be influenced through legislation. We argue that in *Supporting Families*, the government implicitly assumes a universal model of 'rational economic man' and his close relative the 'rational legal subject'. In this view, people take individualistic, cost-benefit type decisions about how to maximise their own personal advantage. Change the financial structure of costs and benefits and the legal structure of rights and duties in the appropriate way, and people will modify their social behaviour in the desired direction. Alternatively, people may make sub-optimal decisions where they lack information about this cost-benefit structure. In this case, simply providing better information, or educating them so that they can access it and act upon it more effectively, will have the desired social effects.

What if this is an incorrect version of how people make important decisions about their moral economies – about how partnerships should be formed, sustained and dissolved; how parenting should be carried out; how this might be combined with paid work; and who does what sort of paid and unpaid work? The assumption of rational economic man, and the theories of neo-classical economics which underlie it, have been vigorously challenged both in general and in their application to complex social decision-making. Rather, people seem to take such decisions with reference to moral and socially nego-tiated views about what behaviour is expected as right and proper. This negotiation, and the views that result, vary between particular social groups, neighbourhoods and welfare states. These decisions are not simply individual, but are negotiated in a collective way. Calculations about individual utility maximisation, and in particular perceived eco-nomic or legal costs and benefits, may be important once these under-standings are established, but are essentially secondary to such social and moral questions. Decisions are still made rationally, but with a dif-ferent sort of rationality to that assumed by the conventional economic and legal model.

Our point is, therefore, that people may take decisions on parenting, partnering and work on quite different grounds to those assumed by the New Labour government. If people do not act according to the model of rational economic man and the rational legal subject, then legislation based on such assumptions may well be ineffectual. The pro-posals in *Supporting Families* are one example. At worst, if government responds to this ineffectiveness by introducing compulsion (as has happened with the New Deal for Lone Parents), then such policies could force large numbers of people to do what they consider morally wrong. Quite apart from the ethical implications, such policy will probably still be inefficient. We label this the 'rationality mistake'.

The 1991 Child Support Act is a good example. This was imposed from above by a government with a clear ideological agenda to mould and change family practices, and simply assumed people would act as 'rational actors' and change their social behaviour in response (Smart and Neale, 1998). The actual result has not only been large scale refusal by both men and women to co-operate with the Child Support Agency, and considerable resentment by many who do, but a wholesale dis-crediting of the legislation for its inefficiency and authoritarianism (see Collier, 1994; Gillespie, 1996; Burgoyne and Millar, 1994; Clarke *et al.*, 1994; Millar, 1996; Davis *et al.*, 1998; Mears, 1998). Will the 'rationality mistake' mean that New Labour – despite a different political vocabulary – will fall into the same trap? In the next section we examine *Supporting Families* from this viewpoint.

The 1998 Green Paper: supporting families or a 'rationality mistake'?

Communitarianism offers New Labour a 'third way' between the neo-liberalism of the new right and the supposedly outmoded social democracy and Marxism of 'old Labour'. Individuals are not seen as asocial creatures but as being and acting through their contextual social experiences and relations – where the communities in which individuals are embedded are especially important. Markets, therefore, are not the natural basis of individual behaviour but are just one more social institution. This perspective has a strong normative tone, where community is regarded as a 'good thing'. Individuals who are 'socially excluded' will not behave in the 'right way', and communities that are fragmented or dysfunctional will produce such individuals. Hence the community as a set of institutions should be fostered and supported (see Driver and Martell, 1997).

Economic efficiency is interwoven with both social cohesion and social morality in this model of society – rational economic actors need a community base (see Figure 5.1, p. 75). Family practice, or rather 'the family' as an ideal form, therefore comes to play a pivotal role (Duncan and Edwards, 1999). The problem is that proper family values (the key to a 'decent society') are in doubt from a New Labour communitarian perspective, given all the changes in families where there is supposedly a growing 'parenting deficit'. Mothers are out at work. Fathers may be absent, and children are left without moral guidance or emotional support. This is exacerbated by a 'moral deficit' where, as Blair (1996a) claims, there is 'indifference to the undermining of family life'. Moreover, it is increasingly difficult for government to manage family life, where partnering, and even parenting, increasingly takes place outside formal marriage. Some commentators even see New Labour's interest in parenting as approaching the status of a 'moral reform crusade' (Coward, 1998); certainly the House of Commons Parliamentary Group on Parenting sees a national parenting strategy as providing foundations for 'social responsibility and self-discipline' which would 'promote important social objectives' (*Guardian*, 9.6.98).

The Conservative government's 'back to basics' campaign during the 1990s proclaimed a moral agenda in favour of the traditional family, and vilified other family forms, most notably lone motherhood

(Smart and Neale, 1998; Duncan and Edwards, 1999). In contrast, New Labour proclaims moral tolerance. Nevertheless, it promotes marriage as an ideal and maintains that living with two biological and preferably married parents is best for children. As Home Secretary Jack Straw put it in July 1998, significantly as part of a speech to launch the government sponsored National Parenting and Family Institute:

> We are not in the business of making the job of lone parents more difficult by blaming them as some have done in the past. ... Yet, whilst not stigmatising other family groupings, there is a presumption that the stability children need is best provided by two participating parents ... Research shows that there is a higher level of commitment between married couples than between those who cohabit; and married couples are more likely to stay together.

This somewhat contradictory position reflects a paradox set up by New Labour's version of communitarianism. On the one hand there is a supposed parenting deficit, but on the other hand all adults below pensionable age have the ascribed duty to take on paid work. Traditional marriage, with two-parent married families, seems to offer the best way of dealing with the contradiction, for this is the family form that best facilitates the combination of parenting with paid work. Lone motherhood, in contrast, epitomises the contradiction between paid work and parenting – there is less disposable time for one parent to achieve either at adequate levels. The intricacies and ambivalences of step-parenting, cohabitation and all the other 'new family forms' just complicate matters and in any case are seen as more likely to lead to family breakdown. Parenting by both biological parents who are also married is therefore the best and most efficient family form in linking social morality, social cohesion and economic efficiency (Figure 5.1).

The Green Paper: *Supporting Families*

Supporting Families makes proposals to operationalize this preference, and this is to be achieved through changing the financial and legal parameters under which parents, as rational actors, are assumed to operate. These proposals are 'good for parents, children, business, the economy and society' (para 3.19). The Green Paper itself is particularly significant as the first 'joined-up' cross-government social policy wholly conceived and developed under Tony Blair's leadership, and lies at the heart of New Labour's values (Travis, 1998; Wintour, 1998). It provides a good indication of the government's intentions. We use *Supporting*

Families to examine government assumptions about social rationality and morality in family practices and about how these should be linked through use of the law.

Parenting behaviour

Chapters one, three and five of the Green Paper, which we discuss briefly here, provide carrots and sticks to encourage proper 'rational' behaviour (see Barlow and Duncan, 1999). Chapter one is concerned with providing better services, information and support for parents and reflects one of the basic assumptions of the neo-classical version of rationality. Suboptimal behaviour is supposedly the result of a lack of information or of the ability to use it. Change this ('change the culture' – para 1.20) and more optimal behaviour will result – in this case desired parenting behaviour. As the chapter makes clear however, particular groups, such as the more disadvantaged in problem council housing estates or the sons of lone mothers, need to be educated or instructed as to what the right information is.

Chapter five shows more of the stick to meet the need for selective inculcation of desired behaviour. At one extreme this takes the coercive form of parenting orders: where parents of children convicted of an offence may be required to undergo counselling themselves, to induce proper parenting behaviour, and may be required to keep a child at home at certain hours or provide an escort to school. This is supplemented by child safety orders, where supervision will be carried out by a social worker, and local child curfews (paras 5.14, 5.17, 5.18).

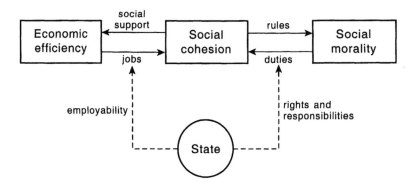

Figure 5.1 New Labour's model of society
Source: Developed by authors from Burkitt and Ashton (1997) and Driver and Martell (1997).

This emphasis on solving social problems (here labelled 'family problems') – through intervention in individual behaviour (here 'parenting' – is a central element of New Labour's version of communitarianism (Driver and Martell, 1997). This may lead to 'victim-blaming'. The activities of employers, for example, in providing low paid or insecure jobs are not questioned. This message is reinforced in chapter three. Here, employers are simply encouraged, in unspecific terms, to introduce 'family-friendly employment', based on voluntary co-operation. No coercion here for those with anti-social behaviour.[1] The point is not only that this policy emphasis results from New Labour's prescriptive and moralistic version of communitarianism which emphasises individual responsibility at the expense of socio-economic reform. Rather, this emphasis becomes 'naturalised' because the sovereignty of individual preferences and behaviour is an axiom of the neo-classical version of social behaviour. Such assumptions lie at the foundations of 'rational economic man'. From this starting point, it makes little sense to see the origins and causes of social problems lying in wider social conditions, still less in the actions of employers and firms.

The guts of the whole project lie in chapter two, on taxes, benefits and employment, and in chapter four, on strengthening the institution of marriage. The latter maps out a basic response to family change, and is the section of the Green Paper with most novel ideas. The former uses the financial levers available to government, bringing together several measures already under implementation. A large increase in Child Benefit, announced in the March 1998 budget, will be accompanied by the introduction of the much heralded Working Families Tax Credit, designed to simplify tax and benefit arrangements and mitigate the poverty trap. This will include a childcare tax credit as part of the 'National Childcare Strategy' also previously announced. The New Deal for Lone Parents, already piloted in test areas and indeed already implemented nationally from October 1998, is applauded. An education maintenance allowance for 16–18 year olds in low income families will be piloted. Finally, administration of the Child Support Agency will be reformed.

A measure which is not mentioned in the Green Paper, although it is implied in chapter two, is the insistence on continuing the previous Conservative policy of cutting lone-parent benefit (a top-up to universal Child Benefit) for new claimants from 1998, despite alienating traditional Labour supporters and saving only a trivial amount of money (some £60 million in the first year). Partly, the new government sought to establish its 'macho' credentials by flouting traditional supporters

(Young, 1997). The changes also give a powerful moral message about the desirability of particular family forms.

The New Deal for Lone Parents

The next section of the chapter, on the New Deal for Lone Parents, combines the ideas that paid work is a moral duty, that the state will support individual fulfilment of this duty through enhancing employability and that some direction is necessary for particular social groups who are perceived as lacking this morality (Lister, 1998). From October 1998, lone parents on Income Support, whose youngest child is over school age, have been invited to interview with a personal advisor in their local job centre to discuss finding paid work. This is supported by improved childcare and information services. A basic premise (Green Paper, para 2.16) is the received wisdom that 85 per cent of unemployed lone mothers say they would like paid work if practical problems could be overcome.

The policy was piloted in eight labour exchange areas from mid-1997. In the furore following the cutting of lone parent benefit, ministers claimed the pilot as a success. A quarter of those participating found jobs (Marsh, 1997) a figure that had risen to a third by April, 1998. The problem is that these figures refer only to those who participated. In fact little more than half the target group was successfully contacted and, of this half, only a quarter actually attended interview. Seventy-five per cent of contacted lone parents did not respond. Just four per cent of the target group (1678 out of 40000) found work through the scheme, a proportion who might well have found jobs anyway. Of these, about half came off benefits. The others simply move from Income Support to Family Credit, a transfer which may even increase spending (House of Commons Social Security Select Committee quoted in the *Guardian*, 17.2.98). A recent evaluation study estimates that the New Deal pilots had helped only one to two per cent of lone parents to leave Income Support by March 1998 (Hales *et al.*, 1999; see also McGlone, 1999).

One reason for low up-take could be that lone parents face severe practical problems in finding day care. Investment in after-school clubs has been increased and raised the 'disregard' for childcare expenses in calculating the amount of family credit to be paid – although early evidence suggests that few lone parents have gained (Daycare Trust, 1997; Roberts, 1998). This is to be replaced by a childcare tax credit when Working Families Tax Credit comes into operation. The childcare constraint, however, would mainly affect those lone parents actually participating in the scheme. For the non-responding majority (seventy-four per cent), it could be that their knowledge of likely wages, usually low and often insecure, coupled with the extra costs of travel to work, school meals, and day care, mean that they see the interviews as a waste of scarce time (Duncan and Edwards, 1999).

Both these explanations would fit into rational economic man type explanations for lone mothers' behaviour – it would just be the case that the government has underestimated the level of constraints and overestimated the quality, rewards and availability of jobs. Lone mothers' cost-benefit analyses, therefore, would usually have a different outcome to that imagined by the government – it would remain most rational, in this neo-classical sense, to remain on benefits. However, more fundamentally, it may be that lone mothers are employing a different rationality to that implied. Thus recent research shows that lone mothers see their moral and practical responsibility for their children as their primary duty and that for many (although not all) this responsibility to be a 'good mother' is seen as largely incompatible with paid work. Interviews with job advisors are at best an irrelevance, and at worst a threat. However, it is *paid* work that New Labour erects as a moral duty, not the unpaid caring which most lone mothers place first. This, we contend, is a 'rationality mistake'. Lone mothers make decisions about taking up paid work on quite different grounds to those assumed in the Green Paper.

By February 1999, with the New Deal now national, Tony Blair was claiming 80 per cent employment take-up for lone parents attending New Deal interviews, although fully 94 per cent of those contacted did not attend an interview in the first place (*Daily Mail*, 10.2.99). This massive non-response has not brought about a re-examination of the policy's behavioural or economic assumptions. Attendance at job interviews is to be made compulsory, under threat of loss of benefits. According to Alistair Darling as Social Security Secretary, this 'harsh but justifiable measure' is necessary to confront lone parents' 'poverty of ambition and poverty of expectation' (*Guardian*, 11.2.99). More generally, as Tony Blair wrote in the *Daily Mail* (10.2.99), the message to claimants is that 'If you can work, you should work'. However, as recent research shows, lone parents in fact have considerable ambition and expectations for their children, and they undertake substantial work in trying to achieve this, albeit unpaid caring work which leaves them formally 'unemployed'. In forcing its own version of rationality upon lone parents the government risks making large numbers do what they consider morally wrong.

Marriage and cohabitation

Chapter four of the Green Paper maps out a basic response to family change. On one level, it claims that intervention aims to help the parenting relationship – whether married or not – to succeed. In any case, government competence is limited where 'families do not want to be lectured about their behaviour or what kind of relationship they are in' (para 4.2). Yet the paper states that the government's preferred parenting structure is marriage. As the preamble makes clear: 'marriage does provide a strong foundation for stability for the care of children. It also sets out rights and responsibilities for all concerned. It remains the choice of the majority of people in Britain. For all these reasons, it makes sense for the Government to do what it can to strengthen marriage (para 4.8).' What is more, the bulk of the chapter (indeed entitled 'Strengthening Marriage') is concerned with how marriage can be supported and encouraged. Other possible partnership and parenting forms are hardly mentioned – despite the fact that in 1996, 21 per cent of children were born to cohabiting parents, with another 14 per cent born to lone mothers. Both figures are increasing, and cohabitation is predicted to double by 2021 (ONS, 1998, 1999). Yet only about half a dozen of the 49 paragraphs could have much relevance to such parents, and only three consider cohabitants. Nothing at all is said about same-sex parenting. What can the Green Paper say to all these parents other than 'get married'?

The chapter proposes measures to strengthen marriage, including better preparation, a clear statement of rights and responsibilities, prenuptial agreements about the distribution of money and property, premarital counselling, modernisation and personalisation of the civil marriage service, access to mediation and counselling to support marriages in difficulty, better information before divorce 'to increase the chance of saving more marriages' and clearer rules on property division on marital breakdown to reduce conflict between married couples.

In contrast only two proposals concern cohabiting families. The first is a non-religious child-naming ceremony which may also be used to stage the public signing of a parental responsibility sharing agreement, where parents are unmarried. This is designed to encourage public assertion of both parents' commitment to a child, whether or not they are living together. Second, the Green Paper grudgingly suggests that 'it might therefore be worthwhile' to produce a guide for cohabitants setting out their legal rights in relations to income, property, tax, welfare benefits, and responsibility towards children. This fails to address the complexity and inadequacies of the law relating to cohabitation. Enforceable prenuptial contracts for those intending to marry are proposed, but the paper is silent on the issue of legally enforceable cohabitation agreements. Nor is there counselling to save cohabitation relationships, in sharp contrast to the proposed efforts to be invested in marriage-saving. The Green Paper therefore fails to acknowledge, let alone address, the need for better family law-based regulation of cohabitation relationships. For lone parents the discussion is hardly about parenting at all (save for the negative assumption that their sons will lack male role models) – the issue is seen as getting lone parents into paid work.

UK policy contrasts sharply with that of some other European countries. In Scandinavia, cohabitation and marriage have long held equality before the law, and same-sex cohabitation, and more recently same-sex marriage, have been drawn into the same orbit. Lone mothers are just another type of 'worker citizen' where all adults below pensionable age are treated as autonomous, and supported in taking up paid work (Björnberg 1992, 1997) . The great advantage is that a large proportion of parents (some 50 per cent) are not legally and policy marginalised. In France the Jospin government is currently attempting to equalise the legal rights of cohabiting and married couples. This change is to be achieved by introducing *Pactes Civiles de Solidarité* – civil union contracts available to all unmarried cohabitants whether heterosexual or same-sex. The French legislation will allow such couples to opt in to legal rights akin to marriage for all purposes including social security benefits, inheritance, maintenance and property division on relationship breakdown.

At the same time the means of carrying through this discourse, of strengthening marriage and reducing the importance of other family forms – or at least the threat they pose – is seen in terms of rational economic man and the 'rational legal subject'. The government appears to believe that changing financial and legal parameters will alter the calculus for decisions about partnering and parenting and lead to desired changes in behaviour. More lone parents will take up paid work, more couples will marry, fewer will cohabit and fewer will divorce. The problem is that the basic assumption about how people make decisions about their moral economies – about how partnerships should be formed, sustained and dissolved; how parenting should be carried out; how this might be combined with paid work; and who does what sort of paid and unpaid work – might be incorrect. The whole enterprise might then become irrelevant – or even oppressive – because of this 'rationality mistake'. The next section reviews recent empirical research on how people make such decisions.

Moral rationalities and family decision-making

Recently family sociology has become more interested in what families actually do, rather than what they ought to do, or are assumed to do, and how deviant family behaviour can then be understood. As David Morgan (1996) has put it, the focus is now on 'family practices' rather than 'family problems'. Among other things, this has meant new research and knowledge about how people make decisions on how to conduct their family life.

Janet Finch's work on family obligations is central to the field (Finch, 1989; see also Finch and Mason, 1993). The empirical focus was how notions of moral obligation and responsibility between kin might be changing in the context of rapid changes in family structures, and other social changes like increasing female employment. Finch found that shared understandings about 'the proper thing to do' emerged over time and in specific contexts – there was no static concept of duty, or pre-given moral rules in terms of abstract principles, and even less a rational economic calculus. This also meant that these essentially moral decisions about care were often ambiguous – there could be more than one 'right answer' depending on the particular circumstances and past histories. The question of moral values, of how they are formed and how they inform action, was then brought back into empirical family sociology.

At around the same time Bill Jordan and colleagues published research on how families make decisions about labour market participation, the allocation of unpaid caring and domestic work, and their family trajectories more generally. These decisions were also set within socially negotiated accounts of what was morally adequate. Thus lone mothers on the deprived public housing estate studied held a stronger desire for paid work than partnered mothers, but they were constrained in following this desire through into action in the face of a strong neighbourhood belief that 'good' mothers should prioritise caring for their own children and only 'fit in' paid work around this moral priority. Child care and other informal support could be withdrawn if mothers transgressed these local norms (Jordan *et al.*, 1992). High income, married parents took seemingly more individualistic and economically rational decisions in terms of career and homemaking, but even so these were strongly gendered through ideas about what husbands and wives should properly do, and set within views about what nuclear families were for. A particular goal was to achieve educational success for their children. Furthermore, respondents saw these decisions within a moral framework; they were making moral judgments about the proper use of family resources (Jordan *et al.*, 1994).

Such work inspired a whole school of family research (see Silva and Smart, 1999) focusing on how moral decisions inform social behaviour. Carol Smart and Bren Neale (1998) in their study of divorcing couples looked at how parents (and their children) were making moral decisions at a time of major life changes and when they were, often quite deliberately, trying to become different people. But again, this new basis for making moral judgments was deeply 'enmeshed' in the context of family histories and responsibilities. Jane Ribbens-McCarthy (1999) and colleagues, looking at how the tension between notions of couple intimacy and responsibility to children is worked through in step-families, place this focus on its head. It is the needs of dependent children that are often necessary to maintain morally adequate identities. Writing more theoretically, Zygmunt Bauman (1993) pointed out in 1993 that 'ordinary people' do not have to be versed in the intricacies of moral philosophy in order to act morally or form moral judgments. In his words, 'To be moral does not mean to be good, but to exercise one's freedom of authorship and/or actorship as a choice between good and evil' (1995, p. 118). Or, as Selma Sevenhuijsen puts in her discussion of the ethics of care, moral and ethical reasoning are 'everyday social and textual practices' (1998, p. 79).

It then follows that how people actually make these moral decisions become crucial in understanding social behaviour and change. As research has shown, such decisions will also vary according to the different contexts of social groups, social places and social histories. This has important implications for the construction of social policy, in terms of both efficiency and ethics. Much social research on families and decision making assumed people were either passive respondents to external stimuli, or rational economic men making decisions in terms of personal costs and benefits. Behaviour patterns were expected to be fairly uniform. Exceptions were in some way deviant. New Labour still seems to hold this assumption.

What, then, does this research say about the social behaviour problematised in the Green Paper? What sort of moral decisions do people make about partnering and paid work? We draw here our own studies of lone mothers' decision-making about paid work (Duncan and Edwards, 1999) and the decision to cohabit or marry (Barlow, 1998).

Research findings: lone mothers and work

The first study combines qualitative and quantitative research; analysis of census data provides information on lone mothers' employment patterns while 95 open-ended intensive interviews explore lone mothers' evaluations of the relationship between motherhood and paid work. These were selected to illustrate the key social divisions of class, ethnicity and culture ('alternative' and 'conventional'), in the context of different types of neighbourhood (inner city, gentrifying, peripheral social housing and suburban) and of the different labour markets and policy environments of Britain, Germany, Sweden and the USA. Here we discuss the UK findings.

A major result of this research is that lone mothers' decisions about whether to try for a job or not are primarily influenced by 'gendered moral rationalities' – that is, their socially negotiated understandings about the proper relationship between good motherhood and paid work. These rationalities provide answers to, or guidance on, questions such as:

- Is it right that I, as a mother bringing up children by myself, should try for a full time job?
- What are my responsibilities, how will my behaviour affect my children?
- What do others expect of me, what do they see as right and how will they treat me as a consequence?

All the interviewees experienced lone motherhood in terms of responsibility towards their children but – crucially – their gendered moral rationalities differed in terms of how this basic responsibility was best discharged.

Some lone mothers, who subscribed to a *primarily mother* gendered moral rationality, gave primacy to the moral benefits of physically caring for their children themselves, based at home. Children's and mothers' needs overlapped, and these mothers saw paid work as contradictory or even inimical to this moral responsibility to be good mothers. Others, with a *primarily worker* gendered moral rationality, gave primacy to a right to paid work for themselves as separate to, and autonomous from, their motherhood. Finally, another group of lone mothers held a *mother/worker* integral gendered moral rationality. They saw paid employment as part of their moral responsibility to their children as good mothers, providing them with both financial security and a good role model. For all the mothers, these moral decisions were not simply established individually, but rested on moral, emotional and practical support – and pressure – from others. Impressions about the financial costs and benefits of taking up paid work or not were still important, but remained secondary to this essentially moral and social evaluation of what was the right and proper thing to do for them and their children.

These different gendered moral rationalities were associated with different social groups living in different types of neighbourhood, as Figure 5.2 shows.[2] In Britain, both white middle class lone mothers living in suburban areas, and white working class lone mothers living in peripheral social housing, were likely to hold a 'primarily mother' gendered moral rationality – despite the considerable class differences between the two groups. Those lone mothers holding 'alternative' views of families and gender roles, usually informed by feminism and living in gentrifying areas, were most likely to hold a 'primarily worker' gendered moral rationality. Finally, it was black lone mothers, mostly living in large council estates in inner city areas, who tended towards a 'mother/worker integral view'.

The generality of these gendered moral rationalities is supported by analysis of the 1991 household Sample of Anonymised Records from the census. This showed that for any given level of constraints or human capital, black lone mothers usually have higher employment rates and, in particular, higher rates of full-time work. Indeed, the least resourced and most constrained black lone mothers (those living in council housing, aged under 30, with more or younger children, with lower educational qualifications and so on) often held employment positions similar to the most resourced and least constrained white lone mothers. The most resourced and least constrained black lone mothers moved towards the (white) 'male norm' of continuous full-time work. Analysis of the longitudinal study census data for 1981–91 showed that these differences are also stable over time. For example, black lone mothers who had (re)partnered by 1991 were even more likely to be in full-time paid work than in 1981. Conversely, (re)partnering white lone mothers were even more likely to be unemployed or to be in part-time work in 1991. This is all the more remarkable since most black lone mothers live in labour market areas that have performed worst in terms of providing jobs.

There are a number of important implications for public policy from this study. Not least of these is that those lone mothers who chose not to take up paid work, far from falling into a deviant sub-culture that abhors self-reliance and social responsibility, did so on the basis of what they believed to be the morally proper thing to do as a mother. Given this strong moral underpinning, their decisions about their non-involvement in the labour market were perfectly rational. Their views are aligned with dominant conventional views about mothering and family life, and in this way unemployed lone mothers are not 'socially excluded' or in some sense 'outside society'. In contrast, those lone

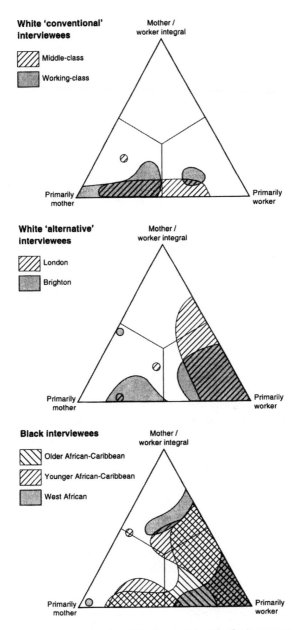

Figure 5.2 Gendered moral rationalities by social and ethnic groups

mothers who did prioritise paid work, or saw it as integral to being a good mother, held views that are alternative to – or even 'deviant' from – dominant conceptions, but are equally moral and rational. The mother/worker integral gendered moral rationality in particular challenges the simple mother versus worker dichotomy which dominates social policy. Furthermore, not only are each of these views both moral and rational, but they are deeply social, mediated through lone mothers experiences of being members of particular social groups in particular areas.

The limited effect to date of the New Deal for Lone Parents, where the vast majority of lone parents do not respond, seems a good example of the 'rationality mistake' in the light of this research. Unfortunately, the response to this weak policy effect has not been to reassess the assumptions but to make interviews compulsory for those lone mothers receiving benefits. This threatens to force large numbers of people to do what they consider morally wrong. Contradicting the values of communitarianism, it also rides roughshod over 'community' norms about parenting and paid work. Policies based on misleading 'rational actor' assumptions about how people make decisions about their moral economy may disregard the way people actually make decisions about their moral economy, and may go badly wrong.

Cohabitation versus marriage

The second study focuses on beliefs about cohabitation compared to marriage. Thirty mothers with pre-school children were interviewed (eleven married, eleven cohabiting and eight lone mothers) in the contrasting social and labour market areas of Great Yarmouth in Norfolk and Merthyr Tydfil in South Wales. The interviews explored reasons for cohabiting or marrying, and also aimed to ascertain respondents' knowledge about relevant family law and its influence on partnering decisions. This study is particularly pertinent to chapter four of the Green Paper on 'strengthening marriage'.

Almost two-thirds of the interviewees saw marriage as an ideal family form, in that it symbolised stability and commitment. Interestingly, this included the majority of cohabitees and half the lone mothers. This ideal view parallels the view of marriage taken in the Green Paper. However, respondents took a different view of the moral reality of their own situations. All the cohabitants had considered marriage. All indicated that most people assumed they were married and that no stigma was attached to cohabiting. They had rejected marriage largely because they thought it made no difference to the success of their relationships or they had previous bad experiences of marriage. About half of these respondents actively saw marriage as in some way threatening to their relationship, because it would change their partners' behaviour for the worse. Lone mothers are more likely to see marriage as a source of unhappiness and disappointment. A smaller group of cohabitants (four of the eleven) wished to marry and saw cohabitation as a trial marriage. While these mothers saw the cost of a 'proper marriage' as a disincentive, they did not doubt the validity of cohabitation as a partnering and parenting form. Marriage was again more of an ideal rather than some superior family form in practice. However, few of the married mothers had actually got married because of its ideal characteristics, and around half had done so because of their wider social position in terms of religious beliefs or pressure from partners or parents. Many respondents saw the ideals of marriage as just that, an ideal not accessible in practice. For many mothers, particularly the cohabiting and lone mothers, cohabitation was seen as equal, or even superior to, marriage. These views are not acknowledged in New Labour's 'social threat'/'social problem' view of unmarried families expressed in the Green Paper. The lone mothers in the sample commonly hated the Child Support Agency, linked to the misconception that acceptance of 'CSA money' would mean that they would be forced to allow fathers contact with their children. This had led two of the lone mothers to refuse co-operation with the agency, despite a 40 per cent reduction in their benefit levels.

The practical advantages of marriage given by respondents, whether married or not, are particularly illuminating. These do not refer to the superiority of marriage for partnering and parenting as the Green Paper supposes, but to marriage as a social symbol. This symbolism is achieved in two major ways – through a change of name and through a full-blown 'white wedding' in church.

The desire by cohabitants to have the same surname as their children and partner was cited as a major reason for marriage, and this had been a major reason for marrying given by four of the five mothers who had previously cohabited. The birth of children commonly precipitated a move. Conversely, most of the cohabiting mothers saw a different surname from their partner and children as the greatest disadvantage of not marrying. (Two had formally changed their surname to their partner's and another two families had all adopted double-barrelled names). Female name-changing is of course not a legal requirement, but is a powerful tradition. Presumably, this is taken as a social signifier of a 'proper family', one which follows accepted gender norms about roles and responsibilities – the very same reason why name changing is actually rejected by many professional married women and by those with 'alternative' feminist views.

The cohabiting mothers were not prepared to marry in a simple register office wedding. If they were to marry, it was on condition that they had a full-blown white church wedding. It was the wedding as a social display and not the institution or ideal of marriage as a partnership or parenting form which was endowed with significance in the context of their lives – underscored by the fact that eight of these mothers had refused their partners' offer of marriage in a register office. Those cohabitees in the 'trial marriage' group fully accepted that this might mean that they never married. These were the only unmarried respondents who indicated that financial incentives would have a decisive effect on their decision to marry – but only if this enabled them to obtain the highly desired 'white wedding' in church.

Marriage was often seen as an ideal state, but in terms of everyday moral adequacy few respondents saw marriage as a superior partnering or parenting form. It was the strength of a mother's relationship with her partner that was decisive, and this was unaffected by whether marriage had taken place or not. Similarly, marriage was seen as largely irrelevant to the welfare of children. Respondents, unlike government spokespersons, did not easily confuse partnering and parenting forms (married, cohabiting and so on) with those processes (love, support and communication) that lead to the success or failure of these relationships. The respondents' moral judgments are rather more sophisticated than those of the government. Rather, the significance of marriage for respondents was more that of a social symbol. The proposals to modernise the civil marriage service are unlikely to influence those seeking the traditional rituals that a church wedding offers. Equally, few respondents saw marriage in financial terms or, if they did so, this was secondary to their socially derived beliefs about the signifying role of marriage. Here again, as with lone mothers' decisions about the compatibility of paid work with good mothering, we can discern a gap between people's actual moral behaviour and that assumed in the Green Paper.

This essentially social signifying role of marriage was buttressed by the 'common law marriage myth'. Nearly all respondents firmly believed that the law treated cohabitants with children of the relationship in all respects as if they were married. This allowed marriage to be dismissed as 'only a piece of paper'. Although the law has not recognised common law marriage since the Clandestine Marriages Act of 1753, both married and unmarried cohabiting couples volunteered this as an acknowledged legal status. Nearly all the cohabiting mothers believed, inaccurately, they would be entitled to a pension or other allowances on the strength of their on their partner's contributions, only one was aware of the different tax treatment of cohabitants, and again only one was aware that cohabitant dependent partners cannot make claims for maintenance or other provision equivalent to that of a spouse under the divorce legislation. Nor was there any understanding that strict property law, rather than family law, applies to owner-occupying cohabitants on relationship breakdown. Unmarried cohabitees thereby have little claim on their family home even when separation occurs after many years, or on death (Children Act 1989, schedule 1, para 2). Nor, when a cohabiting partner dies, does the survivor have an automatic right to inherit any of the estate on intestacy (although a claim may now be made for financial provision, itself less generous than that permitted to spouses – Inheritance Provision for Dependants Act, 1975, amended by Law Reform Succession Act, 1995).

Only one cohabitant in the sample was aware of this. None had taken steps to make their position more secure by making wills, or entering into cohabitation agreements, and remained unaware of any need to do so. In addition there was an almost complete ignorance of the law relating to acquisition of parental responsibility by unmarried fathers. All the cohabiting mothers, together with a lone mother who had jointly registered the birth with the father, believed that unmarried fathers gained the legal status of fatherhood (parental responsibility) through jointly registering the birth. The majority of married mothers (six of the eleven) similarly believed this was the legal position of unmarried fathers. This is also a myth. Unmarried fathers can, currently, only acquire parental responsibility either by entering into a formal 'parental responsibility agreement' (in the prescribed form) with the mother, or by court order. None of the cohabiting mothers had heard of this – not surprising perhaps when this information is deliberately withheld from parents on the birth of a child. Without exception, they had no idea that a partner's legal status was in any way inferior to that of a married father. All of them believed that, should they die, the father would automatically become the legal guardian of their children. In fact, for this to happen it would be necessary for the mother to either have appointed the father as testamentary guardian or to have entered into a parental responsibility agreement with him (Children Act, 1989, sections 4 and 5, McRae, 1993).

This belief in the equivalence of 'common law marriage' is no doubt sustained by developments in the law giving some increased rights to cohabitants (but under which marriage is still clearly privileged), and the fact that the state has it both ways in assessing entitlement to means-tested welfare benefits – cohabiting couples are treated exactly as if they were married and their means are aggregated. Ninety per cent of all respondents thought that any unequal treatment of cohabitees in law was quite wrong. In this context, the Green Paper's cursory suggestion that more information should be made available to cohabitants about their inferior legal position is woefully inadequate. It is interesting that the only substantial change in the law around cohabitation is the proposal, summarised in the Green Paper (paras 4.17–4.18), to give most jointly registering fathers automatic parental responsibility. Rather than any move towards a 'lifestyle choice' view of cohabitation, as in France or Scandinavia, this reform appears more as a reflection of the 'social threat' discourse about the breakdown of traditional gendered families. The proposed change can help create such families *de jure* (Smart, 1987). This may be buttressed by the linked 'social threat' view that children in unmarried families must perforce have weak male role models.

The 'common law marriage myth' is both pervasive and deeply held. In a wider sense the ignorance of the law it displays is quite rational. This is because couples generally see their partnership – and its strength or weakness – in terms of a relationship, not in terms of an institution. Indeed, as we saw earlier, for most the institution of marriage is valued simply as a social signifier of their relationship in their social network. Few mothers share the government's apparent view that the institutional form of partnership governs its success, or tends to make people into better parents. In this way chapter four of the Green Paper on 'Strengthening Marriage' perpetuates the 'rationality mistake' we identified in the New Deal for Lone Parents. People do not decide upon their moral economies according to the model of rational economic man and the rational legal subject.

Conclusion

New Labour is keen to use legislation to encourage what it sees as desirable family practices, and to discourage others. The 1998 Green Paper *Supporting Families* reveals some of the risks of this type of intervention. First of all, the proposals are permeated by what we have called 'the rationality mistake'. The government implicitly assumes a universal model of 'rational economic man' and his close relative the 'rational legal subject'. This does not appear to be how people actually do make important decisions about their moral economies. Rather, people seem to take such decisions with reference to moral and socially negotiated views about what behaviour is expected as right and proper. Such negotiations, and the views that result, varies in particular social contexts. Decisions are still made rationally, but with a different sort of rationality to that assumed by the conventional economic and policy model. Above all, such decisions have a moral content and are taken in a moral framework.

If people do not act according to the model of rational economic man and the rational legal subject, then legislation based on these assumptions might well be ineffectual. This is what seems to have happened with the pilot New Deal for Lone Parents, and the proposals to strengthen marriage seem to be taking a similar course. There are several possible responses to such policy failure. One response is to reconsider the policy in terms of its operation and assumptions. This seems particularly appropriate for the New Deal for Lone Parents, where apparently a massive 94 per cent of eligible lone parents had not responded. Similarly, given the high rates of cohabitation in Britain, and the widespread evaluation that this is equivalent to marriage in most practical and emotional terms, then basing a policy of supporting families almost entirely upon marriage as an institution seems to leave the government with its head in the sand. The government has in fact chosen another alternative to policy re-evaluation – assume that the policy is right and make it compulsory. Implicitly, therefore, they assume that those affected are wrong.

We may call this response to policy inadequacy the 'morality mistake' and it appears on two levels. A first stage is to assume that people are not behaving 'rationally' (in terms or rational economic man and the rational legal subject) because of lack of information or ignorance. Hence, for example, the need for lone parents to have childcare and labour market situations explained to them. If policy is still ineffectual – as seems quite likely – then this 'morality mistake' can move to a second, more authoritarian, stage. People are not behaving 'rationally' because of their own moral or cultural deviancy. Compulsion may be justified as the unfortunate effect of their 'poverty of ambition and poverty of expectation' or as resulting from the 'dependency culture'. The idea that people take what they consider to be morally appropriate decisions in their situation, and that they have worked hard in reaching these decisions, is not considered. As the experience of the Child

Support Act has shown, however, social compulsion is quite likely to be inefficient, as well as forcing large numbers of people to do what they consider wrong. Ironically, in view of the theoretical claims of communitarianism, such legislation also rides roughshod over the varying community contexts in which people reach such decisions. Like the CSA, legislation of this sort will attract widespread resentment as well as remaining inefficient. The alternative is to try to develop supportive and flexible legislative frameworks which do recognise the varying ways in which people take moral decisions.

Notes

1 A basic framework of maximum working hours and extended maternity and parental leave is being introduced through the Fairness at Work Act 1999, partly under the pressure of EU directives. However, the former contain many exceptions while the latter will effectively exclude low earners, since maternity leave over 18 weeks and all paternity leave is unpaid. These low-earners will include many lone parents or those living on inner-cities that the government sees as most likely to display aberrant parenting behaviour.
2 The gendered moral rationalities were identified by taking from the interview transcripts all statements about motherhood and paid work, and children's needs, including contradictory statements within one account. Similar statements were grouped together. In this way the three main forms of relationship between motherhood and paid work were distinguished and the triangular model in Figure 5.2 constructed. The position of each interviewee was then plotted as appropriate.

6
Housing and the Flexible Labour Market: Responding to Risk

Janet Ford

Introduction

One area of social and economic life argued to be 'riskier' now than in the recent past is that of the labour market. The major factors influencing this growing risk are widely discussed and generally agreed. The *extent* of labour market insecurity and risk has, however, been contested and, by some commentators, discounted, as either wholly cyclical in nature or so marginal as to be insignificant. The last three or four years have, however, seen a growing consensus that the impact of structural change in the labour market is significant, and both more widespread and more visible, taking the form of what is often referred to as 'flexible' employment (for example, Gregg and Wadsworth, 1995; Beatson, 1995; White, 1996; Dex and McCullogh, 1997). What is encompassed by the term 'flexibility' is itself contested but candidates include self-employment, temporary work, agency work, part-time work, annualised hours and zero hours contracts. At the same time, *and overall*, positions in the labour market known to be 'riskier' still remain a minority of all labour market positions. Data for heads of households from the Winter 1997/98 *Labour Force Survey* indicate that around a third of all households are headed by someone in a risky position.

The current complement to the risk society is the individualised society. Again, the influences on, and growth of, individualisation and the transfer of responsibilities to individuals are discussed in a substantial literature. The issues for this chapter do not require a reiteration of these literatures and debates (although they are the significant backcloth). Rather, the chapter starts from the recognition that labour market risks have increased alongside developments that have resulted in the individualisation of the responsibility for risk. There are examples of this process within the labour market where employers seek to transfer the responsibilities they previously held for sickness, holiday and pension provision to workers who are recruited not as employees but as nominally self-employed. Similar processes can also be seen in the on-going changes to key areas of social policy whereby the emphasis of the responsibility for risk-management is being transferred from the state to individuals and households (for a general discussion see for example Taylor-Gooby, 1998). Examples of this include, most clearly, the reduction in safety-net provision for unemployed mortgagors Income Support Mortgage Interest (ISMI) and the presumed take-up of market provided insurance cover Mortgage Protection Private Insurance (MPPI), but equally, a series of changes that restrict (in duration and amount) the state's responsibility for income maintenance. These might encourage, and if cut further, require individuals to take greater personal responsibility for the risks of unemployment through market based unemployment, or income replacement insurance. Other current or potential instances include a growing requirement for greater self-provision with respect to pensions and long-term care.

Underpinning these developments in public policy are a set of assumptions about the ways in which individuals will respond to risk and insecurity. In particular, it is assumed that individuals accurately perceive the risks they face and that they are 'risk averse'. As a consequence, individuals will take responsibility for precluding or managing these risks. Those with the highest probabilities of risk will be foremost in seeking to minimize the risk, leading to the fear of *adverse selection* by those who provide market-based insurance, because such a situation reduces their ability to pool risks, (i.e. off-set bad against good risks). Further, once individuals have to draw on the safety-net there is an assumption that they will be less inclined to expose themselves to the same risk again before they have to. This is the *'moral hazard'* that all providers of safety-nets have to guard against. As a consequence, state and market provision have to develop a set of checks and balances to preclude the extension of unintended incentives for such 'naturalistic' or 'economically rational' behaviour. Further assumptions are that individuals calculate risks and returns, and hence cost, along with terms and conditions, can deter the acceptance of insurance. By implication, lower costs will widen take-up.

There are, of course, critiques of the arguments as outlined above. Two are considered here briefly. The first is whether the expectations and characterisations of individual and household behaviour are well founded. The second is the extent to which the risks traditionally provided for by the state are ones that can be accommodated effectively by the private insurance market, and these two issues may well be connected.

With respect to the first issue, there is evidence that both the perception of risk and the preferred ways of managing risk are influenced by cultural and/or psychological dispositions just as much as by 'rational' 'economic' calculation (Lewis *et al.*, 1995). With respect to specific areas of provision and decision-making, Whylie *et al.* (1998) have shown how negative attitudes to insurance are widespread, influencing responses. Ford and Kempson (1997) showed that, against the prediction, there was an *inverse* relationship between the experience of unemployment and the take-up of MPPI. Similar findings are reported by Cebulla *et al.* (1998) with respect to both the current and intended take-up of insurance to replace income following unemployment. In all instances, the writers indicated that personal dispositions and attitudes were important influences on the decisions made and resultant behaviour. Further, distrust of the market has also been identified, for example, in Parker's work on households' response to the suggestion that they should rely on private insurance provision for long-term care. In more general terms there is also evidence from the *British Social Attitudes Survey* of the enduring commitment to state welfare provision (Taylor-Gooby, 1995; Brook *et al.*, 1996), sometimes on principle and sometimes due to enlightened self-interest. It is also likely that continuing evidence of mis-selling in relation to private pensions, and some doubts of the wisdom of endowment mortgages will have had engendered some caution about the desirability of market provision. So even if the private market can provide – individuals may not support the idea.

The second set of criticisms addresses the principles of private insurance and its capacity to take over previously state-provided welfare. Burchardt and Hills (1997), for example, have suggested that the private market may not necessarily be as effective a response as supposed. Centrally, the situations that need to be insured are not necessarily ones where the theoretical requirements of an insurance market can always be met. Costs may also be higher than under state provision. Walker *et al.* (1995) have specifically questioned the ability of the private market to cover unemployment.

This chapter provides an empirically-based consideration of some of the issues outlined above by exploring three questions:

- Are mortgagors at risk in the labour market?
- To what extent are these risks perceived by individuals and households?
- What is their range of responses to labour market risk; firstly, the extent to which mortgagors use private insurance to cover risk and secondly the other options available to and chosen by them?

Data are presented from a study of mortgagor households' response to risk and the nature of their risk management[1] and from a study of families' response to unemployment in the flexible labour market.[2] These two studies make useful complements in so far as the former focuses primarily on the private insurance safety-net while the second focuses on the widest range of ways in which households may mange labour market risk. The first relates only to mortgagors, the second to households from all tenures but with a predominance of mortgagors.

Mortgagors provide a particularly useful 'test case' for some of the ideas under consideration. Historically home-ownership has been relatively risk-free but is now increasingly 'at risk' as labour market opportunities change and the state safety-net for those in receipt of subsistence benefits is curtailed (Ford and Wilcox, 1998; Ford, 1998). As from October 1995, mortgagors with new loans who lose all income and become eligible for Income Support or Job Seeker's Allowance receive no help with their eligible mortgage interest (ISMI) for nine months. Pre-October 1995 borrowers on IS/JSA receive no assistance with eligible interest for the first two months, 50 per cent interest for the following four months and only thereafter, eligible interest in full. The announcement that these cuts were to be implemented was explicitly linked to the expectation that mortgagors would take out private insurance to cover their mortgage payments (MPPI) in the 'ISMI gap'. The recent White Paper on welfare reform affirmed this policy (DSS, 1998).

Risk and the flexible labour market

Analysis of the *Labour Force Survey* indicates that in early 1998 one third of all heads of household occupied a labour market position where, relative to those with a full-time permanent job, the risks were greater (Table 6.1 and below). These risks are ones of unemployment, failed self-employment, temporary working, of poorer terms and conditions of employment, of income volatility and of variable working hours. These might be thought of as 'direct' risks and can be contrasted with 'consequential' risks (see below).

Table 6.1 also shows the distribution of these risk positions by tenure, showing the higher risk to tenants than owners, but that it is only with respect to unemployment that the pattern of risk varies markedly. In total, one in five mortgagor heads of household had a 'risk' position and a further two percent were unemployed.

These data are, however, cross sectional and do not indicate the potential incidence of risk over a period of time. Some indication of

Table 6.1 Employment status of heads of households in, or seeking employment, by tenure, winter 1997–8 (%)

	Mortgagor H of H %	Renter H of H %	All H of H[1] %
Full-time permanent employee	76	51	67
Part-time permanent employee	3	12	6
Full-time self-employed	14	11	14
Part-time self-employed	1	5	2
Full-time temporary employee	3	2	3
Part-time temporary employee	1	1	1
Trainee or unpaid family worker	–		1
Unemployed	2	18	6

[1] In addition to mortgagors and renters this figure includes outright owners, shared owners, those living rent free and squatting.
Source: Labour Force Survey, Winter, December 1997–February 1998.

the incidence of risk was obtained from the *British Household Panel Survey* data (BHPS) for the period 1990–95. Considering all mortgagor heads of household in 1990, the analysis showed that 28 per cent had experienced *at least* one change of employment status over the period. Of all those experiencing some change, 18 per cent had had at least one period of self-employment while 32 per cent were employed or self-employed in 1995, but had had a spell of unemployment at some time since 1990.[3] Thus, continuity of employment status remains the norm, but changes of employment status are not insubstantial and a greater proportion of mortgagor heads of household experienced a risk position over the period 1990–5 than did so at any one point in time.

Associated with these 'direct' risks from particular types of labour market positions are 'consequential' risks. These might take the form of, for example, reduced standards of living (currently and in the future as for example might follow from lack of pension provision), prolonged ill-health (continuing to work when ill due to the lack of eligibility for sick pay), or an inability to pay housing costs and so the risk of the loss of the property. Table 6.2 indicates that the risk of mortgage arrears is consistently and significantly higher for those households where the head of household is unemployed, in part-time work or self-employed (is in a flexible labour market position), compared to those with full-time, permanent employment (see also Burrows and Ford, 1998). It is also the case that labour market 'incidents' (unemployment, reduced commission, re-employment at a lower wage, etc.) account for more than half of the reasons given for mortgage arrears (Ford, 1998).

Table 6.2   Mortgage arrears by employment status of head of household 1993–4
to 1996–7 (%)

	In arrears (% of each group)			
	1993/94	1994/95	1995/96	1996/97
Full-time employees	5	3	3	2
Part-time employees	8	9	7	6
Small business owners	7	4	3	2
Self-employed sole-trader	12	8	6	8
Unemployed	24	19	22	19

Source: SEH 1993–7 (own analysis).

These same categories of mortgagors are similarly ranked if payment
difficulties (i.e. struggling to pay for housing although managing to do
so) are considered rather than mortgage arrears.

Perceptions of risk

If there is a significant minority of risk positions in the labour market,
and associated consequential risks, to what extent do individuals
recognise these risks, in general and, where appropriate, for themselves
in particular? The issue is important for several reasons. Risk recognition is a necessary element shaping the behavioural response predicted
by theories of insurance and embodied in public policy developments.
Equally, long standing work in sociology has noted that perceptions
are real in their consequences, irrespective of the relationship between
objective and subjective assessments, again raising a potential challenge to the normative assumptions about the subsequent behaviour.

There is already some evidence that individuals' perceptions of
employment insecurity *in general* have grown. Evidence from the
British Social Attitudes Survey (Spencer, 1996) indicates that while perceptions of insecurity are clearly influenced by the stage of the economic cycle, the level of their 'recovery' is currently less than would be
expected on purely cyclical grounds. There is also evidence that
respondents' assessment of their own insecurity does not necessarily
mirror their general assessment of the labour market. In short, while
attitudes (generalised, emotional perspectives) to the labour market are
ones that increasingly recognise job insecurity, beliefs (cognitive/situa-
tion specific views) are more variable. Further useful evidence comes
from an omnibus survey of one thousand adults in employment conducted as part of the study of households' response to labour market risk

(Cebulla *et al.*, 1998), other, more detailed aspects of which are reported below. This suggests that individuals' perceptions or beliefs about their job insecurity do not always tally with actuarial assessments that were calculated according to the practice and procedure of credit risk assessment. Individuals were asked to assess the likelihood of their being unemployed for two or more months in the next twelve months. Only 6.5 per cent considered this to be likely or very likely. These responses were then compared with an actuarial assessment of the degree of risk associated with these individuals. This showed that a higher proportion of respondents would be deemed 'at risk' than was suggested by the personal assessment of the individuals concerned. Overall, the available evidence appears to suggest that an individual's perception of their own labour market risk lags their view of both the general position and the actuarial assessment. However, other studies (Doling and Ford, 1996), indicate that this gap or lag is closed, to varying degrees, where respondents have themselves experienced labour market disruption.

Responses to risk – the role of private insurance

Notwithstanding any apparent 'inaccuracy' in the way people assess their vulnerability in the labour market (an issue worthy of unpacking and undertaken elsewhere – see Quilgars and Abbott, 1999), recent changes in the labour market plus those in welfare provision will, potentially, have focussed attention on how such risks are to be managed. This section explores responses to risk. The initial focus is on understanding the extent of take-up and effectiveness of private insurance as a risk management response, the approach assumed by current welfare policy as already discussed above. In this way it is possible to explore the extent to which households' management of risk accords with the expectations and assumptions embedded in current policy. This is followed by a consideration of a wider range of response to risk. As already noted, data are drawn from two studies, one on responses to MPPI and one on families' response to unemployment.

Protection through the market – the take-up of MPPI

The study of mortgagors' response to MPPI had a number of components. One component was a random sample survey of over eight hundred borrowers, drawn from three large mortgage lenders who between them accounted for more than 40 per cent of the mortgage market, and a postal survey of twenty-seven mortgage lenders, designed to identify the take-up of MPPI and to understand the factors that influenced take-up.

In 1997, reported take-up of MPPI ranged from 16 per cent according to lenders to 21 per cent according to borrowers. The latter figure is likely to be the more reliable not least because around 50 per cent of mortgages are sold through intermediaries and the originator of the loan would be unlikely to know if the broker had also sold MPPI. Borrowers might though know what they were sold (or bought) although it is recognised that mortgagors are not always certain of the nature or purpose of their products.

The survey data can be used to make a simple, descriptive comparison between those who had MPPI, those who had considered but not taken the insurance and those who had not considered MPPI at all. Four sets of characteristics were examined: personal and financial circumstances (income, employment status, savings etc); aspects of the mortgage loan (size, date of mortgage etc); the borrower's exposure to labour market risk and their attitudes to risk and insurance. The analysis showed that personal and financial circumstances were not nearly as important in determining take-up of MPPI as some might have expected while characteristics of the mortgage were important with take-up much higher amongst post October 1995 borrowers (suggesting either that lenders were selling more effectively than previously and/or that borrowers were aware of the cuts to the state safety-net).

In relation to the impact of borrowers' exposure to labour market risk on the take-up of MPPI, Table 6.3 shows, contrary to the theoretical expectation, that those at greatest risk were not the most willing to insure. The table provides little evidence to support the fear of adverse selection. Rather it indicates that those most likely to insure were those most likely to be in permanent employment.

Finally, a set of attitude statements allowed respondents to be classified as 'anti', 'pro' or 'neither anti nor pro' insurance. Seventy-two percent were neither anti nor pro with the remainder split roughly between the pros and antis. Those who were pro-insurance were three times more likely to insure than those who were anti. However, being pro-insurance (or anti-insurance) had little if any relationship to material circumstances or risk factors. Those with MPPI were, however, more heavily insured overall, and often MPPI covered them for risks already insured through another of their policies, a finding indicative of a pre-disposition towards heightened risk awareness and risk aversion.

Table 6.3 Relationship between MPPI take-up and risk factors related to claiming (%)

Risk factors	Has MPPI (*n*=171)	Considered MPPI (*n*=191)	Not considered (*n*=476)
In last five years			
Lost job	26	31	43
Own business failed*	28	30	42
Out of work, sickness/accident*	13	13	74
None of these	20	23	57
Redundancies at workplace in last 5 years			
Yes	19	26	55
No	24	24	52
Job security next 12 months			
Very secure	19	20	61
Fairly secure	23	24	53
Fairly insecure	28	40	32
Very insecure*	22	23	55

Source: Borrowers' postal survey, Ford and Kempson, 1997.
* Statistically significant.

Potentially, a number of the factors discussed above correlated with each other, and multi-variate analysis was used to identify the model which best explained MPPI take-up. The first model included all respondents and showed that four factors were significant in increasing the odds of taking out MPPI: a mortgage taken out post October 1995, neither the largest nor smallest of loans, possession of other insurance and positive attitudes towards insurance. A second analysis, excluding those not in employment (in order to include the variables on respondents' perception of their job security and experience of labour market disruption), showed three significant factors increasing the odds of take-up; a mortgage with more than 20 years still to run (i.e. a recent mortgage), a high level of insurance cover and positive attitudes to insurance. Neither of the employment related variables were significant. (For fuller details of the analysis see Ford and Kempson, 1997). Thus, attitudes to insurance along with pre-dispositions towards risk are central in understanding take-up of MPPI. Not dissimilar findings, again stressing the importance of psychological traits (a 'pessimistic' bias as opposed to an 'optimistic' bias), were reported in the study of families' response to unemployment with respect to both current take-up and future intentions to insure against the loss of income due to unemployment. Further, a series of focus group discussions that formed part of this latter study also revealed some negative attitudes towards insurance that were not simply related to market inefficiencies but to whether individuals believed they could 'trust' insurers to pay, an issue discussed with respect to mortgagors and MPPI below.

Other findings from the study of MPPI take-up that cast doubt on the conventionally-argued responses to risk concern the evidence of a relatively poorly developed relationship between the cost of insurance and its take-up. Despite significant reductions in the price since 1995, take-up barely changed between 1994 and early 1997. In the light of the findings reported above, this relationship is perhaps unsurprising in the sense that attitudinal factors form the context within which decisions about insurance are made. Where there are negative attitudes, even substantial reductions in cost may fail to change people's minds. The relatively limited increase in take-up, however, also suggests that the majority of those whose attitudes to insurance are neutral, are not influenced by cost either.

In the light of the finding that take-up of MPPI is significantly influenced by attitudes to insurance, the nature of these attitudes need to be explored further. Before doing that, however, it is important to look briefly at the effectiveness of MPPI, if only because amongst those lacking a principled objection to market provision, this may be an important influence on the way their attitudes to private provision are shaped.

The effectiveness of MPPI

Around the time of the cutbacks to ISMI in 1995, reservations about the likely effectiveness of private sector provision were raised on both empirical and theoretical grounds. Issues raised included the extent of 'exclusions' to MPPI, the costs of policies as well as the fundamental insurability of risks such as unemployment (Walker *et al.*, 1995; TUC, 1996; NACAB, 1995; Burchardt and Hills, 1997), and centrally, whether insurers would pay out when claims were lodged.

As part of the study of MPPI, two further samples of borrowers were used to examine 'effectiveness'. First, a random sample of claimants provided by two MPPI insurers (the MPPI sample). Secondly, a sample of IS/JSA claimants made available by the Department of Social Security, some of whom were now receiving ISMI. A proportion of these people also had MPPI[4]. The reason for the second sample was to enable us to explore the relative merits of the state and private safety-net and the claim that MPPI filled the ISMI gap. (For full details of the study see Kempson *et al.*, 1999.)

Amongst the MPPI sample, seven out of every ten claims made were paid. For those in the IS/JSA sample, and making a claim on an MPPI, claiming was less effective. First, under half of those with MPPI were able to make a claim and second, of this group, only just over five out of every ten did so successfully. Those who had MPPI, but could not claim, were in this position because they had lost income for a reason that was not covered by their policy. Thus the evidence is, amongst those claiming, that those in greatest need (as signified by eligibility for IS/JSA), had the poorer outcome from MPPI.

Claims were usually turned down either because insurers ruled that borrowers had been sacked or had resigned as opposed to being made redundant; or because at the time of the claim borrowers were temporary or contract workers and so not covered by the terms of their policy; or because they claimed for a health condition that was deemed to be 'pre-existing'. Just occasionally, borrowers accepted that the insurer's decision was appropriate, but in many more cases they felt they had been treated badly. Both borrowers who were rejected, and borrowers who found they could not claim, often then cancelled their policies. In addition, a proportion of MPPI holders (particularly amongst those on IS/JSA) cancelled their policies because of the costs.

Arguably, the ultimate measure of effectiveness is whether MPPI precludes arrears. In total, 22 per cent of those receiving an MPPI payout developed mortgage arrears. This situation resulted for several reasons including the length of the deferral period before MPPI paid out and payouts that were less than the borrowers current mortgage payment. This latter situation could arise as a result of borrowers insuring for the payment current at the time they take out the policy. Upward interest rate movements (or the ending of a discounted mortgage) could then leave them with a payment shortfall which could not be met where they lacked savings or a partner in employment to help meet the shortfall. Not surprisingly, those on IS/JSA and receiving MPPI were more likely to be in arrears than non IS/JSA claimants.

Drawing the evidence on MPPI together, one conclusion is that it serves all borrowers relatively poorly, and that the fewer resources (greater needs) borrowers have, the poorer they are served by private insurance. Further, as already shown, these people who took out MPPI were most likely to be those whose attitudes to insurance were positive. These poor outcomes may not sustain such attitudes nor do anything to convince others to take the cover.

Attitudes to insurance

Attitudes and beliefs towards safety-net provision for mortgagors operate at a number of different levels. At the most generalised level, home buyers are likely to have views on the principle of provision; whether mortgagors should be helped at all. The suggestion by Munro *et al.* (1998) that mortgagors often had to balance contradictory views on this matter – noting that home-owners believed they should be 'independent' while at the same time arguing that the state's concern to encourage greater home-ownership meant the state had some responsibilities to support them when they were in difficulty – was articulated by a majority of the sixty borrowers interviewed qualitatively in the study of those claiming MPPI and ISMI. A third of those interviewed thought that the state alone should provide the safety-net while half indicated that in their view there should be mixed safety-net provision through the state and the private market. However, over a quarter thought that individuals should take full responsibility through private insurance.

These findings might be read as indicating growing support for market provision. However, they must be taken in the context of the considerable evidence of dissatisfaction with the market amongst those who, in principle, accept its potential (as well as amongst those who reject it on principle). Such feelings ran from deep distrust *per se* to anxieties about the current operation of the market, sometimes, often the result of the experience of a failed claim:

> I think they're alright while you're giving them money, but when you want to claim they just don't want to know.
>
> ...all they are doing is looking to the interests of their own company, deeply distrust them.
>
> I think there needs to be a major watchdog over these guys because they are trickier than anything I've ever seen...tricky dickies and they know it and they've got away with it.

However, and perhaps surprisingly, the study also showed that a successful claim did not preclude negative attitudes. Amongst those interviewed in depth, most were not as positive after their claim as they had been on taking out the policy. Three-quarters of them expressed serious reservations about the operation of the safety-net, although they did remain positive towards MPPI overall. Support had cooled due to delays in payments and 'ineptitude' on the part of insurers. Other dissatisfactions centred around a lack of transparency in the policies, the time limit on claims (typically twelve months), and the 'excessive' requirements placed on them as claimants for (repeated) documentary evidence of their circumstances.

Thus, the extent of support for private insurance is a more complex matter than sometimes suggested. In particular, even amongst those who see a role for private safety-net provision and support the broad direction of change there are reservations about the current operation of the private market that led a proportion to shun it. As a result, most borrowers facing labour market risks (as well as other risks that disrupt mortgage payments) do so without access to either a private or public safety-net while the minority eligible for IS/JSA have wait periods before help with their mortgage interest is available.

These findings then raise the question of whether and how individuals and households plan to respond to the risks that increasingly jeopardise home-ownership? The study reported above collected only limited data on the way people sought to manage, but this showed the importance of reliance on family and friends, savings, earnings from other household members, benefit payments, other insurance payments and the use of credit. However, these responses related to support once they had lost their jobs and not to earlier, planning to minimise the impact of unemployment should it occur. Detailed information on the widest range of responses is, however, available from the study of families' responses to the risks of the flexible labour market, in particular from a series of focus group discussions and 90 qualitative interviews undertaken in two different locations.

Responses to risk : a wider range of approaches

The term 'response' is used to signify the respondents' approach to managing risk. In considering these responses, there are some important conceptual distinctions to be made. For example, responses may be proactive and planned-deliberate actions taken to minimise the risks of unemployment. Alternatively, responses may be reactive, essentially coping strategies after the event and in the absence of prior planning. The detail and adequacy of these approaches is an empirical matter, but it is likely that there will be both mixed responses and less than adequate responses, not least because the distribution of economic resources will preclude some who are proactive from making adequate provision.

Preliminary analysis of the data indicates at least seven approaches to managing labour market risk. These can be labelled as:

- Occupationally-derived financial security
- Routinization of risk
- Work place positioning
- Domestic positioning

- Self-reliance/self-provisioning
- Security through the state or market
- Fatalism/denial

This typology is preliminary, but incorporates dimensions of both choice and constraint and a recognition that material factors interact with attitudes and psychological predispositions to structure responses. The responses are not mutually exclusive – even those too fatalistic to be pro-active may have occupational provision or routinize risk – and not exhaustive, but they are suggestive of the variety and complexity of risk responses. No attempt is made at this stage to identify a distribution of responses.

Given that this chapter has already provided evidence on market based insurance as one possible response to risk, the discussion here will concentrate on the other six responses. Space precludes a detailed analysis but the nature and content of each approach will be considered, along with some preliminary indications of the extent to which the responses are associated with different socio-economic groups and different orientations to risk. If personal dispositions, attitudinal and cultural factors structure the degree of acceptance of private insurance, it is at least as likely that they will play some part in the other risk management processes that individuals and households devise.

Occupationally-derived financial security

Labour market insecurity can be mitigated by structures of employment. For example, permanent jobs normally have associated with them redundancy rights, sick pay, pension provision etc. Focus group respondents often noted that access to such rights, either through their employment or that of their partner, were key components in their responses to insecurity: 'I've always had the sense that my...wife who works as a teacher gets a good pension...so I know I have this fall back position.' This is not a pro-active response to risk, (although topping up pension provision was noted as a way of ensuring that there would be 'enough'), but it does set the framework in which other planning decisions can be made. This was seen in an exchange between two focus group members about the merits of saving/investing to manage labour market risk where one respondent said:

> It's like you going on about saving and how you did that for a year. There's no way [I could do that]. If I'd had that [the money saved], I'm sorry, I'd have been on that plane and I'd be gone...[but] I've got a pension as well and two life insurances.

In addition, in a core of public sector/blue chip organisations, restructuring has been handled through voluntary redundancy packages. Where respondents had experienced job loss in these circumstances, the nature of the packages had provided the security. Increasingly it is the case that professional and managerial households experience unemployment and temporary contract working. Thus the issue is not that they are immune to risk, but that the historical structure of employment conditions provides many with a legacy of security. The focus group discussions also indicated that around this occupational provision, individuals and households developed other responses, relying significantly on financial investment strategies. Their form and extent was though likely to be influenced by attitudinal factors and their fundamental predispositions to risk, so some 'insured' while others 'saved'.

Occupationally-based provision is differentially available however, with the responses outlined above typically raised by those in professional and managerial positions. Most focus group respondents in socio-economic groups D and E lacked comparable occupational security nor gained much advantage from restructuring packages while the picture for those in the intermediate socio-economic groups was mixed. As a consequence, those in the lower socio-economic groups had to manage risk in different ways.

Routinization of risk

Most of the focus group participants in unskilled employment had at some point in the recent past experienced unemployment or changes in their terms and conditions of work. Given this, there was evidence that such individuals simply saw turnover and poor jobs as 'how things were'. The risk was acknowledged but routinized: 'Well, I'd just go out and get any paid work…it doesn't matter what it is.' This response was also seen in the detailed qualitative interviews where unskilled workers commented that there were plenty of poor jobs around (for the moment) so the issue was less one of re-employment but the nature of that re-employment which might involve lower pay/irregular hours/unsocial hours/nominal self-employment etc. Risk was perceived and experienced, but it was this very risk which provided the basis for continuing employment:

> In some ways I've almost embraced the insecurity which I think is prevalent.

> It's quite secure even inside that insecurity because there's a lot of work going.

The need to work with the grain of labour market insecurity was heightened by the absence of other viable responses. For many in flexible work, wages typically precluded saving, insurance for investments, and where insurance was considered, the very flexibility of their work often excluded them from being accepted for a policy.

'Positioning' at work and at home

Here two pro-active responses are treated together because both involve what can be conceptualised as 'defensive decisions'. Respondents talked about the need to 'keep ahead' at work either in terms of input, training, demonstration of skills or motivation etc. such that they were well positioned in relation to their current work and employer but also in relation to the market if they were unemployed: 'He works extremely hard, not that he's a perfectionist but I suppose he is thinking who's watching me?' They also noted that this response sometimes meant making decisions that would leave you well placed to increase hours, or even to stay in the labour market when you might be expected to leave for a period. For example, one or two women noted that they had retained their jobs after having children just in case it was needed:

> I really kept my job because I'm worried ... if he lost his job ... at least one of us would be continually earning.

> I've kept part-time ... would have preferred to be a full-time mum.

> I've kept part-time simply because its just that little bit extra if he has nothing.

There was also evidence of the importance of defensive strategies in the domestic arena, positioning domestic financial matters so as to ease the impact of any risks that materialised. Sometimes these included insurance provision and saving but more typically they did not and rather were about paying off debts or not accepting credit commitments.

> We don't have anything unless we can [pay] cash for it, we don't have anything on HP. We don't have buy now [1998] pay [1999]. We've structured it like that, deliberately structured it like that.

In response to a focus group member who reported a lack of financial 'positioning' at home because 'I just go through life like in a fog, I suppose because I have great optimism about many things'. Another responded:

> I seem to take a slightly more pessimistic approach in terms of from a financial perspective my finances are structured in such a way that

if I lost my job I wouldn't lose my home. I haven't got a lot of [insurance policies] requiring me to find £200 a month ... we have a repayment mortgage because I used to be in financial services so I didn't trust endowments. ... When I took the mortgage, I was single, and every time I used to have a large bonus I used to pay a couple of thousand off ... so I've got a negligible mortgage ... which really helped us when one of us was made redundant because there was the situation where I could say right we know that all we have to find is X a month and everything is covered. I'm very concerned ... about being old, getting ill ... so I'm going to make it my damnest to do everything I possibly can.

An exchange between two focus group members (one who had already experienced job loss) noted:

Respondent 1 Now we're back on our feet ... we will not stop until we are totally secure ... until I've paid for the house.

Respondent 2 That's exactly our strategy, pay now, pay off the mortgage because I feel at least we'll have a home – they won't be able to take that away from you.

While another said: 'I'd rather take a low life and try and pay off the mortgage and feel more stable that way (than pay insurance)' The evidence that some of the consequential risks associated with job insecurity were given high priority (for example, avoiding mortgage default) was strong, in particular in households with children.

These kinds of defensive responses were found throughout the economic spectrum, but were particularly associated with those who lacked much occupational provision. So these responses were frequent amongst those in lower grade white collar or skilled manual work, groups that now have a relatively high exposure to labour market risk. These are also the groups drawn into taking responsibility for more areas of provision and consumption in the 1980s with the opening up of home-ownership and rising consumer expectations. Thus, for this group, labour market insecurity has emerged against a particular background of relatively new and often substantial commitments.

Self-reliance and self-provisioning

Self-reliance is used here to refer to the reactive position whereby individuals facing a risk situation, deal with when it occurs as best they can.

They may adopt this response because proactive planning is not possible or because they reject such planning. A considerable amount has already been written about the ways in which households with few resources manage (for example, Kempson *et al.*, 1994), showing the reliance on family and friends, on credit, on benefit payments etc. and the associated consequences of poor living standards, ill health and increasing social isolation. All these and other outcomes were reported in the focus groups and interviews by those who lacked financial resources and had experienced unemployment, and these issues need not be repeated again.

Self-provisioning, by contrast, here refers to household financial planning for risk, over and above that directly provided as occupational security (see above). One person, occupying an extreme amongst the respondents, noted that 'I've got insurance to cover my insurance.' He had calculated the likely effect of income loss through unemployment compared with the likely pay-out from the insurance. He had mortgage cover in the event of redundancy as well as income protection against an accident: 'If it came [unemployment] ... I'd say to you I've done the calculations and I think we could make it work' Others too reported self-provisioning, if of a less extreme or precisely calculated nature, through financial products such as TESSAs, PEPs, MPPI, shares and savings. While these responses were most common amongst those in professional and managerial jobs (typically permanent jobs), similar attempts to self-provision were noted amongst less well placed households. One part-time retail manager, for example, set herself savings goals and finance targets each year and had two direct debits into savings plans, one for unexpected short-term things but the other for the long term. She also had some insurance particularly to guard against ill-health. However, not unexpectedly, many respondents reported that whatever their intentions, such self-provisioning was not possible. One respondent who had thought about financial planning and started a pension, but frozen it, said: 'We can't afford to put money aside for no reason really.' Another commented: 'If you can't afford to do it, its no use talking about something that's just a pipe dream.'

Fatalism and lack of concern

This response is best characterised by an absence of planning informed by particular attitudes of pessimism or fatalism. Either circumstances were likely to be so difficult that no amount of planning could affect the situation or people said they would cope with whatever was thrown at them when it happened. This was a different situation from the one in which households wished to plan but are unable to do so.

One respondent indicated such fatalism which she argued had been informed by an earlier experience of divorce which had changed her attitude to planning:

> So no, we haven't got any savings and it don't worry me that we haven't. ... you don't know what's going to happen do you? So I don't really worry too much about the future.

So, responses to risk are also varied and complex. Again, however, material resources constrain the options, but attitudes and pre-dispositions also structure the choices made.

Summary and conclusion

The range of risk situations in the labour market is now considerable, impacting in some way on around a third of all households. There is clear evidence that the implications of these risks, if not 'managed' in some way can be substantial. This chapter has identified the way in which public policy is changing the nature of welfare provision, seeking to reduce state welfare in favour of transferring the responsibility for safety-net provision to individuals with the expectation that they will increasingly rely on the private market to meet their needs. While this process can be seen operating in a number of areas, it is particularly well articulated with respect to support for mortgagors who lose all income.

The empirical evidence presented, which was drawn from two recent studies, suggests that there is a general reluctance amongst a majority of households to behave in the way that is expected of them. With respect to the areas considered, reliance on private insurance is typically eschewed, not least amongst those who run the highest risks of labour market disruption. Caution about taking private insurance cover may be affected by its cost, the operation of exclusions and its perceived effectiveness. However, in a fuller explanation, issues of individuals' pre-dispositions to risk and the extent to which individuals perceive themselves to be 'at risk' (which does not always accord with objective assessments of the risk they face), along with their attitudes to insurance and the private market are also significant. There is a lack of trust in the market which is often expressed in terms of a belief that insurers will be unwilling to pay out. These attitudinal issues sit awkwardly with the current direction of welfare policy.

In the face of a reduction in state support, and the limited engagement with private insurance, the chapter went on to explore the range of ways in which individuals and households 'coped' with the risks they faced and in particular the range of provision that they considered. The responses to risk were seen to be varied and complex, again constructed against a background of personal pre-disposition, attitudes and cultural expectations. Some individuals were pro-active with respect to risk avoidance but others, from inclination or circumstance were reactive, with socio-economic position acting as a further, but not necessarily overriding constraint.

The evidence considered in this paper raises a number of interesting issues. First, it adds to the growing doubts about the assumptions underpinning the current direction of Government welfare policy both in terms of what the market for insurance can provide and in terms of its current operation and effectiveness. At the least, it identifies a set of changes needed in the private market before a greater proportion of households are likely even to consider 'responding' as current policy assumes they will. It suggests that the key questions for policy makers must include a reconsideration of how the appropriate markets should be regulated, and a recognition of the tensions between providing incentives for the further use of the market (or considering compulsion), its currently indifferent performance and the widespread reservations amongst potential users.

Secondly, it indicates that the individualisation of risk responsibility is not necessarily well aligned with the capacity of individuals to accept this responsibility. Even if the market worked well, paying to protect income and committed expenditures either through the market or via self-provisioning is difficult for many households and impossible for some. Further, because of already introduced restrictions to some state provided welfare, individuals, in the end, have to 'protect' themselves either by seeking and taking poor or poorer jobs, or by relying on family and friends. Those who are unable to activate either of these responses face severe poverty. The combination of a flexible labour market, particularly for those in its low paid sectors, and the retreat of the state is, for some, a very harsh combination indeed.

Thirdly, it is important to recognise that as the responsibility for managing risk passes increasingly to households, this is not matched as yet by any equivalent concern or support in the form of financial socialisation. Yet, early experience of privatising the provision of financial security has shown the ease with which mis-selling can occur and that the level of financial literacy in Britain is so poor that in most instances it provides no safeguards at all to individuals. As already noted, there is also a climate of doubt about how satisfactory are the current regulatory regimes. It is clearly the case that expectations about shouldering risks and responsibilities are not currently matched by adequate skills or adequate safeguards.

Notes

1 The research was supported by the Joseph Rowntree Foundation and undertaken with Elaine Kempson and Deborah Quilgars.
2 The study was funded by the Economic and Social Research Council, Grant No. L211252054. The award was jointly held with Robert Walker at Loughborough University. The contribution of the other researchers, David Abbott, Deborah Quilgars, Andreas Cebulla and Sue Middleton is acknowledged.
3 I am grateful to Roger Burrows for the analysis of the *Survey of English Housing* and *British Household Panel Survey*. Full details, including a number of caveats pertaining to the analysis are provided in Ford, 1998.
4 We wish to acknowledge the assistance given by the two insurers and the Department of Social Security.

7
Public Understanding of Financial Risk: The Challenge to Regulation
Peter Lunt and Justine Blundell

Introduction

Since the 1970s an important aspect of welfare policy has been the reduction of welfare dependence. Whether this is understood as rolling back the welfare state, or targeting welfare, it is widely accepted that scope of state contributions to welfare is being reduced. One consequence is that people who would have received state help when facing risks of unemployment, health, education costs or loss of income at retirement will have to rely on their own resources if they want to retain a reasonable standard of living. Notably, the value of the state pension is likely to reduce in the long-term and the costs of higher education, health and residential care will increase. Furthermore, these changes are likely to take place against a background of increased uncertainty in employment and long-term relationships. If, as economists do, we think of these expenses as risks that people face at different points of the life cycle, then there is a need for large numbers of people to save, invest and insure against these risks. However, people have grown up with a different balance between the state and personal responsibility for welfare and need incentives to take greater personal responsibility for their welfare outcomes. In addition, personal financial services of sufficient flexibility and quality will need to be developed to fit the needs and expectations of people wanting to protect themselves against such risks. All this creates new challenges for the regulation of financial services.

Risk society

The focus of our paper is the response of individuals to the changing climate in welfare-funding and the related issues of provision and regulation. We will present an interpretation of focus groups with people of different ages, social grade and gender, discussing the kinds of financial risks that they face and their approach to dealing with these risks. Our aim is to offer an interpretation of the things 'ordinary' people are saying about risk in the late 1990s and to relate our interpretation to the recent theorising of the 'risk society' (Beck, 1992; Giddens, 1991). Sociology has fashioned an extensive critique of technical approaches to risk assessment and risk management. The idea that risks can be given an objective definition based upon expertise and that the role of social science is restricted to an analysis of the comprehension and reception of information concerning risk by the public, is criticised. Social and cultural factors are not seen as secondary factors that influence public responses to objectively-defined risks but are implicated in what constitutes a risk. As a result, the management of risk is understood as a complex process that involves consultation, inclusion and management of trust relationships. A further consequence of the risk society is that expertise no longer takes the form of a unitary authority. Instead, a range of authorities offer partial advice on the problem at hand.

Changes in the market for personal financial services

The growing importance of personal financial services in funding welfare makes the issues of risk, trust and expertise a major concern. There have been significant changes affecting the balance between collective and individual responsibility for insuring against welfare risk. The 1980s and 1990s have seen a rapid expansion in individually-purchased financial services (Lunt and Disney, 1999). This has occurred because government policies such as the liberalisation of financial markets in the early 1980s have allowed greater competition among financial providers and largely eliminated market segmentation where, for example, only building societies offered mortgages and only banks personal loans (Muellbauer, 1990). There has been a political emphasis on 'shareholder capitalism' (predating the 'stakeholder society') in which individual or family ownership of assets is encouraged. Various policies were introduced to facilitate this, including the subsidised 'right to buy' policies for council house tenants and share issues associated with the privatisation of public utilities. Such policies were accompanied by a variety of tax incentives designed to encourage wider ownership of financial assets, such as the introduction of PEPs (Personal Equity Plans) (Banks and Tanner, 1996; Grout, 1987). Collectively-provided welfare plans, such as occupational pension provision and health insurance and trade union and friendly society benefits, have not received the same

support and have tended to decline. A particularly striking development is in the market for employee-purchased Personal Pensions after
1987. These schemes received tax subsidies and contribution rebates
from the government and expanded from zero to coverage of almost a
quarter of employees in the space of five years (Disney and Stears,
1996; Disney and Whitehouse, 1992).

These changes have been accompanied by a greater perception of
social and economic insecurity (Lunt and Livingstone, 1992) concerning the ability, and the willingness, of the government to provide a
Beveridge-style 'social insurance' safety-net against major risks such as
sickness, unemployment and poverty in old age. This arose partly from
the political persuasion of the Conservative administrations of the
period as well as from 'real' constraints on financing such as the
'demographic transition' to a society with an increased number of
elderly dependants (Disney, 1996). In addition, the growing hetero-
geneity of household types and lifestyles, and social trends such as rising divorce rates led to a rapid expansion of new possibilities for
insurance. Naturally the developing financial industry providing personal financial services had every incentive to encourage this feeling of
insecurity and to develop new identifiable risks which 'required' provision of additional insurance products (Lunt and Disney, 1999).

This process is ongoing. In the 1997 General Election campaign, all
the main political parties focused on personal finance welfare as the
long-term means to overcome the inevitable decline in state welfare
and pension provision that will be one result of the demographic
changes over the next thirty to forty years. These have been portrayed
as long term problems that will require greater personal responsibility
amongst citizens and greater provision of privately funded schemes for
savings, investments and pensions to enable people to become more
and more self-sufficient.

These structural changes intersect with life course and ways of living
in complex ways. People on the point of retirement now will be
affected differently from those in their early adult life. Also, changing
gender roles and social class positions will moderate these effects. In
this paper we are concerned with the ways that these different groups
understand the changing nature of welfare funding and how they are
responding to such changes.

Consumption

We will draw on literature that intersects issues of risk and consumption to inform understanding of the implications of the expansion of

personally funded welfare (see Slater, 1997, for a review). The 'risk society' literature reworks the relationship between personal choice, action and the role of expertise. Evidence of these broad social changes in the realm of consumption is provided by a growing range of products that are appropriated by individuals as resources in their active construction of lifestyles. The deregulation of the financial services industry detailed above can be understood as part of this shift from a society based on tradition to one based on the increased autonomy of the individual in a context of decreased regulatory authority. An understanding of the culture of consumption is needed to explain the role of services from the point of view of the everyday lives of consumers. We will use two accounts of consumption as exemplars to think through the role of the culture of consumption in the risks associated with personal funded welfare: the work of Bourdieu (1984) on consumption as the expression of social distinction and the reproduction of social position and the writings on risk and trust by Giddens (1991) which are explicitly applied to consumption by Lash and Urry (1994).

Bourdieu: cultural aspects of consumption

Bourdieu (1984) emphasises the role of goods in the cultural expression and constitution of social class position. Developing Veblen's conception of competitive display, Bourdieu suggests that the intrinsic qualities of goods do not account for their role in the symbolism of social position. Rather, it is the underlying taste structure, instantiating the cultural competence to choose, acquire and use goods in appropriate ways that gives consumption a pre-eminent role in the display and reproduction of social status. This broader, social conception of consumption emphasises that there are competencies learned through education and socialisation that are not reducible to economic capital and which constitute cultural capital.

Bourdieu's work raises specific questions for the proliferation of financial service products as a means of privately funding welfare. The increase of privately purchased plans, savings and investments in this field will make the differential effects of cultural capital more salient. Structures of cultural capital will limit the spread and use of services that insure against risk if this depends upon socially acquired knowledge and practice. In consequence, the management of risk will need to take account of and work on symbolic categories in action if it is to spread the use of vehicles for personal welfare funding. Also, if cultural capital is needed to make use of services in a disciplined way then demonstrating that this cultural capital is in place or that professional advice is readily available will be an important part of the regulation of financial service provision. To leave the responsibility for overcoming the effects of cultural capital to the financial services industry means trusting this to the deployment of marketing and advertising methods.

An alternative is for companies offering personal financial products to approach the issue of the required cultural capital as a technical issue akin to a design problem. Can the requisite expertise be 'coded' into goods and services, thereby managing risks in the background of services that meet the practical needs of actors from different social class fractions? Offering diverse financial service products is important, but these need to be effectively matched to the needs and circumstances of consumers. For both of these methods (offering advice and structuring products) the devil is in the detail – is appropriate advice available and being offered? Are appropriate products available? The inherent dangers of relying on the design of products and the provision of advice are well illustrated by the pensions and mortgage 'scandals' of the 1980s (Disney, 1996). In the context of the increasing importance of personally funded welfare there is a potential contradiction between informed choice on the part of consumers and the restrictions on the take up and use of such services due to the constraints of cultural capital. This opens up a complex indeterminacy: the further development of financial services depends upon engaging and motivating consumers, but the limits of financial literacy require the industry to project an understanding of what is appropriate for a given individual or household. Like it or not, the moral responsibility that was inherent in the mutual principles underpinning collective forms of insurance against welfare risks still applies to the arrangements for the marketing of financial service products. The question is, who is responsible?

Giddens: risk society and reflexivity

A complementary analysis of the risk society which has direct relevance to these issues of the relationship between expertise and practical consumption arrangements is to be found in the work of Giddens (1991) and Lash and Urry (1994). Giddens' great insight was to understand the centrality of the relation between institutional reflexivity and the self as a reflexive project to the social organisation of late modernity. Contemporary institutional arrangements are structured around linking diverse forms of life. Central to Giddens' conception is the indeterminacy of ways of living by such institutional arrangements. Institutions must structure for difference, which creates new problems of self-regulation and accountability. These arrangements are post-traditional in the sense that they are not forms of disseminated expertise that are either adopted or resisted by agents but rather expertise structured around ongoing relations of power/knowledge. People use information available about populations to structure their lives reflexively as a project of the self which in turn feeds back into institutional arrangements. Giddens (1991) discusses the rise of the self-help book as an indication that people are reflexively managing their identities. As Lash and Urry (1987, 1994) describe it, the reflexive attitude is an appropriate response to the disorganisation of capital.

In the past, paternalistic financial institutions operating in a regulated market took a highly constrained approach to borrowing in the context of a welfare culture (Lunt and Livingstone, 1992). This has been replaced by deregulation of the financial services industry and the consequent multiplication and diversification of financial services in the context of increasingly targeted welfare and a political culture that emphasises self-reliance. To this extent, welfare funding has become relatively disorganised and an increasing proportion of the population is an important part of their lifestyle decisions (Chaney, 1996). Giddens (1992) has applied these ideas to the study of personal relationships, arguing that a similar shift has taken place from relationships organised around duty to 'pure' relationships that have value as part of the reflexive project of the self, instead of being structured around traditional conjugal role relationships.

The analysis of reflexive modernity offers a perspective that is sensitive to the complexities of the relationship of expertly structured services and their reflexive appropriation. However, Giddens has been clear in arguing that although these conditions create important new opportunities (for companies to sell financial services and the freedom for individuals to construct their own identities) they also create new dangers for both producers and consumers. For example, the need to know the consumer in order to offer appropriate products places new demands on financial institutions. How are they going to find out about their customers in reliable, secure and unobtrusive ways? The dependency of financial institutions on knowing their customers may create problems of trust and knowledge that are difficult to manage. In contrast, collective and publicly funded methods offer membership of a population to an anonymous public who do not need to be known or understood.

This arrangement is characteristic of public service institutions in a liberal democracy where ideals of citizenship are coded in financial arrangements. In contrast, individual arrangements are intersections between private individuals with personal interests and abstract systems.

Another important issue is the provision of advice. Giddens's example of self-help books is interesting, but what is the equivalent in the area of personally funded welfare? Can financial advice be given in the same way that therapy and counselling is delivered through popular culture? There are many sources of advice about personal financial services, for example, professional financial advisors, consumer associations, financial pages, lifestyle magazines, but is the right advice reaching its target?

Giddens's reflections lead us to some difficult questions concerning the provision of the resources (both material and informational) and structuring of financial services for reflexive subjects. A possible danger is that institutional reflexivity will be driven by the needs of lifestyle, relationship or direct marketing but that the regulatory function will be fixed at the point of accountability of delivery of information. This is the equivalent of having a mass society notion of regulation in a postmodern market. Also, as Beck and Giddens have both emphasised, one characteristic of the risk society is the proliferation of forms of expertise that will often lead to contradictory advice. How is the customer to make informed choices when there are multiple forms of expertise each offering different advice about a different range of products?

Financial services in the new context of consumption

We will now summarise the implications of cultural capital and expression, expertise and reflexivity for developing financial services. One trend in the social organisation of consumption is emulation and the 'trickle down' effect. An underlying policy assumption of the Thatcher years was that the household should be given a status analogous to that of a firm, to act entrepreneurially and autonomously. We are now experiencing the spread of the service culture, which will extend from the new service class to become a highly dispersed way of life. New policies and new personal financial services will demand specific qualities from participants, requiring them to conceive of their lives over the long term and to deploy financial services skilfully, to manage their personal welfare.

Changes in welfare funding illustrate the growing importance of social and cultural factors in both the assessment and the evaluation of risk. The tools of economic analysis become a way of working out the consequences of different arrangements for welfare funding rather than a pre-established form of expertise that sets out to discover the 'right' arrangement. All this highlights the importance of policy in the bringing together of methods to mobilise people to a new way of managing their finances to take account of increased individual responsibility. Risk-management involves not only structuring services to provide resources and incentives for people to insure themselves, but also a cultural influence on people to adopt an appropriate lifestyle – not as a mode of expression but as a necessary response to structural changes in welfare funding.

Consumption culture and the new personally funded welfare

The shift from PEPs/TESSAs to ISAs can be understood as part of the construction of appropriate incentives to assist the spread of forms of saving as insurance against risk. One of the key lessons of the PEP/ TESSA culture was that the saving habit did not spread far enough 'down' the social grades (along with share ownership) and there was a large transfer effect. The main recipients of the new tax incentives were those who would have saved anyway. This experience indicates that there are limits on the effectiveness of fiscal incentives in meeting the aim of spreading the culture of reflexivity in consumption, because certain groups of people are not engaging with the culture of reflexivity.

What has to happen to the practices of everyday life for the policies of increasing personally funded welfare to work? It is clear that on one level this is the spread of the reflexive disposition and the associated cultural capital along with the structured delivery of appropriate financial services. This leads to a variety of empirical social psychological questions concerning whether people can adapt their lifestyles to the demands of reflexive modernisation. A related set of questions concern potential social inequalities in the cultural capital required to make these changes. The shift to reflexive modernisation also places new demands on regulation and expertise. Trust management is not reducible to the accuracy and diffusion of information but involves issues of the reception and appropriation of goods and services. The recent history of the financial services industry is not encouraging from this point of view. The discourse of self-regulation is predominantly a system of accountability based on product design and the availability of information. It is clear that a detailed understanding of the reception of expertise and the way that it is moderated by social influences in the culture of consumption is required.

Ironically, commerce is increasingly concerned with issues of direct marketing and the targeting of specific customer groups – so that appropriate levels of information and appropriate goods and services can be offered to customers. These mechanisms are being developed as marketing tools. Such services require a different type of relationship between producer and consumer based on more detailed knowledge of the consumer. Government policy maintains that it is ultimately in the interests of a developing market to get this right so that the potential for scandals is minimised and confidence is restored. In other words, there are competitive advantages to self-regulation. However, the skills, information and systems required to manage this responsibility are non-trivial. Do companies 'know' what the optimum investments are for a specific individual? Can they afford to train sufficient staff to offer the 'right' advice to the 'right' people? It is conceivable that it may be cheaper to allow 'mistakes' to happen and then compensate later as demonstrated in personal financial service scandals to date. The assumption that a growing financial services industry has the interests of the community at heart and the competence to deal with the increased demand is a plank of current government policy but is highly contestable in the light of recent scandals.

Furthermore, the preferred methods for knowing the consumer and targeting goods and services accurately involve implicit rather than overt techniques. This is to be achieved through the encoding of expertise in the structuring of information, products and offers to customers using increasingly sophisticated data mining and consumer clustering techniques and through careful product design. This idea derives from the development of technological goods where expertise is deployed to deliver complex functions to novice users. For example, the modern digital video camera is built around enormous technological advances that deliver functions that used to be the preserve of expert camera operators into the hands of a public that simply have to look and point. There is indeterminacy between consumers' experience of goods and services and the underlying expertise required in constructing them. This means that customers' evaluations of goods and services are based on their direct experience of them and on a variety of influences related to novelty, fashion and aesthetics rather than on a critical evaluation of the technical expertise that is used to construct the service.

The wide-ranging changes reviewed above constitute the context within which people make their financial decisions. We will now explore the reaction of people to these changes as reflected in focus group discussions.

The focus groups

Ninety-six participants were interviewed across twelve focus groups. Group membership was organised according to three factors: age, social grade and gender. Two different age groups were considered: those at or nearing retirement age (55–64 years) and those just beginning to address issues around saving for retirement (25–34 years). Twelve focus groups were therefore conducted, consisting of one male, one female and one of mixed gender groups for both the ABC1 and C2DE class categories for each of the two age groups. A professional company was employed to recruit participants.

The groups were conducted in an open-ended fashion with one of the authors acting as moderator. The groups started by everyone introducing themselves and then the moderator gave a schematic outline of the purposes of the group. This was restricted to using general terms indicating that we were interested in what people had to say about personal financial services and the kind of risks they faced now and in the future in their everyday lives. Other areas to be explored were intergenerational patterns of giving; how people deal with periods of uncertainty; if and how needs are expected to change after retirement; what value people placed on various assets such as home-ownership, savings and pensions; whether people expect to require private nursing/health care and whether any steps are being taken to provide for this; attitudes towards credit and debt across the generations such as the increased use of borrowing and credit facilities and the rendering of household allocation. In the conduct of the focus groups the emphasis was placed on encouraging participants to give their own views and to discuss them freely with the other participants. The moderator had a check list of the areas mentioned above and more direct questions relating to these areas were raised towards the end of the sessions only if they were not addressed spontaneously by the participants themselves.

What are the different people we have talked to been saying about these issues of risk and savings? What are their various responses to the incremental shift from collective to household-level responsibility in welfare funding? We will offer an interpretation of the differences and will finish with some broader observations about the story that emerges from the analysis.

The views of middle-class participants

The older, middle-class participants are conscious of good fortune. They came to adulthood during the late 1950s and early 1960s. Having lived their lives through a period of extraordinary change, they talked openly of being the first generation to do many things. This was reflected in wide ranging discussions about the shift from the 1950s to the 1960s and the changing social conditions of the time. In the area of personal finance this included being first-generation homeowners and shareholders. In many ways they have lived a golden life and that is reflected in comments about how much more difficult things are for the generations that followed them. They are a confident, self-made generation who grew up in relative affluence compared to their parents.

Through the course of their adult working lives they have experienced the change in political economy from the welfare state to the current arrangements and they have a strong sense of everything getting harder. They are consequently worried for their children and grandchildren. They anticipate future generations having less fun, less flexibility, less money, but they do not, generally speaking, extend this to helping their children financially. Intergenerational transfer within families is reserved for emergencies and specific expenses such as helping with the deposit on the first flat or with childcare expenses.

Interestingly, the structuring of the distribution of assets within the family is not being discussed and systematically worked out by families. People give specific financial help when their children or their parents have specific needs. As families, as opposed to individuals or households, people are using a traditional approach to allocation: helping out according to need especially in emergencies.

Gender and age differences among the middle class

There are highly salient gender differences in the older middle class groups. The older women repeatedly speak of having been ignorant of the consequences of their consumption decisions – a psychology of not wanting to 'worry' or think about the future, coupled with a financial strategy of spending according to resources and need. They didn't expect to live so long, they didn't anticipate the changes in collective provision. Although they were aware of the decreasing value of benefits and public services from the 1970s onwards they did not take any steps to safeguard against this. It would appear that the older women lack the cultural capital necessary to make use of services available and were, for the most part, happy to let their partners take care of financial matters outside the family budget (Pahl, 1989).

In contrast, the older middle-class men display considerable cultural capital in relation to issues around personal financial services. This group is considerably sceptical about the potential for personally funded welfare. They are particularly sceptical about the potential of insurance-based savings schemes and personal pensions and point to the pensions scandal and other examples of 'mis-selling' (Disney, 1996).

In all this the value of property plays a crucial role. Participants talk about the sacrifices they made to get into property in the first place.

This generation talked about how, when they were entering the house-buying market there seemed to not be a clear view of the advantages of home-ownership. They did not anticipate the levels to which house values would rise. Consequently, as a result of lack of foresight, a failure to anticipate changes in welfare funding and the desire to spend and enjoy life, they have not developed a range of savings and investments – pensions and houses have been the order of the day. This strategy interacts with gender in an interesting way. Essentially, men assume that they will die before their women, and that the house will provide the resources needed for the remainder of the woman's life. The asset tied up in the house is considered enough to provide for her needs until she too dies.

Women see this very differently. The idea of selling the 'family home', possibly to pay for private nursing or health care, does not appear to be an option. Continuing to live in the house and then leaving the house to their children is the preferred choice. This raises some interesting issues, concerned with gender differences in understanding of nature of the asset provided by home-ownership.

There are also gender differences for the older, middle class participants in relation to their sensibility to and strategies towards their children and grandchildren. It was very difficult to get the men to talk about their (financial) relationship with their children. When they did, the rhetoric was one of standing on their own two feet. Women talked freely about these issues amongst themselves, they made it clear that they had not discussed this in any depth with their partners/husbands. There were also some interesting contradictions in the views of older, relatively wealthy parents concerning their children. Their predominant view was that 'life is now more difficult than it was for us'. However, they are proud and impressed by the achievements of their children and surprised at the size of some of the salaries and mortgages that their children have. Added to this, the changing position of women makes dual incomes more likely for their children. Thus, there is a lack of clarity about the underlying financial position of their adult children. It is clear that these issues are not normally discussed within families and, again, the traditional model of 'helping out in emergencies' is adopted.

The younger middle class groups, although well aware of divorce statistics and of decreased job security and the end of the life-time career (the contours of late modernity are clear), fall short of being able to plan for divorce and to discuss it with partners and spouses. They see such an approach as in direct contradiction of their romantic view of relationships. Although the conditions that require a reflexive orientation towards developing a pure relationship are widely understood, it appears that there are social psychological barriers to the development of the appropriate response.

These different cases are interesting, not only because there seems to be continuity across cohorts who are actually facing quite different circumstances, but also because the consequences of a failure to discuss these issues seems to be different in the different cases. In the older group the men clearly think they have resolved the problem successfully. The asset represented by the house will support their wives after they have gone and they will live on their pensions in the meantime. They have found a solution that does not require them to talk to their spouses and to negotiate. However, this will not do for the younger groups where rising divorce rates and changing needs due to shifts in welfare provision may require a more explicit dialogue within relationships.

Here, the structuring of relationships on traditional romantic lines cuts across the requirements of reflexive management of personal finances. The older, relatively wealthy men have adopted a tactical resolution to these issues – but the requirement of contemporary conditions means that, for the younger groups, a solution can only be found through open negotiation and communication with partners, which they do not appear to engage in. It appears that the modernisation of personal funding for welfare has not necessarily been accompanied by a corresponding shift in the way that finances are managed within the family. This means that the allocation of household resources for insuring against risk and building up precautionary assets is uneven and that it is missing in areas where there are social psychological barriers to adopting a method of saving and insurance. The lack of planning for divorce is an extreme example, but similar issues emerge in the failure to plan for the differential life-expectancies of partners of different sexes, or for the difficult issues of how to weigh the different contributions of the partners to the household budget. This may explain the preference for using the house as the primary asset. On a psychological level, the rationale for concentrating on home ownership is provided by the use value of the house as shelter and accommodation and the rapid growth in the asset value of owner-occupied housing during the post-war period. However, the issue of liquidity and the problems around the loss of employment incomes, divorce, retirement or the death of a partner do not seem to be discussed by households.

Working-class participants: gender and age differences

The 'lower' social class groups had a strong sense of the unfairness of the retreat of the welfare state. On one level they simply feel that they do not have the resources to save. The younger groups were quite aware that they face job insecurity and they fully expect a continuing decline in the value of pensions and a reduction in the standards of public services. They feel they have more pressing matters to worry about than future financial security and anticipate an old age lived in poverty.

There were gender differences in the expression of this sense of unfairness. For the women, unfairness was expressed towards what they termed 'having to pay twice' for pensions and health care through private pension or insurance schemes and through taxation. They wished to be in a position to choose whether to pay taxes and National Insurance contributions to state schemes or to opt for private provision. There was also some misunderstanding of the state pension system: the younger group had assumed that the money paid by them in taxes was somehow saved by the government and given back to them in the form of a pension when they retired. However, the consensus in the younger group seemed to be that money isn't everything and values are more important, especially in relation to the family. They expressed strong commitment to the value of mutual family support and of offering help in times of trouble both within and between generations.

For the men, their feelings against the targeting of welfare were strong – expressed in a racist discourse against immigrants and asylum seekers. This indicates that the group who are going to experience the greatest difficulty in engaging with reflexive modernisation are, in the main, men from lower class social groups. (Interestingly, the women in the younger lower social class group did produce racist discourse when in the company of men in the mixed group.) This reflects Bauman's (1998) conception that the changing nature of welfare provision and the consequent risks that people face create a structure which favours a particular culture – that of reflexive autonomy. Our findings indicate that there are clear social class and gender differences in embracing this new culture. In particular there is a group of people in early adult life who are resistant to the reflexive stance even though they see it as a necessary response to current and future arrangements.

This group has strong preferences for redistributive systems of welfare. They expressed strong opposition to compulsory savings schemes. These strongly expressed views indicate the potential social problems that are likely to be experienced by those who will not be poor enough to receive benefits if the welfare state retreats to a safety-net approach, but who have neither the resources nor the cultural capital to take full advantage of the risk society. In terms of their life course, this group see themselves as likely to live on relatively low incomes and to experience repeated spells of unemployment. They are not convinced that the gradual, incremental acquisition of assets is open to them, or that opportunities for such practices will work in their interests. They will build up few assets for retirement and anticipate living on social security in their old age.

Participants indicated the importance of occupational provision, particularly in relation to pensions. This is reflected in the memories of older participants who emphasised that they had not made explicit choices about pensions and savings but had gone along with work-based schemes. A combination of the occupational provision and normative pressure from peers were the key influences in their adoption of pensions and savings schemes. In contrast, the younger groups expect their employers as well as the government to retreat from welfare funding and administration.

Conclusions: the future of personally funded welfare

What are the barriers to people taking personal responsibility for precautionary saving and insurance against welfare risk? Amongst our participants there is a strong feeling that the external structuring of contributions to savings and insurance schemes by state or employer makes them work better than private commercial schemes. For example, people do not regard National Insurance schemes as an imposition even though they are compulsory, but see mandatory membership as part of the cost of belonging to a scheme that has the benefits of mutuality and some redistribution. The same people are very much opposed to compulsion to join private-sector commercial saving schemes. People regard investment in state and work-based schemes as participation, but compulsory savings as an imposition. It is difficult to see how the feeling of goodwill towards the state pension can be reproduced for compulsory savings schemes given the regret that is expressed about the loss of state-funded welfare.

Two barriers to the development of personally funded welfare are particularly significant. First, there is scepticism concerning the motives and capabilities of the financial service industry even among the middle-class men who were most knowledgeable and experienced in personal financial affairs. Poor performance on investment and saving and potential problems in obtaining flexible and appropriate products and cover were among the reasons for these reactions. There is a potential problem in institutional reflexivity resulting from the possibility that 'knowing the customer' may become an aspect of marketing technique rather than a part of a broadly based self-regulation in the financial service industries.

The scepticism about personal financial services is grounded in some of the high-profile failures of this sector. There was little sign that people thought that these were specific problems with particular products. Rather these examples were taken as symptomatic of the potential dangers in pensions, investments and insurance-based schemes. There is now a growing concern that people who have planned and saved hard are being disappointed by the level of income generated by annuities in a period of relatively low interest rates. It appears that people do not have a clear view of what their income will be on retirement. They tend to look to the schemes they have and make a global judgement of whether it will be 'enough'. Low interest rates mean that people need a higher lump sum to get a reasonable income. Alternative methods of managing their assets may combine fixed interest investments, which carry a low risk, such as Gilts or National Savings Bonds, with investments which yield a higher return at some risk to the capital sum, for example, corporate bonds.

The potential problems for people retiring in the near future on lower than expected personal pensions may be taken as further evidence of the inadequacy of the personal financial services industry in providing appropriate products to cope with the risks of living in modern society. These problems may not be as dramatic as the pensions scandal, but it remains the case that the personal financial industry has difficulty in providing the security that people expect at prices they are prepared to pay. If the industry cannot avoid more complex financial arrangements which carry a measure of risk in the mechanisms available to it to cope with a fall in the interest rates on annuities, it is expecting a high level of public trust. It is probable that large numbers of people will prefer to adopt conservative strategies rather than live with the risks of current approaches to personal investment in providing security for their old age.

The second barrier concerns the availability and distribution of the appropriate cultural capital to handle the complex issues of personal financial welfare. This is illustrated in the case of the older middle-class men who were knowledgeable but who had clearly avoided explicit discussion of financial matters with their partners. If we measure cultural capital as knowledge we may get a misleading conception of people's ability to manage sensitive topics such as saving for retirement. Issues such as differential exposure to job insecurity, the possibility of divorce and the impact of having children were all topics that were considered too sensitive to talk about. This raises the issue of potential conflicts over the take-up of individually purchased financial services within households. One approach to conflict is avoidance.

A similar picture emerges for the role of the state and the firm. It is clear that people are, to a large extent, inclined to respond to circumstances rather than taking control of them. Far from seeing the state as the nanny-state and their employers as interfering they preferred to have services structured for them. In contrast people are sceptical about the role of the personal finance industry in managing savings and insurance and they show a preference for the active involvement of the state.

The younger working-class participants tended to regard the new welfare policies as an attack on their own position. They are now expected to bear the cost of risks that, in their view, should be covered by the state. The development of individually purchased financial products is perceived as part of a general loss of communal ethic and government responsibility. These changes are linked in the public imagination to concerns about decreasing social cohesion and feelings of belonging and responsibility.

The increasing individualisation implicit in the growth of personally funded welfare pushes people in the direction of rational planning. However, personal financial planning develops slowly under the influence of the practices of everyday life rather than as the result of well informed, 'rational' decisions. People manage their finances through tacit agreements rather than through explicit discussion and negotiation. This strategy depends upon expertise in a number of important respects – through the arrangement of workplace pension schemes and state funded education and health services. The welfare state may be in retreat but whether families have either the wealth or the cultural capital to be financially autonomous across the life course remain unclear.

8
Insights into the Uncertain World of the Consumer: Reflections on the Risks of Non-Prescription Medicines

Paul R. Ward, Paul Bissell and Peter R. Noyce

Introduction

Academic debates within sociology concerning risk as a conceptual and thematic framework have largely neglected the more everyday, taken for granted or mundane aspects of human behaviour. Within the discipline of sociology, the focus on environmental hazards (Williams and Popay, 1994; Phillimore and Moffatt, 1994), toxic waste (Brown, 1992), or radioactive contamination (Wynne, 1992) has been at the expense of other areas of health, social and welfare policy. Within this chapter, we focus on consumer perceptions of the risks of non-prescription medicines. The use of non-prescription medicines for the treatment of minor ailments is a commonplace activity and as such, represents a useful example of lay people's interaction with modern medicine. Therefore, the study on which this chapter is based represents a contrast to the more macro-scale issues referred to above thus, an attempt to plug some of these gaps identified within the sociological literature on risk.

It is interesting that the absence of engagement with research into the risks of non-prescription medicines is occurring against a background of heightened interest in the notion of risk within the sociology of health and illness. To our knowledge, the debate concerning non-prescription medicine use has largely been conducted in the absence of any theoretical input or discussion of the core themes in the sociology of risk. This seems surprising given the prolific output of this body of work (Beck, 1992; Gabe, 1995; Lash *et al.*, 1996; Alaszewski, 1998; Heyman, 1998). In order to provide a theoretical and conceptual framework for our findings about the risks on non-prescription medicine use, we briefly outline some of the central theoretical considerations that have emerged over the last decade. In this brief description, we draw chiefly on the work of Beck (1992) and Giddens (1990; 1991) although we recognise the contribution made by psychologists such as Paul Slovic and others (Slovic, 1987; Slovic *et al.*, 1990; Renn *et al.*, 1992; Alhakami and Slovic, 1994) in the construction of theories of risk perception and anthropologists such as Mary Douglas (Douglas and Wildavsky, 1982; Douglas, 1986; Douglas, 1992) in the development of cultural theories of risk.

During the twentieth century, public discourse around risk has focused largely on the negative outcomes of industrial expansion (Douglas, 1992) and contemporary public policy has been framed by expressions such as 'risks from technology', 'industrial risks', or 'risks to the environment'. A social issue would be difficult to find that is better known to people than the harm to the natural environment or the human body attributed to modern technology (Dake and Wildavsky, 1991).

This increase in interest about risks within the late modern era, it has been suggested, may have occurred as a consequence of populations within industrialised nations living longer and healthier lives than any other people, at any other time in history (Douglas and Wildavsky, 1982). However, if this is the case, what are the factors leading to this proliferation of risks within society and why are people more worried or aware about risks now? These questions prompted researchers in America to ask, 'what are Americans afraid of?' with the answer being, 'nothing much really, except the food they eat, the water they drink, the air they breathe, the land they live on, and the energy they use' (Douglas and Wildavsky, 1982). Whatever the reasons may be for the increased interest in risk within contemporary society, whether because of personal experiences, the media, industrial expansion, or social and political influences, there is a sense in which: 'many ordinary citizens view themselves as the victims rather than the beneficiaries of technology.' (Dake 1992, p. 22) One of the most important and influential contributors to the debate on risk has been Beck who proposed the idea that in the late twentieth century, we are all living in a 'risk society' (Beck, 1992). Beck suggests that a prominent theme of life in late modernity is the centrality and heightened awareness of risk. Beck proposes that in a risk society, humans become increasingly vulnerable to major socio-technical dislocation as a result of growing interdependency. In this way, risk is seen as an inevitable and inescapable consequence of global modernisation and the multiplication of risk cannot be avoided (Beck, 1992). Indeed, Dake suggests that 'concern about risk pervades every aspect of our lives' (1992, p. 23).

Beck's thesis has been drawn on by numerous writers and represents a major cultural critique of the existential contours of life in late modernity. Beck's argument hinges on a critical analysis of modern science and technology whereby the production of wealth has been matched or overtaken by the production of risk. Beck argues for a re-framing of the traditional concerns of 'class' and 'industrial society' found in much modernist sociology, towards an emphasis on the quest for safety in the late modern era. The main themes of Beck's argument can be succinctly stated. As a result of increasing personal and societal reflexivity, the modernist social project is now overwhelmed by an awareness and identification with risk. Beck's emphasis has been on demonstrating that the very success of industrialization and science has lead inexorably to ecological and environmental disaster, but his critique can clearly be extended to other areas such as agricultural practices, pharmacology, the housing and employment market and the welfare state (Taylor-Gooby *et al.*, 1998). Beck himself has suggested that medicine and risk are now intricately and intimately connected with the one effectively feeding off the other:

> in more and more fields of action a reality defined and thoroughly structured by medicine is becoming the prerequisite of thought and action ... not only is the spiral of the medical formation and decision-making twisted deeper and deeper into the ... reality of the risk society, but an insatiable appetite for medicine is produced, a permanent expanding market for the services of the medical profession whose ramifications echo into the distant depths (Beck, 1992, p. 211).

One of Beck's key arguments concentrates on the problem of the interpretation of evidence about risks – an issue clearly relevant to the concerns of medicines users faced to make evaluations about the risks and benefits of the non-prescription medicines that they customarily use. He suggests that partly because of the speed of dissemination of this information, and the reflexive nature of risk, it makes it more and more difficult to establish factual information with certainty. The recent outbreak of BSE in cattle in the UK represents a good example of this in practice, as does the outbreak of narcotizing fasciitis in May 1994 (Gabe, 1995).

Essentially, what these cases highlight are not only divergent perspectives on risk but also the extent to which scientific experts can no longer provide objective guidance on matters of public health and safety. This, Beck suggests, has led lay people to question and contest the knowledge base on which medical science rests. Beck suggests that the contested nature of medical knowledge necessarily allows or facilitates more and more groups of (lay) people to comment and act as 'experts'. Similarly Giddens (1990; 1991) suggests that we are all living in a period in which judgements of experts are constantly open to scrutiny or 'chronically contested' and are either accepted or rejected by lay people on the basis of pragmatic calculations about the risks involved. As a result of the contested nature of expert knowledge, Giddens suggests that the trust and faith invested in experts by lay people is being eroded. Lack of trust in expert authority, according to Giddens, is a central theme in the late modern era.

The observations from commentators on the sociology of risk may be pertinent when the views of consumers of deregulated medicines are considered, specifically in the context of new and changing information about the risks of non-prescription medicines. The arguments developed in the brief description above – the globalisation of risks, enhanced perceptions of risk, mistrust of expertise and social reflexivity – will be discussed in the light of some empirical evidence about lay people's ideas about medicines that challenge the wholesale adoption of these notions and also form the theoretical framework against which this study was undertaken.

Aims of the chapter

In this chapter, we attempt to locate debates on the risk society in relation to one specific area – that of non-prescription medicine use. Specifically, we consider lay people's use and views of a specific type of medicines, which may only be purchased from the community pharmacy in the UK (known as pharmacy medicines). Drawing on data from a qualitative study, we suggest that non-prescription medicine use is a very everyday or routinised activity, with consumers making few conscious assessments of the risks of medicines. In addition, we identify a common discourse centred on notions of lay expertise in the use of medicines for the treatment of specific minor ailments.

In addition, using the case study of the non-prescription medicine terfenadine (which was reclassified from pharmacy status back to prescription-only status in August, 1997), we describe how new information about the risks of terfenadine unhinged some of the findings we outlined above about the absence of reflexive thought with regard to non-prescription medicines. We show that the re-classification of terfenadine to prescription-only status stimulated a broader discourse about the failure of modern medicine and its concomitant risks, providing some evidence for the notion of a reflexive consumer of medicines. We argue that whilst this discourse was important in shaping lay views about risk and safety with regard to medicines, it did not translate into widespread disaffection or disuse of non-prescription medicines. Rather than providing wholesale support for Beck and Giddens' view of the reflexive consumer, we suggest that these findings lend credence to Lupton's (1996; 1997) thesis that increasing scepticism of medicine goes hand in hand with increasing acceptance of its risks and dependence on it as a medium of healing.

Background

Non-prescription medicines: the policy and professional framework

Within the UK, medicines are categorised into three distinct classes: prescription-only medicines which can only be obtained with a prescription from a doctor, pharmacy medicines which can only be purchased from a community pharmacy under the supervision of a pharmacist, and general sales list medicines which may be purchased from any retail outlet, including a community pharmacy.

Interest in research around non-prescription medicines has been stimulated by the changing policy framework affecting the availability of medicines and the increasing use of community pharmacy as a forum for the treatment of minor ailments. Self-care activities have been facilitated by the rapidly expanding number of medicines deregulated from POM to P status. Since 1983, over 50 medicines have been re-classified from prescription status to pharmacy status (Blenkinsopp and Bradley, 1996). A range of medicines for the treatment for dyspepsia, vaginal thrush, cold sores, and hay fever are now available without prescription.

The deregulation of medicines has lead to many more medicines being available to purchase in the pharmacy, thereby providing consumers with increased choice about whether to visit the doctor's surgery or self-medicate when experiencing minor ailments (Thomas and Noyce, 1996; Blenkinsopp and Bradley, 1996; Payne *et al.*, 1998). Extending choice necessarily widens the scope for encouraging personal responsibility for health. However, the expansion of self-medication highlights the potential for inappropriate use of medicines and raises wider questions about the appropriateness of risk management and communication strategies employed within the pharmacy, with one commentator suggesting: 'in this risk-benefit equation, only the benefits are clear; the risk and the burden of harm that may accrue, are hard to predict.' (Barber, 1993, p. 640) Another commentator suggested that whilst the benefits to consumers may be substantial, there must also be some degree of risk, since medicine use typically expands but general practitioner supervision decreases (Oster *et al.*, 1990). Thus the growing awareness of the possible risks accruing from mis-use of non-prescription medicines, their potentially harmful interaction with prescribed medication and the potentially negative impact on public health and levels of iatrogenic morbidity has stimulated research into community pharmacists' supervisory activities (Consumers Association, 1994; 1996; Krska and Kennedy, 1996; Bissell *et al.*, 1997a, 1997b; Bower and Eaton, 1998).

Within the UK, there is a legal requirement that community pharmacists must supervise the sale of all pharmacy medicines in order to ensure both safe and effective medicines purchases (Appelbe and Wingfield, 1997). In addition, in 1995, the Royal Pharmaceutical Society of Great Britain (RPSGB) stipulated that all community pharmacies draw up protocols governing the sale of medicines and the provision of advice to consumers. These are intended to offer guidance to staff on the procedures to be followed when advising consumers on the sale of non-prescription medicines and the management of minor ailments. In this way, protocols carry an implication that medicines should be seen as essentially different to other items of commerce available in the pharmacy, requiring both specific expert surveillance and expertise in their choice and use, emphasising their status as bearers of risk as well as concrete entities which carry therapeutic benefit. These developments are founded on an attempt to provide a more consistent service and at the same time to differentiate the pharmacy from other retail outlets selling medicines such as supermarkets.

This emphasis on risk and benefit in the policy arena has been matched by a professional discourse centred on the irresponsibility of marketing and advertising of medicines as 'ordinary' items of commerce. For example, the director of the National Pharmaceutical Association (National Pharmaceutical Association, 1998) referring to non-prescription medicines stated:

> The special nature of medicines, with their considerable potential to do harm if taken inappropriately, means they do not sit comfortably in an environment conducive to the sale and marketing of fast-moving consumer goods (1998, p. 1).

Thus, there is a developing sense in which the policy, professional and research agendas in this area are being framed around issues concerned with risk and the management of risk. On the part of the pharmacy profession, medicines are viewed as potential sources of risk, which require expert supervision. Against this view, the pharmaceutical industry is keen to encourage self-medication and to promote medicines as bearers of benefit as opposed to risk (Avorn *et al.*, 1982; Vuckovic and Nichter, 1997). Indeed, Vuckovic and Nichter (1997) point out from the US, that these contradictory ideologies serve mainly to engender contradiction and confusion for the consumer of medicines.

Lay views of medicines, health and risk

Research on risk and risk perceptions in the field of health and illness have tended to focus on health risk behaviours, such as sexual risk (Holland *et al.*, 1992; Lowy and Ross, 1994), the transmission of genetic diseases (Parsons and Atkinson, 1992), the risk of accidents (Green, 1997) and reproductive risks concerning childbirth (Handwerker, 1994). Of the studies which have explored risks in relation to specific medicines, the vast majority have focussed on prescribed medicines (Lively *et al.*, 1981; Britten, 1996; Gabe and Bury, 1996; Morgan, 1996; Barter and Cormack, 1996), as opposed to non-prescribed medicines.

Within the sparse literature on lay views of non-prescription medicines, research within the US has postulated an inverse relationship between perceptions of risk and benefit for a whole range of health-related issues, including non-prescription and prescription medicines (Alhakami and Slovic, 1994). This finding has been reiterated by Vuckovic and Nichter (1997), who, in a review of the literature on pharmaceutical use in the US suggest that prescription medicines are generally thought to be stronger than non-prescription medicines, leading to an opinion that non-prescription products are weak medicines, or for some, 'not really medicines at all'. Within the UK, Luck and Jesson (1992) found that a medicine which is prescribed by a doctor is often thought to be more powerful than one which can be bought non-prescription, thus emphasising that the route of supply may be important in shaping views of the risk and benefit. However, although seemingly a widespread view that prescription medicines might be considered 'stronger' than non-prescription medicines, this has not, until now, been subject to empirical testing in a systematic manner.

Whilst there has been work from the US which has began to make connections between pharmaceutical use and the sociology of risk

(Vuckovic and Nichter, 1997) there is a dearth of similar work in the UK. To our knowledge, there has been no published study which has explored consumers' views of the risks of deregulated medicines, or pharmacy medicines. In a recent review of the literature on self-care and the role of the pharmacy, Ward and Tully (1998) called for further research to be conducted into lay people's perspectives on non-prescription medicines. Similarly, Blaxter and Britten (1996) in a wide-ranging review of the research into lay perspectives on medicines, highlight the dearth of research into lay or user views of non-prescription medicines.

In addition, the majority of research within pharmacy practice has failed to consider the views and self-defined expertise of lay people in their use of non-prescription medicines. Much of this research is founded on the paternalistic assumption that the consumer of medicines is not sufficiently educated or knowledgeable to manage their use of medicines and requires expert assistance in this matter. The consumer is seen as essentially un-reflexive and uninvolved or disinterested in the process of care – a 'docile' rather than a 'reflexive' body (Williams and Calnan, 1996). In this paradigm, risks must therefore be managed by experts in order that the passive user of medicines might be shielded from danger and responsibility.

The study and method

The data on which this chapter is based forms part of a larger study, which set out to explore the nature and extent of communication about the risks of medicines between pharmacy staff and consumers purchasing deregulated medicines. Within this chapter, we focus specifically on consumer views about the risks and benefits of these medicines.

Given that little was known about the area under study, it seemed important to adopt a qualitative approach, which allowed for an understanding of the lay or consumer voice (Mason, 1996). Although we had a specific research agenda, our intention was to enable consumers of deregulated medicines to provide accounts of their non-prescription medicines use within their wider health maintenance activities. A central element of the research was concerned with tapping into consumer perspectives on the risks and benefits of medicines available in the pharmacy and their use of these medicines as treatment modalities.

Throughout this study, a dual approach to data collection was employed. Non-participant observational methods were used in conjunction with focus groups and interviews with consumers of deregulated medicines, pharmacists and medicines counter assistants. The research was conducted in the spring and summer of 1997 in 7 independent and 3 large chain pharmacies. The researcher (PW) visited each pharmacy for five working days and adopted a purely observational role. Field notes included details of interactions involving consumers, supplemented by data from informal discussions with pharmacy staff. Interviews (94) and focus groups (7) were conducted with a sample of consumers purchasing deregulated medicines from the research sites. In addition, we also conducted 21 depth interviews with a sample of consumers who presented with symptoms of hay fever during the study period in order to explore their views about the new information about the risks of terfenadine. The findings presented in this chapter are based on the interviews and focus groups with consumers purchasing deregulated medicines and interviews with hay fever sufferers.

The rationale for using focus groups, in addition to interviews, in this study was that they are particularly useful in studying issues which participants may not have previously thought about. Focus groups provide a rich seam of data about the perceptions, thoughts and feelings of those taking part (for a fuller appreciation of focus groups see Desvousges and Smith, 1988; Morgan, 1993; Kreuger, 1994; Kitzinger, 1995). Morgan (1993) argues that focus groups are particularly useful because participants can be asked to consider issues that they had not previously thought about, and that discussion will help them to construct and argue their view. This point was particularly pertinent for studying the views of consumers, who may not have given a great deal of consideration to the risks of non-prescription medicines. For these reasons, we believed that by using focus groups, consumers would be able to explore and clarify their views, comment on each others' experiences and create discussion in a way which would be less easily accessible in a one to one interview.

Findings

The findings from this study are divided into two main sections. Firstly, we highlight consumer views about the risks of non-prescription medicines in general. We then go on to look at the views of hay fever sufferers to the new information about the risks of terfenadine which ultimately lead to its reclassification back to prescription-only status.

Consumer views of non-prescription medicines

One of the main themes identified in this study was the emphasis on the idea of benefit rather than risk in consumers' accounts of the usage of medicines. We found consumers were far more likely to talk about the benefits of non-prescription medicines, and rarely talked about the risks or dangers of medication until prompted by the researcher. As one hay fever sufferer said: 'Look, when my eyes are streaming and my nose is streaming, how can I teach? I need some relief. And I need it fast, so I'm glad I can just nip to the chemist to get my tablets.' Asked if he had ever considered if his hay fever remedy presented any risks or dangers, this respondent commented: 'Apart from drowsiness, which I know about and I don't buy that one. No, to be honest I hadn't thought about the risks.' These views were echoed by a number of respondents who claimed not to have considered the issue of risk in relation to non-prescription medicines. Their focus was very much on alleviating symptoms or 'getting better' rather than making evaluations of the differential properties of medicines they were using. When asked if a consumer thought there were specific risks associated with the non-prescription medicines he customarily used, he responded:

> I thought someone sorted all that out anyway. We know they're not going to put anything unsafe on the shelves are they? Well, not something really dangerous anyway. To be honest, I hadn't given the issue that much thought.

Thus, our analysis of consumer views of non-prescription medicines is characterised by a privileging of benefit rather than risk and a focus on 'getting better' as opposed to making evaluations about the properties of medicines. As the above quotations demonstrate, consumers felt that risk was not an issue that exercised their minds in relation to non-prescription medicines. In addition it was not an issue that had been given much consideration, since the general impression seemed to be that the regulatory authorities would not allow 'dangerous' medicines to be available in the pharmacy.

As a result of the seeming absence of consideration of the risks of non-prescription medicines, we specifically tried to explore this point in relation to medicines recently deregulated from prescription-only status to pharmacy status. At the outset, we found some ambiguity around whether recently deregulated medicines carried risks or not. For example, some consumers thought that because deregulated medicines had previously been available on prescription, they must therefore be 'stronger' and carry some degree of risk. On the other hand, others thought that because they were now available 'on the shelves', they must – by definition – be safe. The following accounts neatly illustrate these beliefs:

> Well, if they've been on prescription, then you'd think they were stronger I suppose. And more dangerous. And that's why you can only get them in the pharmacy is it?

> I suppose, if they're for sale, like. That must mean they're safe mustn't it? They wouldn't do it otherwise.

It is possible that the relative absence of talk about risk was related to the high level of 'expertise' over medicines usage expressed by consumers. Many consumers had a strong sense of their own ability to self-manage specific minor ailments using non-prescription medicines. Their confidence in self-management stemmed in part from long personal experience of successfully managing minor ailments. For example, one woman described her experience of managing vaginal thrush using a non-prescription medicine. She suggested:

> I don't have a problem with it because I've been using it [Canestan cream] for years, and I know how it works and what it does to my body...I might not know the chemistry of it or what not, but I know where to put it and how to use it. It works.

This finding was replicated for a number of different non-prescription medicines for the treatment of hay fever, dyspepsia and other minor ailments. Lay expertise around specific medicine use appeared to limit the extent to which there was a discourse about risk. Thus, *personal* experience facilitated responsibility and control over medicine use and effective management of it, limiting a discourse based on risk.

Within this section we have outlined consumers accounts of their general perceptions of the risks and benefits of non-prescription medicines. In general, consumers were far more concerned to emphasise the benefits accruing from medicine use, rather than making assessments, or indeed, thinking about the possible risks of non-prescription medicines. In this way, non-prescription medicine use may be conceptualized as a relatively ingrained and taken for granted practice. In terms of debates about reflexivity and the notion of a risk society, consumer attitudes represent something of challenge given the absence of reflexive thought.

Against this relatively sanguine background, the next part of the chapter looks at how new information about the risks of the non-prescription hay fever remedy terfenadine affected consumers risk perceptions and their health-related behaviour.

Introducing information about the risks of medicines – the case of terfenadine

Background to the re-classification of terfenadine

During data collection for the present study, new information emerged into the public sphere about the non-prescription hay fever remedy terfenadine (commonly known as the branded product Triludan) which resulted in its re-classification from pharmacy status to prescription-only status. This reclassification occurred as information became available to the regulatory authority (the Medicines Control Agency) about previously unreported or unknown interactions between terfenadine and a commonly-prescribed antibiotic (erythromycin). In addition, an interaction between terfenadine and an enzyme in fresh grapefruit juice was also reported. These interactions accounted for approximately 14 deaths within the UK and numerous incidents of cardiac arrhythmias. According to the chair of the Committee for the Safety of Medicines, the interaction with grapefruit juice had been the 'final straw' (Anon 1997). The institutional response to the new risks of terfenadine was therefore, to limit the availability of terfenadine to the doctor's prescription.

The reclassification of terfenadine provided us with a unique opportunity to explore risk perceptions about non-prescription medicines in the context of a specific case where new information had been made available in the public sphere. In other words, the terfenadine case provided us with a concrete opportunity to explore in greater depth some of the issues around the risks and safety of medicines. In order to do this, we carried out an additional set of depth interviews with 21 consumers who presented with symptoms of hay fever during the study period.

Responses to the new information about the risks of terfenadine

The new information about the risks of terfenadine had, not surprisingly, raised anxieties about the use and adverse effects of terfenadine. Consumers reported being keenly aware of checking any other medication they took at the same time as terfenadine and ensuring they did not drink grapefruit juice at the same time. In this sense, consumers presented themselves as active, reasoned decision makers who were aware of the putative danger of medicines.

A further element of consumer anxieties centred on an acknowledgement of the essential uncertainty of medical knowledge. It was suggested that the new information about the risks of terfenadine had underlined to them how little medical science knew about the dangers of the products and technologies that were being customarily used. For example one consumer said: 'Well [I'm] obviously very worried. We didn't know about the risks did we? And by the sound of it, neither did the doctors.' Another respondent reported similar experiences: 'I used to take Triludan and three friends rang up and said don't eat any grapefruit. ... It's worrying to find out that suddenly there are all these things wrong with the drug isn't it?' In addition, some consumers suggested that their anxieties about the new risks of terfenadine were accentuated because terfenadine had been available to purchase in the pharmacy, thus being easily available and, in consumers eyes', considered less potentially dangerous than prescription medicines. One respondent, for example, questioned the monitoring of medicines for specific dangers. She suggested:

> You would have thought they would have already sorted this sort of thing out before they started selling it over the counter, or even putting it on prescription. It makes you wonder how they monitor these things, how they know whether they are safe or not.

Many respondents reported being worried about the risk status of terfenadine and had concerns that additional information might come to light in the future. Most respondents, however, had taken note of the new information – and were mindful of not taking antibiotics with their hay fever tablets. What was of particular concern to many respondents, however, was the interaction between terfenadine and grapefruit juice. Concerns centred on the argument that interactions were unexpected between natural products – such as grapefruit – and a drug – such as terfenadine. As one respondent stated:

> I don't know ... about chemistry, but I know that there are likely to be interactions – is that right, what you said – between different chemicals 'cos they are man made. But between a fruit and another drug? Now that is something you don't expect. And neither can you expect drug companies to be checking whether their medicine interacts with all the natural products we eat. I mean, what's next?

Strawberries and aspirin? Pineapple and paracetamol? It just shows how much we don't know, how little we really know about medical stuff and nature... and how little they know.

Reflecting on the risks of medicines

Our respondents suggested that for most of the time, pronouncements made by medical authorities were generally accepted and acted upon. However, when new information about the risks of a medicine occurred, respondents suggested that it forced them to reassess or reflect on claims made about the safety of modern medicine in general. One respondent suggested that the safety of medicines was not an issue that they had needed to consider in her lifetime, but that the case of terfenadine had forced her to reassess this point:

A whole load of us have grown up expecting to get what we wanted and life to be quite straightforward I think really. And that's how it is with drugs, you expect them to be quite straightforward and when they're not it makes you worried.

Another respondent put the case in more detail:

I think you do tend to go along thinking they get it right most of the time. And because these things are on sale in the chemists, they can't be that bad for you, can they? And to be honest, its not something you think about that much is it? But, the problem is, when things like terfenadine happens, well, its like, its like, you start to remember all the other bad apples we've had ... you know. I'm old enough to remember thalidomide. And there were others as well. I suppose it's experience isn't it? You accept it all until something goes wrong. And then you realise they don't always get it right.

Thus, the suggestion in the above quote was that people accept the claims of medical authorities about the safety of medicines until new information emerges which arouses their memories about past medical calamities and compounds people's fears about risk. For example, participants linked the new information about the dangers of terfenadine to the previously unknown dangers associated with the thalidomide and Opren controversies of the 1970s. Participants also linked these concerns to anxieties about the over-prescribing of sleeping tablets and tranquillisers. These concerns, coupled with respondents own experiences of heath services, combined and manifested themselves in a general discourse about the problems with medical technology and medicines specifically, as the following dialogue highlights:

It's not the first time, is it? Look at Thalidomide. Look at the problems they had with that. They didn't know about that either.

Yes, and look how slapdash they've been about Valium and tranquillisers. They used to prescribe them willy-nilly. I don't know if it's the same now but these drugs were just given out weren't they, without any thought for the consequences. So, you do have to be aware of the risks and the possible problems. You, as a person taking these things.

Acceptance of the limits of medical knowledge and dependence upon medicine

It is apparent from these accounts, that notions of uncertainty about medical science and medical knowledge underpinned consumers' views about medicines in general and contrasts markedly with the views about the benefits of non-prescription medicines as revealed earlier in the chapter. However, significantly, the uncertainty and anxieties generated by the terfenadine case had *not* fed into a overall rejection of medicines or medical authority. We found that consumers in this study were still using non-prescription medicines to treat minor ailments and many were still using terfenadine for their hay fever. It was suggested that for people who were already 'drug-averse', the new information about terfenadine would have merely serve to reinforce existing doubts and attitudes about safety. As one respondent said:

I think if you're already anti-drug then this will just add to that. I know a woman who is reflexology this, aromatherapy that: she wouldn't touch a drug from the chemist. But she was already like that. The terfenadine thing hasn't made me like that. It just makes you more wary. You just know that doctors don't know everything, we've got our doubts. But it doesn't make you give up on them.

The overwhelming majority were still using non-prescription medicines of one sort or another for treating their hay fever, despite the widespread awareness of deaths resulting from use of terfenadine. Some individuals were still requesting terfenadine in the pharmacy *after* the announcement of drug interactions. Indeed, several respondents reported that they had merely gone to obtain terfenadine on prescription after its re-classification because for them, no other product worked as well.

In this sense then, consumer dependence on medicine and relief from symptoms appears to be a more powerful factor than fear of risk. As one participant said about the overall impact of the terfenadine episode on his beliefs and behaviour:

> We know they don't know everything, doctors and that. They make mistakes. But medicines work as well, and I want something that works at the end of the day. I know there are risks of some sort from medicines – there's got to be. But you're prepared to take that risk in order to get better. And this Triludan thing won't alter that.

Crucially, whilst this account emphasises an awareness of the limits to medical knowledge in terms of its uncertainty, this awareness had *not* translated into a rejection of medical knowledge and authority. Thus, consumers showed themselves to be active decision makers, able to absorb and act upon new information.

Conclusion

Consumers' attitudes towards non-prescription medicines

Within this chapter, we have suggested that consumers view medicines available from the pharmacy as possessing fewer risks than prescription-only medicines. These attitudes are associated with a greater focus on the benefits accruing from non-prescription medicine use, at the expense of making evaluations about the risks or dangers of medicines. In this way, non-prescription medicine use may be conceptualized as a routine, taken for granted activity.

The seeming absence of assessment of the risks of non-prescription medicines is also shaped by the extent of lay expertise over the treatment of minor ailments using non-prescription medicines. Frequent experience of successfully treating a minor ailment provides a sense of lay expertise or mastery over medicine use. Where such mastery exists, there seems a consequent reduction in considerations of risk. To an extent, our data loosely supports the assertions of Vuckovic and Nichter (1997) and Luck and Jesson (1992): there does seem to be evidence from this study that non-prescription medicines are considered to possess fewer risks and also be less powerful than prescription medicines. In addition, these data suggest that deregulating medicines from prescription-only to pharmacy status leaves people unclear whether these medicines have the same risks as prescription medicines, or whether, because they are now available in the pharmacy, they must be relatively harm-free. This complex web of ideas about risk does not lend itself easily to policy makers or practitioners who may wish to present deregulated medicines as different from other items of commerce.

Similarly, our data suggests clear limits to the sociological enterprise described by Beck (1992) and Giddens (1990; 1991). The idea of the multiplication, globalization and continual assessment of risks is not reflected in consumer accounts about non-prescription medicines. In this way, we suggest that evaluations of risks and benefit are not reflexively produced and neither are they a central motif of lay discourse around the area of non-prescription medicine use.

Responses to risk – the case of terfenadine

In the context of consumer attitudes to new information about the risks of terfenadine, it is possible to see the production of a different set of accounts to those outlined above. Consumers presented themselves as risk-aware individuals who could assimilate and act upon information about the risks of terfenadine. Consumers were keen to highlight their awareness of the uncertainty of medical knowledge and the degree to which risks often remained unknown. However, this had not translated into a sense that all scientific knowledge was incorrect or somehow unknowable. Rather than seeing medical knowledge and all forms of risk assessments as unintelligible, consumers actively assimilated the new information about the risks of medicines and acted upon it, showing themselves to be responsible, risk-aware medicines users.

In a sense then, we can see two levels of reasoning at play here which produced two sets of accounts. The first set of accounts revealed the everyday cognitions about non-prescription medicines which emphasised their routine, safe and beneficial nature. Consumers suggested that they did not think about the risks of non-prescription medicines because they were more concerned with alleviating their symptoms and that medicines available in the pharmacy were presumed to be devoid of risks. Thus, we may conceptualize this as an essentially unreflexive approach to understanding in this context.

The second set of accounts revealed that, at a time of relative crisis, consumers had been forced to re-assess their everyday habits in the face of new information. What we found, not surprisingly, alongside the fear and anxieties of consumers was the linkage between the new information about the risks of terfenadine and other more reflexive and durable concerns about the uncertainty of modern medicine. The new information both caused and reinforced these sets of concerns, producing the distinctive discourse reported. This may be conceptualized as a more reflexive approach to understanding.

Although this second set of accounts provides some justification for the Beck (1992) Giddens (1990; 1991) position, highlighting the emergence of the 'reflexive consumer' in late modernity, the extent to which consumers in this study went along with medical authority and continued using non-prescription medicines shows clear limits to this thesis. Rather, we would suggest that consumers in this study bore closer resemblance to the position adopted by Lupton (1996; 1997). Lupton suggests that western medicine at the end of the twentieth century is characterised by a central paradox, which is illustrated in this study. Medicine is characterised by increasing challenges to its ability to deliver safe, risk free and effective therapies even though it has assumed the position of a secular religion in western societies in a time of post-traditional order. It is assailed by criticism for its lack of certainty and yet at the same time, people are increasingly dependent on it as therapy.

The dependence on medicines as a form of therapy may be seen as a central theme within our study. Although consumers presented themselves as reflexive actors in the aftermath of the new information about the risks of terfenadine, this did not lead to disuse of terfenadine or non-prescription medicines in general. Consumers in this study were aware of the risks of terfenadine, but were prepared to accept these risks because of their dependence on the benefits of terfenadine. Thus, these findings reveal that consumers may occupy both consumerist and paternalist, or reflexive and docile spaces.

The case of non-prescription medicines and the new information about the risks of terfenadine highlights the dynamic and shifting nature of consumers' ideas about risks. Consumers may be seen to be in a state of flux, occupying, as it were, spaces within both docile and as reflexive bodies, in a similar way to that outlined by Williams and Calnan (1996), who suggest that: 'lay people are not simply passive or active, dependent or independent, believers or sceptics. Rather, they are a complex mixture of all these things (and much more besides)' (1996, p. 264). On a normal, everyday level, consumers did not think about the risks of the non-prescription medicines they were ingesting. However, new information about the risks of one non-prescription medicine prompted them to reflect on the risks of all medicines and the expert status of medical knowledge. In this way, mapping the contours of consumer ideas about risk becomes a complex project in which people may be seen to be shifting back and forth along a continuum between the production of docile and reflexive approaches to understanding in this context.

9

Riding the Roller Coaster: Household Responses to Changing Housing Market Risk

Moira Munro

Introduction

This chapter uses recent survey evidence to examine the way in which people understand and respond to the risks they encounter when they are making decisions about buying and selling their homes. Housing may be argued to occupy an ambivalent position with respect to public policy and the welfare state in Britain. On one hand, a significant element in the post-second world war welfare revolution was direct state intervention in the provision of council housing to make good quality, affordable housing available for the ordinary working population (Malpass and Murie, 1995). The conception of housing as a basic necessity, and something therefore that the Government 'ought' to take responsibility for, is still discernible in many aspects of the public policy debate around housing. Although there have been very significant changes to the financial and management structures in council housing, few commentators would take the position that there is no need for *any* social rented housing. Similarly, there appears to be a broad consensus around the principle of giving assistance towards housing costs as part of the broader welfare safety net for families and individuals in need.

Yet, despite an apparently broad acceptance of the public responsibility for many different aspects of housing problems, the provision of housing in Britain is now overwhelming in the private sector. By the beginning of 1997, 67 per cent of households in Britain were owner-occupiers (Council for Mortgage Lenders, 1998). Significant shifts in the tenure distribution occurred through the 1980s, particularly as a result of the right-to-buy policy which enabled council tenants to buy their homes at a discounted price (Forrest and Murie, 1992). However, the evidence suggests that owner-occupation is, for most people the strongly *preferred* option and this preference does not chiefly depend on direct policy support (SEH, 1997). It is difficult to argue that the privatisation of the housing system, unlike other areas of welfare reform, was forced upon an unwilling population. To the contrary, owner-occupation is associated with a range of very positive characteristics; access to better quality housing and neighbourhoods, long-term financial advantages (both because, unlike renting, mortgage payments tend to fall in real terms over the life of the mortgage and eventually cease, *and* because of the access to capital gains and wealth that owner-occupation can bring), and independence from any interference by a landlord.

In this context, policy projections in such areas as analysis of the future housing and land requirements arising from recent household forecasts assumes the continued dominance of the private sector (Breheny and Hall, 1996; Holmans, 1995). However, there are two major areas in which the role of the public sector in housing remains contentious. First, the appropriate boundaries between public and private responsibilities are subject to debate. For example, there is scope for considerable disagreement as to exactly which groups should be entitled to social housing or the extent to which government should interfere with private sector provision, in relation to construction standard or planning controls. A second set of contentious issues reflects considerable concern about the appropriateness of the private sector option for at least some of those who are choosing to take it. The so-called 'residual-isation' of the social rented sector has made it an option of last resort both because it is increasingly difficult to gain access to good quality housing in this tenure and also because to do so is to be excluded from the advantages of owner-occupation enjoyed by the mainstream majority (Cole and Furbey, 1994). There is a danger, then, that people are effec-tively 'forced' into owner-occupation, when their personal circum-stances make this a relatively risky option for them.

As the owner-occupied sector becomes ever larger and consequently contains a greater proportion of more marginal households, the inci-dence of mortgage arrears and eventual repossession has risen signifi-cantly. Data from 1997 for the Council of Mortgage Lenders indicate that 2.4 per cent of mortgages over a quarter of a million house buyers were 2.5 per cent or more in arrears. In 1997, a further 32 770 properties were taken into possession (Council for Mortgage Lenders, 1998) a total that excludes those households which abandoned owner-occupation at some point *before* that ultimate sanction was exercised. These figures represent a reduction compared to the problems experienced at the depth of the early 1990s recession, but can be taken to indicate that some degree of mortgage difficulty is inevitable in this much expanded sector. Even where lenders are keen to reach arrangements with those who find themselves in difficulty, ultimately the commercial imperative of the relationship cannot be overruled permanently. Mortgage lenders ultimately do not have to make housing available to those in difficulty, but *do* have to make a profit on their lending activities.

The loss of the home is a serious adverse risk which owners face, and the extent of the risk is argued to be exacerbated by increasing uncertainty and flexibility in labour markets (Maclennan *et al.*, 1998; Ford, chapter 6 in this volume) and the inadequacy of the benefits safety net available to owner-occupiers who become unemployed (Ford and Kempson, 1997; Ford and Wilcot, 1994). The reduction in state support for owners in financial difficulty is a clear example of the ambivalence surrounding the extent of Government responsibility for what is, arguably, a wholly private decision. The difficulties in sustaining owner-occupation faced by the growing number of people in marginal and fragile labour market situations cause some to believe that any continued increase in the proportion of owner-occupiers is unlikely and even to doubt whether current levels are sustainable (Forrest *et al.*, 1995).

However, in addition to these most extreme risks (of major debt and loss of the home), it is clear that owner-occupation presents owners with a range of uncertainties that create risks, although with less dramatic consequences. These uncertainties result directly from the instability of both property and finance markets. The anticipated advantages of owner-occupation mentioned above depend on particular outcomes in these markets (at least for the great majority of owners who finance their purchase with a long-term mortgage loan). The trend to increases in real wages combined with stable or falling interest rates leads repayments to fall in relative and absolute terms. Capital gains have resulted from a faster real inflation rate in house prices than in the prices of other goods and services. It is clear, though, that these conditions have not always been sustained in the housing market and may by no means be assumed to be inevitable and inherent characteristics of owner-occupation.

The research reported in this chapter was designed to examine how owner-occupiers understood the risks they face and created strategies to cope with them. It focuses particularly on those engaged in housing market transactions, either buying for the first time or trading (involving the co-ordinated sale of one property and the acquisition of another). The work does not, therefore, concentrate particularly on those who are the most vulnerable to the extreme risks of the housing market, but instead examines how a broad cross-section of owners cope with a situation which is inevitably uncertain. The decisions made have real consequences at least in the sense that buying a house is one of the biggest financial commitments that most people make and ultimately for most it becomes their largest asset. This would suggest that most people have an incentive to give the decision-making processes serious consideration and to arrive at the best choice that they can. As Maclennan (1982) argues, economic theory is not well adapted to the real world complexities of the housing market and so it is hard to set up in practical terms a comparison of actual behaviour with what would be 'economically rational' behaviour in any situation. However, the instability of the housing market creates a situation in which the reaction of people to very different contexts can be examined and compared. This enables a better understanding of the effect of uncertainty on the choices made in this important aspect of consumption. In addition, it provides insight into more general strategies that can be adopted in response to an increasingly risky social environment and the decline of welfare support.

The unstable housing market

This study makes possible the comparison of housing market experience and outcomes across two of the most important established dimensions of housing market instability and inequality; namely through time and across space. The spatial contrasts were designed to capture the strong regional and local differences that are apparent within the British housing market, in both price levels and patterns of price appreciation (Hamnett, 1989). The variation in house price levels and price inflation across the country was captured in the choice of two contrasting city case studies, Glasgow and Bristol. These cities provide strongly contrasting contexts in terms both of absolute price levels and recent experience of price instability allowing the researchers to compare both the perceptions of riskiness and reactions to it in these circumstances.

The first phase of analysis concentrated on the cross-sectional differences between the cities in 1995 in relation to measureable outcomes in the housing markets (for example, how much was borrowed) and also qualitative evidence from buyers in both cities as to how they perceived the risks and options they faced and how they articulated their choices[1]. This work found that overt differences in reactions to the housing market slump were less discernible between the two contrasting housing market areas than had been expected (Munro *et al.*, 1998). Much greater price instability was experienced in Bristol; witnessed in a very rapid boom in house prices in the late 1980s followed by falling prices first in real then absolute terms in the early 1990s. A different pattern was found in Glasgow, where a relatively modest but steady upward trend in prices meant that most buyers neither enjoyed very large capital gains nor were subsequently exposed to the risks of negative equity and falling prices. Despite these contrasts, the attitudes expressed and the perceptions of the potential risks attached to home ownership were relatively similar in the two locations. This consistency was explained partly in relation to the apparently low priority given to any kind of explicit calculation of 'economically rational' behaviour in most aspects of housing market decision-making. Instead, qualitative interviews revealed a range of important, non-economic considerations that underpinned decisions in the housing market, particularly to do with expectations of the ways in which housing careers and family changes 'should' mesh together.

The qualitative interviews revealed a considerable awareness of the many uncertainties and risks in the housing market and there was a broad acceptance that risk and uncertainty were an inevitable feature of modern labour markets. However, the research identified a range of more or less pragmatic strategies for dealing with (or often ignoring) those risks, that were not obviously linked to respondents' own experiences in the housing and labour markets (Madigan and Munro, 1999; see also Ford, chapter 6 in this book). Uptake of options which are, in principle available to help deal with risks, particularly through the ever-expanding range of financial and insurance products available, also showed few contrasts between the areas. Indeed the qualitative work revealed that many people did not fully understand the complex financial choices available to them. In these circumstances it is clearly impossible to expect a 'rational' economic response to different risks, as buyers are often unable to identify what such a response would be. A final possible explanation for finding relatively fewer contrasts between the two cities than expected is that the *national* picture, as prevailing in the media, is more important in provoking responses than the *local* picture.

The intention in this paper is to extend this earlier cross-sectional analysis by focusing more explicitly on contrasts through the national boom-bust cycle. In particular, this draws into the analysis survey evidence available for the two cities on housing market behaviour and choices in 1988[2]. These snapshots in 1988 and 1995 are taken first at the height of the boom in the southern housing market, when house prices and turnover levels reached a peak, and second in the stagnant condition following the housing market recession of the early 1990s.

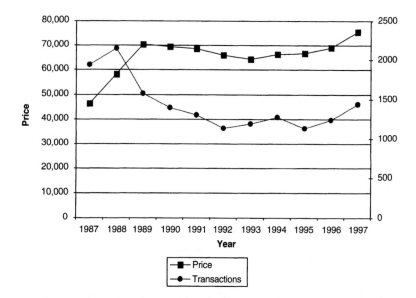

Figure 9.1   House sales, 1987–97, price (£) and number of transactions (000s)
Notes: *Price* is the mix-adjusted price at mortgage completion stage for all UK.
Transactions are all property transactions in England and Wales.
Source: Council for Mortgage Lenders, 1998.

Figure 9.1 shows the rise and fall in house prices across Britain as a whole and the associated rise and fall in the level of transactions. It shows how large year-on-year price rises in the late 1980s were followed by falls, even though general retail price inflation continued through the period. The level of property transactions also fell dramatically from a peak in 1988, by 26 per cent and 12 per cent in the two following years. The diagram shows how the housing market recession was characterised by falling prices and low transaction levels, while the (modest) market recovery of 1996 and 1997 is associated with an increasing turnover in the market.

Comparing these two surveys provides rich opportunities to consider the effects of national housing market instability and local variations from that pattern. In particular, it allows an examination of the different housing choices made in the 'boom' and the 'bust' and, implicit in this, the response to the different risks which dominate under different market circumstances.

Research approach

The two surveys which provide the main new empirical evidence presented in this chapter were carried out with different primary purposes.

The later study was specifically concerned with expectations and beliefs in the owner-occupied market, while the earlier research was more explicitly *financial* in focus, as part of a larger project designed to investigate the levels of subsidies enjoyed by people in different tenures (for full details of this earlier survey and the results for Glasgow see Hancock *et al.*, 1991, and for Bristol, Bramley, 1989). An overview of the programme is given in Maclennan (1991)). The stratified sample designs used mean that valid comparisons can be drawn between the two cities and in comparing different 'types' of buyer (first time buyer, recently trading owner and non-mover, where recent traders and first time buyers are those that have moved within the previous three years). However, this very specific design means that care should be taken before drawing more general inferences about *all* owner-occupiers. The main advantage of using these original surveys is that more sophisticated analysis is possible than would be the case with published data, for example, as each survey contains considerable detail about the financial, demographic and housing market characteristics and choices of owners at the individual level, that would not generally be available elsewhere. Three salient aspects of the decision-making process are explored in this chapter; first, borrowing behaviour, second, the characteristics and motivations of movers and third, the extent to which changing conditions in the housing market appear to reduce people's ability to make the housing moves that they would wish to make.

Comparing housing choices: the boom and the slump

Borrowing behaviour

A central element of the risk that people take as part of the house purchase process is in taking on a long-term mortgage debt. It would be expected that a range of complex considerations would enter into the decision as to how much to borrow; limited on one hand by the willingness of the financial institutions to lend the amount that the household might ideally wish to borrow and on the other by the household's calculation of how much debt it would wish to take on. This would be expected to result from some consideration of the likely risk and return in taking on housing debt, presumably based on expectations of the future, which might involve considerations of:

• Future labour market prospects: are wages likely to rise rapidly in real terms? Is there significant job uncertainty or risk of redundancy?

- Future household changes: are there plans to start a family? Will this lead to the loss of or reduction in one's partner's income?
- Future housing market trends: are prices expected to increase rapidly?

In addition, households are likely to vary in their aversion to risk; some will be more uncomfortable than others at the prospect of coping with unexpected changes, such as those that would arise from a rise in interest rates (and of course households will differ in the extent to which they have already experienced such changes and in the extent to which they understand or anticipate such risks). These factors are obviously very personal and unique to each household (at which level choices may also reflect the outcomes of negotiations concerning these factors between partners in a couple) and are probably impossible ever to model in a quantitatively satisfactory way. However, in aggregate, the large change in the context from the boom to the slump in the housing market would be expected to change borrowing behaviour measurably.

In the popular imagination the boom was associated with some reck-lessness on the part of buyers, reflected in a willingness to borrow as much as possible and probably more than would be seen as rational with the benefit of hindsight. Beckman (1997) takes a radical and rather pessimistic view of the future of the housing market and argues that there should be no expectation of any reprieve from the housing market slump over the next 20 years. He specifically rejects the argu-ment that the boom and bust was caused by more immediately 'rational' considerations, such as increased fears about job security:

> buyers...were blinded by the media hype for ownership during the 1980s. During the height of the house buying boom, job security was no more a consideration than whether the house would survive for the duration of the mortgage. To understand the sequence of booms and busts you must recognise and acquiesce to the forces of unreason. There can be no rational explanation for an irrational environment (Beckman, 1997, p. 206).

In this interpretation, the boom is fuelled by speculative irrationality, which may be self-sustaining in the short-term at least. It is useful in reminding us of the prevailing climate of boom (Saunders, 1990). At least two rationalisations can be given for being willing to borrow more when caught up in a house price boom:

- A belief that accessibility to owner-occupation is constantly retreating, so that as affordability is continually being eroded by ever higher prices, one must jump on the ladder now (or never).

- A belief that it is *worth* taking on major debt to gain maximum access to the benefits of capital gains that are available – and, apparently, assured and significant.

The chief implication of these perceptions is that in the boom people will be willing to buy a more expensive property – by maximising their borrowing from formal sources *and* by increasing the use of any alternative sources of funding (capital gains, savings, informal borrowing) that they can access. In contrast, a slump would be expected to be associated with more caution in borrowing behaviour as gains seem smaller and uncertain.

The information available in the surveys enables various aspects of the financial decisions taken by buyers during the boom and the slump to be compared. As with the cross-sectional analyses, these investigations reveal considerably fewer significant differences in apparent actual behaviour than would be expected in the light of the accounts given above. Table 9.1 presents average mortgage to income ratios for each city and type of buyer in the 'boom' and 'bust' years. Every effort is made in the analysis to maintain comparability between the two surveys but given that they *were* differently designed and focused, the analyst would wish to see strong and unambivalent evidence of trends and patterns before drawing strong conclusions. Table 9.1 can be interpreted to indicate that there was more *variability* in borrowing across the boom and

Table 9.1 Mortgage to income ratios: Glasgow and Bristol (%)

	1988	1995
First-time buyers		
Bristol	2.19	2.03
Glasgow	1.97	2.05
Trading owners		
Bristol	1.58	1.49
Glasgow	1.53	1.63
Stayers		
Bristol	0.67	0.94
Glasgow	0.78	0.98

Notes: t-statistics reveal no statistically significant differences in the average ratios between the cities in each year. The table excludes owners who purchased council rented dwellings under the 'right to buy' scheme from the analysis.

the slump in Bristol, suggesting a greater experience of disequilibrium experienced in this housing market, but the clearest message from the table appears to be of relative *stability* in the choices made by buyers in the boom and the slump with recent first time buyers borrowing about twice their income and trading owners just over one and a half times. As these are less than the maximum ratios typically allowed by lenders we can assume that for most households borrowing outcomes are a result of choice rather than being constrained by lenders.

Perhaps unexpectedly, the biggest difference in current mortgage to income ratios is seen amongst the *non-traders*, who on average owed considerably more relative to their incomes during the slump than the boom. This outcome is obviously not the result of *direct* decision-making, but a consequence of decisions made four or more years earlier. The difference in the relative size of outstanding mortgages may partly reflect the differences in the characteristics of those *not* trading in the boom and the slump (discussed in more detail below), but is also a direct product of the lower inflation environment that characterised the early 1990s in which mortgage debt was not eroded so rapidly by generally inflating prices and incomes as had been the case in the years prior to the 1988 boom.

Table 9.2 examines another aspect of the financial decision, namely the proportion of the price borrowed in the two contrasting time periods. Again, it would be expected that if people were 'stretching' themselves' more during the boom they would be keen to borrow as much as possible. Given the evidence above, that they were *not* on average borrowing markedly more in relation to incomes, then the alternative way of maximising access to housing equity is to put more money into the purchase from other sources (whether savings, cashing existing assets or further borrowing from alternative formal and informal sources). If borrowers were indeed attempting to maximise their speculative investment in housing, it would be expected that primary mortgage borrowing would be somewhat *lower* in relation to purchase price in the boom than the slump. The table shows some indicative evidence that this was so. For first time buyers, the very great majority take out loans for over 80 per cent or over 90 per cent of the purchase price in both time periods, while there is a much broader spread evident amongst those who are trading owners (many of whom will have some equity accumulated from their previous house available to help them in the trading process). In Bristol the proportion of all buyers taking the highest value loans is typically less than in Glasgow. In both cities, a greater proportion of buyers borrowed over 90 per cent of the purchase

Table 9.2 Proportion of price borrowed (%)

	1988		1995	
	Glasgow	**Bristol**	**Glasgow**	**Bristol**
First time buyers				
<50%	2.7	4.5	3.2	6.4
−60%	2.7	5.7	1.6	2.5
−70%	2.7	3.4	3.3	1.7
−80%	2.7	10.2	1.6	5.8
−90%	10.8	25.0	9.0	16.5
90%+	78.4	50.0	81.1	66.9
Trading owners				
<10%	12.5	14.9	0.8	−
−30%	7.0	12.6	3.4	5.7
−50%	8.3	17.3	13.4	17.0
−70%	16.6	27.4	17.6	18.0
−80%	22.2	14.9	12.6	10.4
−90%	20.8	9.1	16.8	19.8
90%+	12.5	4.0	35.3	29.2

Note: The table excludes owners who purchased council rented dwellings under the 'right to buy' scheme from the analysis.

price in the slump, and this shift towards higher proportionate loans is particularly marked for trading owners.

It is also interesting to note that the number of trading owners taking the very lowest proportionate mortgages reduces considerably from the boom to the slump. This group is likely to be dominated by those who are trading *down* within the housing market, perhaps extracting considerable amounts of accumulated housing equity to use for other purposes. This is a relatively little examined aspect of the housing decision-making process in Britain (although there is some limited work on retirement migration and mobility in old age – Karn, 1977; Warnes, 1992) but it might be expected that such moves would be highly discretionary in their timing and would be particularly attractive at, and even encouraged by, those times when house price inflation had made owners' previous property accumulate value particularly quickly and also when, at the height of the boom, there is a great difference in absolute prices between high and low priced parts of the country. In these circumstances trading down for a retirement move can net considerable profit.

In summary, then, the evidence on the proportion of price borrowed reveals more interesting changes from boom to slump than are evident in mortgage to income ratios. Local differences may also influence the extent to which different borrowing strategies are viable. For example, in times of rapid local inflation, the valuations of properties which constitute the notional '100 per cent' against which institutions are willing to lend, are likely to lag behind the prices that actually prevail in the market. Buyers in such cases, may be forced to find additional sources of capital to make up shortfalls. Ultimately it is difficult to be sure whether the shift in the slump towards a reduced use of non-mortgage funds in house purchase results from buyer choices or constraints imposed by lenders or is structured by market conditions. In either case, though, increased use of saving and other money during the boom years would support the perception that people are willing to 'stretch' themselves more financially to capture greater possible gains.

Characteristics of movers in the boom and the slump

The unstable housing market arguably presents a range of risks for traders at all points of the housing market cycle, perhaps particularly for trading owners who have to judge the likely risks and returns associated with buying and selling properties more or less simultaneously. Figure 9.1 showed that a key characteristic of the transition from boom to slump was a large fall in the volume of trading. It is possible that there is a reduced willingness or ability to trade in a slump across all types of buyers, but more specifically this might be reflected in changes in the motivations of purchasers in the two periods:

- The boom is associated with speculation: it might be expected that financial motives would drive the desire to trade, to capitalise on the opportunities presented to use accumulated equity to trade up within the housing market.
- The slump provides fewer opportunities for profit and so it might be expected that those moves which do take place are more driven by housing consumption.

Further, there would be expected to be differences in motivation for first time buyers and trading owners. To take advantage of any lower priced 'bargains' that might be available in a slower market, current home owners must also sell their own property, which can be difficult and may not bring the profit they expect. For first-time buyers there would be expected to be positive *advantages* in buying during a market slow-down; prices are likely to be relatively lower and there is less competition amongst potential buyers for any particular available property.

However, desire to buy may be undermined by any lack of confidence in future price levels and a relatively smaller supply may limit effective choices. Detailed investigation of the two surveys provided little evidence of major motivational shifts for buyers in the two time periods. Reasons given in each time period were overwhelmingly to do with family and related 'normal' lifecycle reasons. Clearly this evidence needs to be treated with some caution, since people may not always feel able to express their true motivations in an interview situation. They may perhaps suppress what seem to be 'greedy' or avaricious motives in favour of presenting what are believed to be more 'legitimate' reasons for moving, such as wanting to move to a bigger house because of starting a new relationship or because children are growing older and need more space.

The qualitative interviews in 1995 however confirm the emphasis placed by most respondents on family reasons for moving. When asked why people had decided to move at that time, even though the market conditions were difficult for many, the following are typical responses:

Ms Gibson 'I'd moved in with (partner), so we want to be in our own house basically' (Trading owner, Bristol)

Mrs Todd 'Well we want something bigger... I don't know, we'll probably, we might start a family in the next couple of years' (Trading owner, Bristol)

Mrs Irvine 'Because we need something bigger, because we now have two children... we've just kind of out-grown the house' (Trading owner, Glasgow)

Mrs Brown 'This house is now too big for us. It's a house of spirits, that's full of memories. We brought our children up here, we've had hundreds of guests, we've had lots of parties... but it's now too big for us' (Trading owner, Glasgow)

A further way of examining whether buyers' main motivations had indeed changed relatively little between the boom and the slump was to compare the socio-demographic characteristic of buyers in the two periods. In each period, the characteristics of buyers in Glasgow and Bristol were found to be the same (as no statistically significant differences could be found), suggesting that the differential local experience of booms and slumps did not cause strong local differences to appear in the types of trader. Therefore, in Table 9.3 the localities are aggregated together to focus on comparisons between the boom and the slump.

Table 9.3   Characteristics of traders in the boom and slump (%)

	First-time buyers		Trading owners	
	1988	1995	1988	1995
Age of respondents				
16–19	2.3	1.3	–	–
20–29	67.8	63.9	22.3	14.8
30–39	22.6	27.4	42.6	46.0
40–49	5.1	3.9	18.5	18.1
50–59	0.6	2.2	8.3	8.4
60+	1.7	1.2	8.3	12.8
Main household types				
Single adult	44.3	37.2	11.2	7.7
Couple no child(ren)	22.9	25.1	19.4	21.6
Couple & infant(s)	19.0	15.2	27.2	24.6
Couple & child(ren)	4.3	11.7	19.9	19.7
Other	9.5	10.8	22.3	26.4

Note: 'Households' excludes those who have bought using the right to buy.

The table shows some relatively minor shifts in the characteristics of buyers between the two time periods. The average age of both recent movers and first time buyers tends to rise in the slower market conditions. This shift is confirmed using exact ages, but is shown to be relatively slight, effectively the average age for first time buyers increased from late twenties to early thirties. Amongst first time buyers, there are fewer single adult households buying in the slower market, and also a reduction in the proportion of couples with infants. At the same time there is some increase in the number of childless couples buying and in the number of couples with children. Similarly for recent traders, there is the greatest proportionate fall in the single adults category comparing boom to slump.

These changes, though slight, are consistent with the hypotheses advanced about the 'frenzy' effect of the boom. In the calmer conditions of the market slow down, buyers are delaying purchase somewhat. Single adults are perhaps the classic group who might be expected to defer purchase when the prospects of immediate financial gains are not so great. There are two main possible reasons for this: first, young first time buyers perhaps have the easiest access to alternative accommodation either in the private rented sector or with family. Second, it is less profitable to buy when rapid, short-term gains are not assured. This group may well have a relatively shorter period in which they will definitely stay in the purchased property, since it may be possible to anticipate relatively quicker changes in household circumstances or in their labour market position. Analysts have also pointed to broader changes affecting younger people, that may make it harder for current and future generations to enter owner-occupation, particularly because of greater student debt requiring repayment in the early working years (Council for Mortgage Lenders, 1998). These factors would be expected to make younger single people contemplating owner-occupation more sensitive to prospects of immediate financial return that would generally seem less appealing in a slower market.

However, in relation to these and the other socio-demographic factors investigated it should be stressed that the absolute size of the changes is relatively small. This would tend to confirm households' own accounts that family and demographic factors dominate their decision-making process, with considerations of financial conditions very much secondary. The evidence of only small changes in trader profile is also consistent with the qualitative evidence gathered in 1995 which showed that most people see buying a house as a relatively long-term choice. Typically, they choose a property that they hope will suit them for some considerable time (Madigan and Munro, 1999). This strategy can allow a reduced concern about potential resale value or shorter-term capital losses in the 'new' property (as these are much less relevant when the intention is to stay in the next house for the foreseeable future) and is also consistent with the emotional investment that is tied up with settling into a 'home'. However, for some respondents it seemed clear that seeking to make a very long-term choice was associated with the frustration caused by an inability to move house as quickly as had originally been planned. The evidence presented here suggests that these considerations do not disproportionately disadvantage some particular types of buyer, but instead apply more or less evenly to dissuade movers across the board.

Frustrated mobility

It is difficult to give an entirely convincing account of the evidence presented so far. The puzzle lies in the fact that changes in the behaviour of home-buyers seem to be relatively minor, yet as Figure 9.1 showed there was a very significant fall in the level of housing market transactions overall. A part of the explanation for this lies in recalling that the market imposes constraints as well as providing opportunities for choice. The final aspect of behaviour examined in this chapter focuses on the extent of frustrated mobility, to examine the extent to which the change in market condition made it difficult or impossible for people to pursue their preferred options.

As well as the direct constraints that may be placed on household choices by institutions (for example, in relation to borrowing limits) indirect constraints are created by the market conditions that prevail at the time. For instance, in the slower market, particularly in Bristol, it was clear that many people found it difficult to find a buyer for their houses, and there were some potential movers apparently trapped in houses that were particularly unpopular (in the slower market conditions the smallest 'starter' homes appeared to be 'leapfrogged' by buyers in favour of bigger houses that could be expected to meet changing household needs for longer but which were now affordable – Munro *et al.*, 1998). In these circumstances, there was relatively little individuals could do to pursue their plans; most were limited in the extent to which they were able to drop their price because of the limit to the loss that they were able to bear and at this selling price there were very few willing buyers. Such circumstances are clearly most difficult for those who also find themselves in financial difficulty. Without the option of trading on, they have no choice but to remain in a situation which continues to increase their debt. The inability to pursue a chosen strategy is important to analyse directly because it is an important adverse consequence of the risks inherent in the housing market, as in many others. It would be expected that such problems would be more prevalent in the slow market compared to the more fluid, though inflationary, context of a booming market.

Regrettably, the comparisons that can be made between the surveys concerning detailed matters of motivation and choices can only be indicative because the exact questions in each were different. A further fundamental problem arises when attempting to capture any frustrated aspiration by means of an administered survey; people may be reluctant to admit to the desire to move when they feel they have little possibility of doing so. Housing surveys typically find quite high levels of overall expressed satisfaction with housing circumstances, a finding which can be interpreted in the light of the importance that most people attach to their home environment. To admit a deep dissatisfaction with something so important as 'home' is to admit to a significant area of unhappiness and perhaps failure. It would be expected that similar sentiments would reduce the propensity of people to say that they would like to, but cannot, move house.

Table 9.4 compares the proportion of people who, respectively say they 'intended' to move in 1988 or 'would like' to move in 1995.

Table 9.4 The extent of frustrated mobility in the boom and the slump (%)

	'Intend to move' 1988		'Would like to move' 1995	
	Glasgow	Bristol	Glasgow	Bristol
Non-mover	10.9	9.9	34.2	36.5
Trading owners	6.6	12.0	20.6	15.3
First time buyer	19.0	16.8	25.7	26.4
Total	11.3	11.2	25.2	24.9

Note: The table excludes 'right to buy' owners.

The differently phrased questions will no doubt exaggerate the apparent differences between the two years as the 'intention' to move suggests firmer plans than implied by simply 'liking' to move. Even so, there seems no doubt that there was a considerably greater degree of frustrated mobility in the slower market in 1995, as would be expected.

Striking contrasts emerge from this table. During the 1988 boom, first-time buyers (who had all bought in the previous three years) were most likely to say they intended to move at the time of the survey. This would suggest that they had made their first purchase with the intention of staying a relatively short time, or were persuaded by market conditions that it was worth moving on quickly. Around one in ten of owners across the survey intended to move in total. Overall, the levels of frustrated mobility increased markedly in the 1995 survey so that about one in four owners then said that they would like to move. It is particularly notable that over a third of the longer-term residents in each city say that they would like to move in 1995. There seems no doubt that the 1995 housing market slump has stopped many people pursuing their preferred choices, particularly for longer-term residents over a third of whom would like to be moving on.

Another way of examining the extent of frustrated mobility is to see how long people have stayed in their current house. If owners become less able to fulfil their aspirations to move average stays will become longer. Table 9.5 shows an increase in frustrated mobility across all groups of non-mover comparing boom to bust. During the boom in 1988 there is a sharp contrast between a very low desire to move amongst the longest-standing stayers, and a higher desire to move amongst those who are less long-standing residents and perhaps still in the process of trading up to their preferred longer-term home. A very much greater proportion of all 'non-moving' households say they would like to

Table 9.5   Intention to move by length of stay (non-movers, %)

Length of stay	'Intend to move' 1988		'Would like to move' 1995	
	Glasgow	Bristol	Glasgow	Bristol
4–6 years	19.5	13.5	27.8	51.7
7–10 years	16.4	9.6	29.2	54.2
10 + years	3.2	8.8	34.1	27.0
Total	10.1	10.1	30.7	38.8

Notes: The table excludes 'right to buy' owners. 'Non-movers' are those who have not moved in the three years prior to the study.

move in 1995. A particularly striking increase is seen in the proportion of those resident for ten years or more who would like to move. Perhaps the most striking finding is that over a half of owners in Bristol who have been in the same house for 4–6 years or 7–10 years would like to move. This very high level of dissatisfaction is certainly related to the more extreme market slowdown experienced in Bristol making it very hard for many people to sell in 1995. It can also be speculated, however, that it also reflects the disequilibrium created by the *boom*. These buyers bought around the most unstable time of the mid to late 1980s and it may be that the high levels of dissatisfaction expressed in 1995 reflect to some degree pressure to make hurried and short-run decisions at that time. The legacy is thus long-term discontent for some owners.

Discussion

The key focus of the evidence presented in this paper has been on the ways in which choices have varied in very unstable housing market conditions, both nationally and locally, over the last 'boom–bust' cycle. To some extent, this analysis has tended to confirm earlier work, suggesting that the differences in household choices do not vary as greatly in different market conditions as might have been expected. This may in part be a beneficial outcome of some of the checks and balances that operate particularly through the financial institutions. These institutions have a long-term commercial interest in the security of their loan and probably better, more comprehensive knowledge on which to base lending decisions than is available to ordinary owners.

It may however also be that households are not particularly sensitive to the sources of risk in the housing market or motivated by the possibility of speculative returns. For most people housing is most important as a *home*, in which role it carries considerable ideological resonance. The primacy of house as 'home', as a refuge and locus of family life echo in reasons that people give for wanting to move. Even when owners are persuaded of the seductive possibility of large capital gains to be made through trading it is perhaps not surprising that the main motivation for embarking on a potentially uncertain and costly move is that there is (also) a strong desire to change the consumption characteristics of their home, typically connected with family imperatives.

The main changes in behaviour identified from boom to bust in this paper can be argued to be associated with the time horizon and flexibility of market choices perceived by owners. Several strands of evidence point to differences in the (implicit) assumptions made about the potential and constraints existing in the housing market. It seems clear that choices were made in the boom that were only expected to be suitable in the short-term; the greater degree of fluidity in the housing market, buoyed by capital gains, made it seem reasonable to those buying in 1988 to plan to trade again within a relatively short period. In 1995 the slower market has created considerable frustration amongst those who have *not* been able to fulfil these intentions and who have become trapped in circumstances that they had not expected to suit them for so long. In addition, of course, the slower housing market also thwarts access to more suitable housing by those facing *unanticipated* changes in their preferred housing solutions, whether because of labour market change, the separation from a partner or the arrival of a new baby.

It seems evident, however, that *within* this reduced overall level of activity, buyers do not 'fine tune' the financial aspects of their decisions to reflect more detailed expectations about housing market risks and returns. This is witnessed in the relatively small differences in choices between the boom and the slump and in the general lack of strongly significant differences identified between the two cities – despite apparently significant differences in market characteristics. In the qualitative work, respondents clearly expressed their understanding of the considerable risks involved in house purchase and so it was initially surprising not to see clearer evidence of significant behavioural change in response to this risk. But it may be that there are simply too many unknowns – future job stability; future interest rate changes; the future course of house price inflation – for people to undertake a rational calculus of how to shield themselves against all these risks. In the end, housing is a sufficiently important part of family life that a decision *has* to be taken, even it entails the optimistic hope that the worst will

not happen to them. This is not to support the Beckman argument of
pure irrationality of decision making in the housing market. However, it
does suggest that there are very real limits to the extent to which people can really respond to the risks that they perceive or protect themselves from adverse outcomes.

Conclusions

What lessons does the experience of the unstable housing market have
for the introduction of market-like incentives in other areas of public
policy? Each public policy area is very different and it would be unwise
to translate experiences from one to the other too directly. As argued
at the beginning of this chapter, housing is distinct from many other
areas of the welfare state because market-led private provision is long-
established and increasingly preferred by the majority of British people.
The potential advantages of being in the private housing market are
widely accepted and even market instability is embraced – it is note-
worthy that popular coverage of housing issues continues to present
house price inflation as a factor to be welcomed, while any hesitation
in the upward march of prices is seen as a marker of economic and
consumer gloom.

Yet even within this context, this work points to the difficulties that
most people have in developing and pursuing strategies in response to
the uncertainties that they face. Although people are aware of risks, they
are also aware of the limited extent to which any action of their own
can ameliorate those risks. It seems clear that market instability *does*
create situations in which buyers are exposed to and consequently suffer
from the consequences of risk; in the boom they may have to make
hurried, short-term choices and use their savings and other resources
for this, while in the slump they suffer the legacy of such decisions,
becoming trapped in housing circumstances that no longer suit them.
The risky housing market created 'losers', suffering adversities caused
by market circumstances that are not favourable to them but which
they feel they could not have anticipated or avoided. In such circumstances considerable frustration can emerge. It is unsurprising that, at
this point, many will blame the Government for their plight, because
they believe that the Government *encouraged* people to enter the market.
Even though there is a general acceptance of and preference for market
provision in housing, people believe that they cannot protect themselves against all possible risks. In this situation many expect the
Government to share the responsibility of providing a safety net when

people get into difficulty. They may also blame the Government for problems created by the risky market.

Notes

1 Two closely related original surveys were undertaken in 1995 in each city. The first was a structured survey of a total of 800 house-buyers, stratified by quota to compare recent traders in the housing market, recent first-time buyers and longer-term stayers (of four or more years). This enabled a quantitative comparison of key socio-economic characteristics of different buyer groups, attitudinal questions and various choice outcomes. The second element consisted of 45 semi-structured, in-depth interviews with recent and current traders in each city (including first time buyers) to explore attitudes and motivations in more detail.

2 The survey evidence from 1988 was collected as part of a Joseph Rowntree Foundation financed programme on housing subsidies and costs. Extensive survey evidence was gathered from households in all tenures in six cities – including Glasgow and Bristol. The analysis in this paper is based on new analysis of the subset of respondents who were owners in Glasgow or Bristol, with the original data reworked to provide consistency of core definitions (especially 'recent' traders, and first time buyers). The original survey sought to achieve a representative sample of households in each city – hence the sample of owners is about twice as big in Bristol (1168 respondents) as in Glasgow (611). 'Stayers' are also in the great majority (67 per cent of the sample). However, the total size of the survey population (1779) allows confidence in results for the smaller subdivisions. Fuller details of the 1988 survey can be found in Maclennan *et al.* (1991).

10
Risk and the Need for Long-Term Care
Gillian Parker

Introduction

Most people know that average life expectancy has risen consistently in the recent past – in fact, since the middle of the nineteenth century. Indeed, Benjamin Franklin's duo of inevitabilities – death and taxes – could well be argued in the developed world now to be a trio, adding old age. The average life expectancy for a boy born in the UK in 1994 is 74 and that for a girl 79 (Office for National Statistics, 1997). However, what none of us can be wholly certain of is how long our own life will be and we have even less idea about what condition we will be in at the end of it. As a consequence we have no way of knowing whether we will need personal or domiciliary care services or to be admitted to residential or nursing home care and, if so, for how long.

This is not a new type of uncertainty, of course. Older people without substantial resources of their own have always been at the mercy of family, church or state for meeting care needs, and until very recently their financial needs (Parker, 1995). However, recent demographic, social, political and economic changes have altered the odds. The first set of changes relates to the need for care and individuals' ability to pay for it themselves. This includes uncertainty about whether longer years of life are also longer years of healthy life, and extended periods of retirement, during which financial resources accumulated during working life diminish. However, set against this is the perception that older people are more affluent than in the past and therefore able to pay for care needs. Secondly, there is the increased emphasis in politics on individual responsibility for welfare. A third cluster of changes concerns the 'traditional' source of care – the family. Reductions in average family size, potential changes in patterns of inter-generational responsibility as a result of higher levels of divorce and remarriage, geographical mobility and married women's greater participation in the labour market have all raised questions about the continued ability and willingness of the 'family' to provide care at the current level. A fourth cluster relates to changes in health and social care policy – the reduction of 'free' long-term care provision in health settings, the increase in the 1980s of social security spending on residential and nursing home care, and the subsequent NHS and Community Care Act (1990) which introduced assessment of the need for care, as well as the ability to pay for it, into the publicly funded system.

Individuals attempting to make decisions about their care needs in old age thus face four major types of uncertainty – about their personal risk of the need for care, about the role of the state, about the future shape and responsibilities of the family, and about the adequacy of their incomes and capital in older age.

Our research on paying for long-term care has revealed some of the ways in which (if at all) people recognise and deal with these uncertainties (Parker and Clarke 1997a, 1997b and 1998). This research was in two stages. First, we carried out a nationally representative sample survey of 957 men and women aged between 25 and 70 years in England and Wales in late 1995 (fieldwork by Social and Community Planning Research). The interviews included questions about the balance between the state and the individual for financing care and about respondents' views of private insurance for long-term care, as well as their beliefs about the 'best way' in which care should be funded. Basic socio-economic information was also collected, along with more detailed information about individuals' experiences of chronic ill-health or disability, of providing informal care and about their and their households' financial circumstances.

In the second stage we re-interviewed a sub-sample of 102 people from the first stage in June 1996 to investigate their planned and actual behaviour for securing care in older age. The interview was structured, but included a higher proportion of open questions than in the first stage. Among other things, it explored respondents' perceptions of their own and others' risks of the need for care, and asked more detailed questions about their views on the use of housing capital, on inheritance, and on inter-generational responsibility for the provision of care.

In what follows we discuss the four different sets of uncertainties identified above - the risk of the need for care; the role of the state; uncertainties about the future shape and responsibilities of the family; and the role of income and capital.

Risk and the need for care

Recognising risk

In order to respond to our own need for care, we need to be able to judge how likely we are to need it. It is difficult to do this. There are no UK-based longitudinal studies which can predict the individual, life-time risk of needing care in old age and the UK insurance industry relies heavily on US actuarial calculations. However, even if we knew about population risks this would still leave us as individuals relatively uninformed. At the least, we would have to take into account a number of individual behavioural, environmental and genetic factors which might influence our length of life and its quality, but about which science currently knows relatively little. Further, the psychological literature shows consistently that we have a tendency to under-estimate our own risk of 'negative' events and over-estimate our risk of 'positive' events (Hoorens, 1995; 1996) thus, presumably, reducing our ability to respond appropriately.

We found that those surveyed consistently over-estimated the proportions of people over the age of 85 who might currently need different types of care – help with domestic tasks, help with personal care, or care in a residential or nursing home. Estimates for help with domestic tasks were higher than current levels, but not excessively so. By contrast, respondents gave very exaggerated estimates for the need for residential or nursing home care and, particularly, the need for personal care. We also asked respondents how likely they thought it that they themselves would need help of the sorts described by the time they were 85. For domestic tasks and personal care individuals over-estimated their personal risk to a similar degree as they had the current population risks. For admission to residential or nursing home care, by contrast, their estimates of personal risk were lower than those they gave for the current population (although still substantially higher than the current actual levels). Respondents also substantially over-estimated the likely length of stay in residential or nursing home care.

As predicted by psychological theory (Hoorens, 1995), then, there was a tendency for people to estimate their own risk of the most 'serious' form of care as lower than their estimates of the population risk. This suggests that in the area of long-term care risk is interpreted as both endemic (for other people) and not (for oneself). However, as we see below, there was substantial variation between individuals in their propensity to respond to risk by taking action that would, if not protect

them from the risk, at least protect them from the financial consequences of experiencing it.

Dealing with risk

Despite having these exaggerated perceptions of risk, people were not
universally likely to feel that any action on their part towards securing
care was warranted. The research demonstrated a persisting and strong
attachment to the belief that the state had a fundamental responsibility for the care of older people, albeit with some degree of means-testing, although few believed that this should require them to use their
own means for paying for care. As a consequence, there was little spon-
taneous enthusiasm for long-term care insurance as a way of preparing
for old age. However, we did find evidence that giving people information in this area, where most are operating in conditions of considerable uncertainty, could influence their responses.

After the questions which had elicited their own estimates of risk for
different types of care, we gave respondents a range of risk figures for
admission to residential or nursing home care at the age of 85, and asked
them, at each level, how they now viewed long-term care insurance.
Even at our lowest risk level (which, at one in four, was itself lower than
the average risk level respondents had estimated in the earlier question) more people now felt positive towards insurance.

As throughout the two surveys, the question split the sample, although
it provoked more elaborated responses than did some other questions.
Almost half the sample said that, if they could afford it, they would
be inclined to take out care insurance at a risk figure of one in four.
The most commonly mentioned rationale was that insurance would
give peace of mind, spreading the cost of care and ensuring a degree of
choice. Another important group of reasons given hinged around the
desire to avoid dependency on the state or the family, or simply, in
general terms, the wish to remain independent. A small group saw care
insurance as a good investment – allowing them to pass on money to
their families – or as a good bet – the odds of needing care were seen as
high enough to warrant the cost of the insurance, if one lived long
enough to claim.

For the half who remained negative about the idea of care insurance,
even at the highest risk level of three in four, the main objection, as in
so many other parts of the interview, was about the state's perceived
obligation to provide care and the fact that respondents felt that they
had already 'paid in' and would thus be paying twice. However, there

was also an important sub-group of answers which suggested that the negative perception of care insurance came from the willingness to take a risk on not needing care – answers which gave the impression that individuals did not expect to need care or to live long enough, that they would rather take a 'gamble' than pay out or that they did not see insurance as a sufficiently attractive 'bet'.

A smattering of respondents spoke of its being 'too soon' to be thinking about the need for care or that they 'would cross that bridge' when they came to it. This was linked to wanting to keep control over their money or not seeing care as a priority at the moment. Two respondents simply disliked the idea of insurance, while another completely failed to grasp its principles, arguing that it would not be possible to 'save enough' for care by this method.

Here, then, in addition to people's political orientations we picked up responses which reflected personalities as much as anything else. Some were risk averse – and therefore susceptible to 'expert' information which apparently increased their knowledge of risk – while others were not and would be unlikely to respond to any information of this sort, no matter how high the apparent risk. Further, people clearly tempered the information we gave them with their personal experience and knowledge, for example, referring to their parents' current age and level of independence as reasons why average risk levels would not apply to them.

Risk and the state

Social, rather than health, care in residential settings has not been 'free' to those with more than very modest means since 1948, so it could be argued that individual responsibility has always been a feature of this area of policy. Support for social care, particularly that provided in residential settings, has its origins in the Poor Law and still demonstrates that background (Baldwin, 1994; Means and Smith, 1998). As a result, people wishing to enter residential or nursing home care who do not have sufficient resources of their own have to look to the state for partial or complete subsidy. A capital test for state assistance with the costs of residential or nursing home care has existed since 1948 and was subsumed into the NHS and Community Care Act 1990. However, relatively few people are aware of this and most have assumed that care will be available when they needed it in old age; not knowing that the system requires them to pay for it if their resources, including the value of their homes, are above a certain level. This was not really an issue when the bulk of older people who might need care were not home-owners. However, another key plank of social policy in the 1980s and 1990s – the extension of home-ownership – has pushed this issue into the limelight because housing capital has become an important factor in older people's wealth.

The division of responsibility between individual, family and state

The first stage of the research revealed that most people felt that the state should still have responsibility for the care of older people, in some general sense, but that this responsibility should be shared with the individual. Only a third were prepared to contemplate increased taxation to ensure care for all older people when they needed it and most felt that some kind of means-testing or basic level provision which individuals could top up if they wished was the best model. However, direct questions about which means people might be prepared to dedicate to the shared purchase of care showed that most were also generally reluctant to contemplate using any of their own means to ensure provision (see Parker and Clarke, 1998 for detailed discussion).

People's ability to make decisions about their own care needs in older age, rather than their opinions about what should be done for 'others' is, of course, determined by their knowledge of what is currently available and their judgement about how that might change in the interim. In the second stage we were able to explore some of these issues in more depth and asked both about views of current state support for residential and nursing care[1] and people's expectations about how they might have their own care needs met if it came to it.

Just over a third of our stage two respondents felt that the current, means-tested system was reasonable, most referring to the fact that if people had that level of resources then they should be expected to pay, that the 'line needed to be drawn somewhere' and the current limits seemed reasonable, or that most people needing care would be likely to have less than £10 000 anyway. A few were surprised to find that individuals were able to keep any assets and therefore were more positive about the current scheme than they had expected to be. Others referred to the need to accept a division of responsibility between the state and the individual, given that the state could not be expected to pay for everyone. A small sub-group felt that the principle of the means test was right but that the capital limit was too low.

The two-thirds who felt that the current system was not a good one tended to give a number of inter-related reasons. First, there were those who felt that no one should be required to pay for their care in old age, often linked to the feeling that provision had already been paid for. Secondly, there were those who felt strongly that assets should be retained in order to pass them on and that one should not be forced to sell one's home. The third group of reasons given related to the feeling that the present system penalised thrift or meant that some people were paying for others who had not worked or saved. The fourth main set of reasons referred to the low level of capital limits with the feeling that respondents would have been more positive about the present system had it left rather more capital intact.

Among those who had mixed views, three made a distinction between different sorts of capital: 'I've got mixed views on this – stocks and shares they won't need but to have to sell their home, when they've worked hard for it and also paid NI is not good – it should go to their children.'

Plans for one's own care

We also asked people how they thought care would be paid for if they themselves reached 85 and needed care. These questions again divided the group fairly evenly. First were those who, in line with their answers throughout the questionnaire, felt that the state should pay and who, consequently, were unwilling to consider any alternative. A similar proportion said that they expected to pay themselves or that relatives would provide or pay for required assistance. A further group either acknowledged the need for some form of partnership between the individual and the state, dependent on the individual's resources, or who simply recognised that they would be likely to have to contribute to the costs of care because of the level of their income or assets. The proportion of answers that fell into each of these groups varied somewhat with the type of care concerned. Support for state help was highest in washing/dressing and residential/nursing home care scenarios and weakest in relation to help with shopping and cleaning. However, the question about residential and nursing home care also prompted the greatest proportion of answers about having to use one's own assets.

The apparently clear division between responses to these questions disguises a somewhat more complex picture. Despite the wording of the question, which was about who would pay, in all three scenarios there were those who stated that the state should pay (but did not necessarily believe that it would) and those who still believed that the state would pay. Similarly, among those referring to individual responsibility, there were some who felt that this should be for reasons of principle and those who believed that there would be no other option.

In addition, in all three scenarios there was a small group of people unable or unwilling to acknowledge that these issues might ever affect them personally - those who said that they did not expect to live to 85 or to need care if they did, who found it difficult even to contemplate 'not managing' or who optimistically expected their families to provide the care that they would need.

To sum up, questions in this section revealed a growing realisation that the state is unwilling or unable to provide care for most people. When asked whom they thought might provide or pay for different types of care for them if they needed it in old age, between a quarter and a third believed that they or their families would have to do so. Generally, these responses reflected a grudging recognition either that personal resources would take them out of the reach of state assistance, or that by the time they were that old, everyone would be expected to be making a personal contribution to the costs of care. But there was also the group who persisted throughout the survey in a particular vision of state responsibility for the care of older people that reflects neither the position as it actually is at the moment nor, indeed, the likely future political agenda.

Risk and family care

The third set of issues that we explored with people in the second stage centred around inter-generational responsibilities for care. Most of the personal and domestic help provided for older or disabled people comes from family and friends, especially from family. Until the 1970s most of this help went unnamed and largely unrecognised until a series of political and economic changes combined to promote 'care in the community' as an explicit policy objective (Parker, 1990). This emphasis raised anxieties among feminist commentators in particular who began to unpack the equation: 'care in the community' = 'care by the family' = 'care by women' (Land, 1978). While more recent research has shown that men are also involved in providing care (Parker, 1993) reliance on the family to provide the majority of care-giving remains unchanged. However, a number of factors, outlined in the introduction to this chapter, call into question the continuing ability or willingness of the family to provide the amount of care that it currently does. However, the extent to which people make judgements about their need to prepare for future care provision on the basis of their expectations about the availability of family care, and the extent to which these expectations may be changing, is not clear.

Caring for parents

We explored this issue in a number of ways. First we established that just under a third of the group had provided help or care for more than a few weeks for a parent in the past or were doing so currently. Further, of those who still had at least one parent alive (77 of the 102 surveyed) over half expected that they would have to provide help or care in the future. We then asked those with a parent still alive about their views about caring for their parents. This question distinguished clearly between three main groups – those who felt that they would (or already were) caring for their parents 'under any circumstances', those who would care 'if circumstances allowed it' and those who felt that they would want to provide a degree of care but who would not want to be completely responsible. Two very small groups said either that they could not care in any circumstances as they did not get on with their parents or that, if they could afford it, they would pay for some-one else to provide care. A follow-up question explained that it is possi-ble to pay for care, whether at home or in residential or nursing home care, and asked, if care was needed for their parents, whether respon-dents felt it would be best to care themselves or to pay someone else to do so. This question elicited much more support for the payment option (around a third) and somewhat less for the option of caring directly (around a quarter). The mixed option of paying for some care and providing the rest directly was also less popular in responses to this question.

An open question explored why respondents had replied as they did. For those who had preferred the option of paying for someone else to care (30) if this was affordable, diverse and multiple reasons were evident. Some were related to change in society and family life - families were felt to be more geographically dispersed than in the past, people (women) needed or wanted to work and not to give up that work in order to pro-vide care personally. Other answers related to parents' perceived desire to remain 'independent' or to children's inability or lack of desire to pro-vide care. Both these latter reasons were sometimes related to the feeling that it would be better to pay a 'professional' to care 'properly'.

For those who felt that they would prefer to provide care personally (25), most simply said that that was the way they wanted it and/or that their parents had cared for them and, therefore, they wanted to recip-rocate. Another strong strand of reasoning was that this was what par-ents would themselves wish, particularly as they would not want to be cared for by 'strangers'.

The much smaller group who felt that a joint approach to providing care was preferable (13) mostly referred to the difficulty that doing 'everything' could create – the lack of a break, having to provide types of care that were personally off-putting, needing to feel supported and so on. In general, this approach seemed a good compromise between appearing uncaring and shouldering the whole burden.

The small group expressing other opinions were largely opposed to the idea of providing or paying for the care of parents at all, either on political principle or because of the poor quality of their relationship.

Children's responsibility to care

People who had children were then asked a similar set of questions about what they would like to happen if they themselves needed care. Here we found a higher proportion who did not want their children to be involved at all (18 per cent) and a smaller proportion wanting them to care in any circumstances (2 per cent) or if circumstances allowed it (19 per cent). As a corollary, more said that they would prefer their children to pay for care (18 per cent) or to provide care but not be entirely responsible (43 per cent). Asked to imagine that they would need care when older, these parents were then asked if they would prefer their children to look after them themselves or pay for someone else to look after them (if they – the children – could afford it). Here again, there was a somewhat higher level of support for paying someone else to provide care (42 per cent) or for a mixture of payment and personal caring (22 per cent) and a lower level for children providing care themselves (22 per cent) than in the parallel questions about providing care for parents.

Those preferring their children to pay were most likely to refer to not wanting to feel dependent or a burden on their children and this was often related to statements about children having their own priorities or their own lives to lead. A few had experienced or observed caregiving in their own families and said that they would not want their own children to experience the same. Others referred to principle – they did not feel that it was a child's responsibility to provide care.

The smaller group who felt that they would prefer their children to care were most likely to mention not wanting to be cared for by 'strangers' in an impersonal way or to be dependent on others outside the family. Three said outright that families should care and one that it should be expected and two simply expressed the hope that their children would wish to care for them.

As with the questions about caring for parents, most of those who preferred a mixture of paying and providing care talked about not wanting their children to carry the whole burden for care or that children would need a break or could not do it all. Others referred to sharing the load with professionals. Again, there was a small group for whom the whole issue was simply out of the question – they did not feel that children should be expected to provide in any way for parents in old age. This was the state's responsibility in return for tax and national insurance paid over a lifetime. Others mentioned changes in families' sense of responsibility or estrangement.

Finally in this section, people with children were asked whether they felt that relationships between parents and children had changed over recent generations. Over a half said that they believed relationships had changed and were asked in what way they believed this had occurred. The predominant explanation given was that children had become more selfish or showed less respect than earlier generations (14). Related to this in some respondents' minds was the fact that children were less likely to care because they could afford to pay for it in ways that previous generations could not or because the state now provided it. Several felt that family life had changed in ways that meant that children were more independent and that parents themselves did not expect or wish their children to provide care. The distance apart at which some family members lived was also mentioned.

One somewhat unexpected line of reasoning was that relationships had changed because parents actually help children more or for longer than was the case in the past. This was perhaps because parents were relatively better off than their own parents had been and wished to help out, or because their children were unemployed and/or worse off than they were themselves.

These responses do not, in themselves, paint a particularly startling picture of expected change in family responsibilities. As with studies of 'women in the middle' (Brody, 1981) they show that the theoretical commitment people express to providing care for their parents is stronger than their wish to be cared for by their own children. There is little to suggest that, in years to come, their own children may not hold similar views. Rather more respondents felt that relationships between children and parents had changed over recent generations than not – but it has probably been ever thus!

The implications for actual care-giving are difficult to judge. Those with some experience of caring, either directly or as observers in their own families, were perhaps more reluctant to contemplate their children's involvement. The practical impact of such sentiments is uncertain. Recent national data show that there has been no marked change in the proportions of adults who become involved in providing substantial amounts of care since 1975 (Rowlands and Parker, 1998). However, there is some suggestion that younger married women are less involved in informal helping activity such as shopping or cleaning, than they were; how this will play itself out over the longer term remains to be seen.

What may be more influential in relation to family care in the future is not inter-generational but same generational relationships, about which we did not ask. For the current generation of older people, marital partners are a major source of care (Parker, 1993). As higher rates of marital dissolution begin to work their way through the generations, the absence of this source of support in old age may make the role of any children even more important.

Income and capital

The income and capital that we take into old age may be crucial in determining how we meet care needs or, in some cases, whether we ever develop any. Those who have the resources to ensure appropriate housing or adaptations as they age or to buy in small amounts of assistance may be less at risk of developing full-blown care needs over and above any protective effect that a higher income may have conferred over their lifetime.

Older people's financial resources, on average, have improved over the past 20 years or so, but this improvement has not been uniform between different groups. For example, for those largely reliant on state benefits, improvements in average disposable household income have been much lower – around 8 per cent and 17 per cent in real terms for single person and two person households respectively – than for those reliant on other sources of income, where the relevant figures are 37 per cent and 36 per cent (Parker, 1998).

As mentioned earlier, state provision has always had an interest in people's income and capital holdings when providing long-term care outside of the health service, due to the Poor Law origins of such provision. Recent policy has, similarly, started to look explicitly to individual's personal financial resources – whether as income, capital or insurance – as a source of support for care (Department of Health 1996, 1997). This approach is attractive for a number of reasons, including the fact that it leaves the power about how to meet care needs in the hands of those who actually need it. This is an argument developed in most detail by younger disabled people (see, for example, Oliver, 1990) but one which applies just as well to those who encounter impairment in older age. The problem is that not everyone will have adequate resources and, even if they did, it may be unfair to ask them to contribute to costs which occur for reasons over which they have little or no control. It is this last argument which has been particularly influential in the thinking of the Royal Commission on Long-Term Care (Royal Commission on Long-Term Care, 1999). We explored the extent to which people had thought about and planned for their retirement income in some detail.

Pensions and savings

About a third of the respondents thought that they had done as much as they needed to for the present about their pension and plans for retirement and about half who felt that they had not. The former fell into two main groups – those who referred to what they felt were secure pension arrangements, additional voluntary contributions, savings and insurance and those who were 'putting things off until tomorrow'. This latter group said that they felt that it was 'too soon' to be doing anything, that they would be able to save or prepare in the future, or that they expected to be able to continue earning after pensionable age. Others seemed simply to have their heads in the sand – claiming that their family would look after them, that they should not be expected to save for their own old age, or that they would 'only need enough to live on' when they retired. A small but important group said that, even if they had wanted to do more, they could not afford to.

Among those who felt that they had not done enough responses ran along similar lines (although rather more of this group said they could not afford to do more) and were related to fractured work histories and current unemployment. Again there was a sub-group who had simply 'never done anything about it', 'left it too late', or, at the other end of the age distribution, felt that it was too soon to be planning.

An interesting set of comments came from people who spoke about the difficulty of predicting how much one might actually need in retirement, or wondered if they had done enough, having latterly become more aware of the potential costs of retirement and care.

Only half the group said that they were currently saving, over and above any pension contributions. However, a more specific question revealed that only a third were actually doing this in a systematic and regular fashion; the remainder saved as and when they had any money to spare. Further, the sample was split between longer- and shorter-term priorities for saving; the first priority for saving cited most often was paying everyday bills and expenses while the second most frequent priority was to provide money for retirement. Overall, saving for holidays came out more often among respondents' top three priorities than did saving for retirement or for care in older age.

When asked to imagine what their priorities for saving might be in ten and twenty years' time, people did express a greater need to think about retirement or care, indicating again the distant nature of perceptions of the need to prepare. However, as with perceptions about family responsibilities for care, it is difficult to judge how such long-term intentions will work out in reality.

After reviewing retirement income and savings, we then asked how confident people felt about having enough to live on after they had retired. Only 15 per cent said that they felt very confident, followed by 45 per cent who were 'fairly confident'. The remainder were not very confident (23 per cent), not at all confident (12 per cent) or did not feel able to judge (6 per cent). For the third of respondents who said that they did not feel confident, the main reason given was the belief that by the time they retired the state pension would be inadequate, that the state would be making no better provision for retirement income than it does at present or that their occupational pension would be inadequate. The difficulty of judging the future was also mentioned, both in relation to inflationary pressures and the likelihood of there being fewer young people to pay for more pensioners in the future. One respondent pointed out how difficult life became when so many responsibilities had been transferred to individuals: 'We don't have enough money to pay out for the children's education and future, *and* pay the mortgage *and* take out adequate insurance for our future' The inability to save or contribute to a pension during working life was important for some while others felt that although they were making some plans, these were inadequate. A sprinkling of people reported that they had no plans or were not making any because they did not know how long they would live.

The impact of information about risk on decisions

We had interviewed people in some depth in the first stage about care in older age and ways in which it might be financed. We were keen to see, when we returned in the second stage, if this experience had sensitised people to the issue so that they had actually changed their plans or behaviour. First, we asked whether, during the previous year, respondents had been feeling more or less confident about the financial provision they had made or were making for their retirement. The majority either felt no different (41 per cent) or did not know one way or the other (5 per cent). Only 17 per cent were feeling more confident while 38 per cent were feeling less confident.

Among the few (17 in all) who were feeling more confident, the main reasons given were related to new financial products that they had bought, money that they had invested or pension schemes that they had joined. A few also reported an improved level of income which was allowing them to save more and one, currently a mature student, was looking forward to getting a job with the increased income and pension opportunities that this might bring. A sub-group talked about having sought advice in the past year. One had discovered a larger pension entitlement than previously expected, but the others had merely 'looked into it' without apparently doing anything about it.

The reasons given by the much larger group of 39 who felt less confident fell under three main headings. First, there were those who were getting close to retirement or getting older and becoming more aware of the issues. One spoke about observing others' circumstances change as they retired and reflecting on this in relation to themselves. This group also spoke about their anxieties about not having saved or 'paid in' enough, pensions not being index-linked and consequently not being worth as much as expected, and simply not having a pension. The second group of reasons given were less well-defined but no less likely to provoke anxiety – general worries about the likelihood of their income decreasing in the future and about what state benefits and government policy might be by the time they retired. One person assumed that individuals would be expected to pay more for themselves in the future. Thirdly, there were those whose anxieties were linked to their inability to make any or much provision for themselves for the future because of their current financial circumstances – money was tight, they could not afford to contribute to a pension, or short-term employment made it difficult to think long-term.

As the final question in the interview we asked people whether they had given any thought to the issue of care for older people since the last interview and, if they had, whether it had influenced any plans they might have had about paying for care in their own older age. Just over half (54 per cent) of respondents said that they had given the issue some thought – and just under half of these said that they had given it a lot of thought. However, few had followed this up with any kind of action. Of the 54 people who had given it some thought, 30 said that while they had done nothing specific as a result. Others referred to other priorities, asserted that they had 'thought about' pensions or insurance, or that they might do something in the future. We had clearly depressed a couple of respondents, one of whom was thinking of emigrating! A tiny group of people, however, had been galvanised into action – three had increased pensions contributions or savings and one had sorted out a mortgage and thought about a will.

Overall, then, the evidence of this part of the research is that while one can get people to think about a risk issue it is much more difficult to get them to do anything about it, even when they recognise that they are currently not well protected. For some, the problem was that their income was too low to do anything about protecting themselves; others had an adequate income, but matters other than retirement and care had a higher priority. A relatively small group were (or perceived themselves to be) well-prepared and still others would never be prepared to make provision either because they were ideologically opposed to the idea of individual responsibility or because they simply did not perceive a risk.

Housing as capital

Between 1971 and 1995 home-ownership increased from 49 per cent of households in Great Britain to 67 per cent (Rowlands *et al.*, 1997). While the greatest change has been among younger generations, we are already observing an increasing proportion of people moving into retirement with capital resources in the form of housing. In 1980 47 per cent of households containing at least one person aged 65 or over were in owner-occupied accommodation; by 1991 this had increased to 58 per cent (Goddard and Savage, 1994, table 7). Figures for younger age groups suggest that this proportion might eventually 'top out' at around 70 to 75 per cent of households. While up-to-date figures are difficult to come by, Johnson and Falkingham (1992) cite a study by Mackintosh, Means and Leather which showed that in 1986 over three-quarters of older people who had housing capital had equity of more than £25 000 – well over the *current* capital limit for assistance with the costs of residential or nursing home care.

Housing is the pre-eminent means of capital holding for the bulk of people in the UK. One result is that housing capital has become a key factor in the political debate about paying for care. Media stories about 'selling the family home' to pay for care increased the political temperature about long-term care during the 1990s. The Conservative Party attempted to address this issue in its consultation documents on 'partnership' between the individual and the state (Department of Health, 1996, 1997) while the Labour Party promised to establish a Royal Commission on long-term care if it won the 1997 election. The issue was consequently much in evidence when we carried out our research.

Both stages of the research explored the role of housing capital in means-testing and as a potential source of money to secure care provision and details from this have been covered elsewhere (Parker and Clarke, 1997a, 1997b, 1998). In this chapter, we concentrate on any evidence that views are changing about whether housing should (or should not) be seen as a capital resource for use in older age.

In the second stage, those who were already owner-occupiers or who were seriously thinking about buying were asked what they felt was the most important reason for owning their own home, over and above providing somewhere to live. For just over a third, the most important reasons was as an investment for the future. Providing security for old age came next in importance, though mentioned less than half as often. Only one in ten mentioned having something of value to pass onto their family.

We then asked whether respondents felt that people of their generation bought homes expecting to be able to pass them on to their family in the same way as had 'older people'. Despite the apparent lack of interest in the potential for bequest as a reason for home ownership given in the previous question, over half (58 per cent) felt that there had been no change in this view. Those who believed that their generation did feel differently were most likely to refer in some way to knowledge about having to pay for care out of capital. Almost as many also referred to the expectation that younger generations would more independent because it had been easier for them to buy homes. Others felt that family life had changed. People simply did not feel so deeply about bequeathing their homes, because the family was not as 'strong' as it had been in the past or because people were more mobile and did not expect to have a 'family home' which was passed on. A related line of reasoning was that younger generations did not look as far ahead or lived more for the present than the future. However, one respondent pointed out that one's views on this might change during the life-course. Finally, a few people referred to the increased tendency to see housing as more of a financial than an emotional investment or that it was not the only way in which one could invest.

Just under a half of the 78 per cent of the stage two sample who were current home-owners said that they had personally bought their home expecting to be able to pass it on to their family and most still felt this way. The handful whose views had changed gave no single reason for this change – two referred to the state 'taking property' to pay for care, but others no longer saw their home as an asset, wanted to trade down to release capital for themselves, or felt that children should not expect a 'silver spoon' from their parents. As we saw in an earlier section, however, people's awareness that they might have to use their housing capital to pay for care was much more evident in responses to direct questions about this issue.

Conclusions

The emphasis on increased individual responsibility for assessing and reacting appropriately to risk in everyday life has become a persistent feature of political thinking in the UK, regardless of which party is actually in government (Meikle, 1998). However, if people are to be expected to prepare optimally for such risks we have to be sure that the risks are properly understood and that the means of reacting appropriately are actually available. The empirical evidence presented in this chapter indicates that factors which influence knowledge about and reactions to the risk of needing long-term care, and consequently the degree of preparation for it, are complex.

First, it is clear that political persuasion, of itself, influences whether or not people feel they should have to prepare for this risk at all. However, strongly held views about the 'sanctity' of housing capital cut across traditional political divisions, so that even those who believe that people with reasonable levels of resources should make some contribution to paying for care baulk at having to 'sell up' to do so.

Secondly, people have varying access to the financial resources which might enable them to prepare individually for care needs in old age and to the family resources which might (or might not) ensure them a degree of informal assistance when needed. Coupled with the, at this stage, largely unpredictable effect of marital dissolution on informal care, we thus face the possibility of new divisions between people who are 'asset rich/poor' and 'family rich/poor' in older age.

Thirdly, people's knowledge of current policies and provision for long-term care varies and is mostly inaccurate. They have even less idea of how these may alter in the future. Unless the state withdraws completely from ensuring a basic level of care for older people in the future or commits itself to providing care for everyone (neither a likely scenario for the 21st century) then it must give a clearer view of the maximum it is prepared to provide now and of the least it is going to provide in the future. Only with this type of knowledge can people make appropriate judgements about future income, savings and other forms of provision, many years in advance of their likely need.

Finally, while we all underestimate our risk of negative events, such as the need for care in old age, some underestimate it more than others. In addition, even if aware of their real risk, some people are simply constitutionally averse to long-term planning. Insurers have always recognised this, and it is not a trait associated with any particular group in society.

All these factors suggest a continuing role for the state in paying for or providing long-term care: whether to even out inequities created during younger life or arising from regional imbalance in the housing market, to acknowledge that we will never have perfect knowledge of the future and, even if we did, human nature suggests that some of us will never be prepared, or to allow, as a matter of social justice, that those who incur 'catastrophic' care costs that are largely unpredictable should be compensated, regardless of their existing resources.

Note

1   At the time of the second stage survey the upper capital limit for assistance with the costs of residential or nursing home care was £16 000, above which amount no state assistance was available. Between £10 000 and £16 000 a sliding scale operated which meant that the individual would make a contribution, with the remainder was topped up by the state. Below £10 000 the state met the whole costs of care. The position for charging for domiciliary-based care (care delivered in people's own homes) is more complicated than this, depending on who delivers the care (NHS staff deliver care free at the point of use for all) and where people live if they use social care services (different local authorities have different charging policies, some making no charge at all, some using the same capital limits as the means test for residential/nursing home care, others using an income test, and so on). We did not attempt to judge people's views about this element of the care system.

Appendix: The Economic Beliefs and Behaviour Research Programme – Projects, Researchers and Publications

Programme publications

Taylor-Gooby, P., 'Markets and Motives: Trust in Welfare Markets', *Journal of Social Policy*, 27, 1, pp. 97–115, 1998.

'"Things can only get better": Expectations and the Welfare State', *Policy and Politics*, 24, 4, pp. 471–6, 1998.

'The Obsolescence of Consumerism', *Journal of Economic Psychology*, 19, 5, 1998.

Taylor-Gooby, P., Dean, H., Munro, M. and Parker, G. 'Risk and the Welfare State', *British Journal of Sociology*, 50, 2, 1999.

Taylor-Gooby, P. (ed.), *Choice and Public Policy*, Macmillan, 1998.

Taylor-Gooby, P. (ed.), *Risk, Trust and Welfare*, Macmillan, 2000.

Publications by the research projects

Attitudes and Behaviour towards Financial Planning for Care in Old Age
Gillian Parker, Jeremy Jones and Harriet Clarke

Clarke, H., 'Attitudes and Behaviour towards Purchasing Long-Term Care', *Insurance Trends*, October, 1997.

Clarke, H. and Parker, G. 'Long-Term Care Survey', *The Actuary*, 26–7, July, 1998.

Clarke, H. and Parker, G. 'Funding options for long-term care', *Elderly Client Adviser*, 3, 2, 26–29, January/February 1998.

Parker, G. and Clarke, H. 'Attitudes and Behaviour towards Financial Planning for Care in Old Age', *Nuffield Community Care Studies Unit*, University of Leicester, Working Paper No. 58, November, 1997.

Clarke, H. 'Ethnicity and Ageing: Preliminary Analysis of White and Non-White Respondents' Attitudes Towards the Funding and Provision of Care in Old Age', *Nuffield Community Care Studies Unit*, University of Leicester, Working Paper No. 72, September, 1998.

Parker, G. and Clarke, H., 'The Development of Long-Term Care Insurance in Britain', *Nuffield Community Care Studies Unit*, University of Leicester, Working Paper No. 42, September, 1995.

Parker, G. and Clarke, H., 'Attitudes towards Long-Term Care for Elderly People: Evidence Submitted to the Health Committee', *Nuffield Community Care Studies Unit*, University of Leicester, Working Paper No. 38, January, 1996.

Parker, G. and Clarke, H., 'Attitudes and Behaviour towards Financial Planning for Care in Old Age: Results of a National Survey', in C. Roland-Levy (ed.), *Social and Economic Representations*, 2, 1166–1175, proceedings of the International Association for Economic Psychology XXIst Annual Colloquium, Paris: Académie de Paris, Université de René Descartes, 1996.

Parker, G., Editorial – 'Can't Pay? Won't Pay? Finance for Long-Term Care', *Journal of Health Services Research and Policy*, July, 1997.

Parker, G. and Clarke, H., 'Will you still need me? Will you still feed me? Attitudes towards long-term care', *Social Policy and Administration*, 31:2, 119–135, 1997.

The project also contributed chapters to both programme books.

Beliefs, Perceptions and Expectations in the UK Owner-Occupied Housing Market

Moira Munro, Kenneth Gibb, Duncan Maclennan, Ruth Madigan and Clodagh Memery

Munro, M. and Madigan, R., 'Housing Strategies in an Uncertain Market', *The Sociological Review*, 46:4, 714–34, 1998.

Madigan, R. and Munro, M., 'Housing Ladders and Household Strategies', *Sociology*, 1998.

Memery, C., 'Beliefs, Perceptions and Expectations of U.K. Homeowners', in *Mortgage Weekly*, 10.11.95.

Munro, M., 'Rationality and Choice in House Purchase', in C. Roland-Levy (ed.), *Social and Economic Representations*, 1, 473–486, proceedings of the International Association for Economic Psychology XXIst Annual Colloquium, Paris: Académie de Paris, Université de René Descartes, 1996.

Munro, M., 'Perceptions of Uncertainty and Risk in the Housing Market', *Housing Finance*, 36, November 1997.

The project also contributed chapters to both programme books.

British Asian Self-Employment: The Interaction of Culture and Economics

Tariq Modood, Satnam Virdee and Hilary Metcalf

Metcalf, H., Modood, T. and Virdee, S., *Asian Self-Employment: The Interaction of Culture and Economics in England*, London: Policy Studies Institute, 1996.

T. Modood, 'Asian Self-Employment: Do the Differences between South Asian Ethnicities Matter?' in R. Barot and T. Nichols (eds) *Economy, Ethnicity and Social Change: South Asian Business Enterprise in Britain*, Aldershot: Ashgate, 1999.

The research contributed to: Modood, T. *et al.*, *Ethnic Minorities in Britain: Diversity and Disadvantage*, Policy Studies Institute: London, 1997.

The project also contributed a chapter to the first programme book.

A Distributed Artificial Intelligence Simulation of Budgetary Decision Making

Nigel Gilbert and Edmund Chattoe

Chattoe, E., 'The Use of Evolutionary Algorithms in Economics: Metaphors or Models for Social Interaction?', in E. Hillebrand and J. Stender (eds), *Many-agent Simulation and Artificial Life*, Amsterdam: IOS Press, 1994.

Chattoe, E., 'Why Are We Simulating Anyway? Some Answers from Economics', in K.G. Troitzsch, U.G. Muller, N. Gilbert and J.E. Doran (eds), *Social Science Microsimulation*, Chapter 4, 67–8, Berlin: Springer-Verlag, 1996.

Chattoe, E., 'A Simulation of Budgetary Decision Making Based on Interviews with Pensioners', in C. Roland-Levy (ed.), *Social and Economic Representations*, 2, 1114, proceedings of the International Association for Economic Psychology XXIst Annual Colloquium, Paris: Académie de Paris, Université de René Descartes, 1996.

Chattoe, E., 'Modelling Economic Interaction Using a Genetic Algorithm', in T. Back, D. Fogel and Z. Michalewicz (eds), *The Handbook of Evolutionary Computation*, New York: Oxford University Press/IOP Publishing, G7.1 1–5, 1997.

Chattoe, E. and Gilbert, N., 'A Simulation of Adaptation Mechanisms in Budgetary Decision Making', in R. Conte *et al.* (eds), *Simulating Social Phenomena*, Berlin: Springer, 1997.

Chattoe, E., 'What Simulation Has Done for Economics and What It Might Do', in Sydow, Achim (ed.), *Proceedings of the 15th IMACS World Congress on Scientific Computation, Modelling and Applied Mathematics, Volume 6: Applications in Modelling and Simulation*, Berlin: Wissenschaft und Technik Verlag, pp. 757–62, 1997.

Chattoe, E. and Gilbert, N. (forthcoming) 'Talking About Budgets', *Sociology*.

Gilbert, N. and Doran, J. (eds), *Simulating Societies: The Computer Simulation of Social Phenomena*, London: UCL Press, 1994.

Gilbert, N. and Conte, R. (eds), *Artificial Societies: The Computer Simulation of Social Life*, London: UCL Press, 1995.

Gilbert, N., 'Simulation as a Research Strategy', in K.G. Troitzsch, U.G. Muller, N. Gilbert and J.E. Doran (eds), *Social Science Microsimulation*, Berlin: Springer-Verlag, 1996.

Gilbert, N., 'Environments and Languages to Support Social Simulation', in K.G. Troitzsch, U.G. Muller, N. Gilbert and J.E. Doran (eds), *Social Science Microsimulation*, Berlin: Springer-Verlag, 1996.

Gilbert, N., 'Holism, Individualism and Emergent Properties: An Approach from the Perspective of Simulation', in R. Hegselmann *et al.* (eds), *Modelling and Simulation in the Social Sciences from the Philosophy of Science Point of View*, Dordrecht: Kluwer, 1996.

The research contributed to: Gilbert, G.N., 'Computer Simulation and the Social Sciences', *Report for ESRC*, 16 October (17pp.).

Gilbert, G.N., 'The Simulation of Social Processes', in T. Coppock (ed.), *Information Technology and Scholarly Disciplines*, London: British Academy, 1997.

Gilbert, N. and Troitzsch, K., 'Social Science Micro-simulation', *Bulletin de Méthode Sociologique*, 56, pp. 71–8, 1997.

Gilbert, N. and Troitzsch, K., *Simulation for the Social Sciences*, Milton Keynes: Open University Press, forthcoming.

Economic Learning and Social Evolution

Ken Binmore, Robin Dunbar, Henry Plotkin, Robin Seymour, David Ulph and Richard Vaughan

Binmore, K.G., 'Rationality in the Centipede', in R. Fagin (ed.), *Theoretical Aspects of Reasoning about Knowledge: Proceedings of the fifth TARK conference*, Morgan Kaufmann, San Mateo, California, 1994.

Binmore, K.G. and Samuelson, L., 'An Economist's Perspective on the Evolution of Norms', *Journal of Institutional and Theoretical Economics*, 150, 45–71, 1994.

Binmore, K.G. and Samuelson, L., 'Drift', *European Economic Review*, 38, 851–67, 1994.

Binmore, K.G., Samuelson, L. and Vaughan, R., 'Musical Chairs: Modelling Noisy Evolution', *Games and Economic Behaviour*, 11, 1–35, 1995.

Binmore, K.G., Gale, J. and Samuelson, L., 'Learning to be Imperfect: the Ultimatum Game', *Games and Economic Behaviour*, 8, 56–90, 1995.

Dunbar, R. and Spoors, M., 'Social Networking, Support Cliques and Kinship', *Human Nature*, 6(3), 273–90, 1995.

Dunbar, R., Clark, A. and Hurst, N., 'Conflict and Co-operation among the Vikings: Contingent Behavioural Decisions', *Ethology and Sociology*, 16, 233–46, 1995.

The research contributed to: Binmore, K.G., *'Playing Fair'*, *Game Theory and the Social Contract I*, MIT Press, Cambridge, Mass., 1994.

Dunbar, R., 'The Mating System of Callitrichid Primates: I. Conditions for the Co-evolution of Pair Bonding and Twinning', *Animal Behaviour*, 50, 1057–70, 1995.

Dunbar, R., 'The Mating System of Callitrichid Primates: II. The Impact of Helpers', *Animal Behaviour*, 50, 1071–89, 1995.

Dunbar, R., 'Neocortex Size and Group Size in Primates: A Test of the Hypothesis', *Journal of Human Evolution*, 28, 287–96, 1995.

Entrepreneurial Behaviour amongst General Practitioners

David Whynes, Christine Ennew and Teresa Feighan

Ennew, C., Whynes, D., Jolleys, J. and Robinson, P., 'Entrepreneurship and Innovation among GP Fundholders', *Public Money and Management*, 18(1), pp. 59–64, 1998.

Ennew, C., Feighan, T. and Whynes, D., 'Entrepreneurial Activity in the Public Sector: Evidence from U.K. Primary Care', *Public Money and Management*, 1998.

Whynes, D. and Reed, G., 'Fundholders' Referral Patterns and Perceptions of Service Quality in Hospital Provision of Elective General Surgery', *British Journal of General Practice*, 44, 557–60, 1994.

Whynes, D., Baines, D. and Tolley, K., 'GP Fundholding and the Costs of Prescribing', *Journal of Public Health Medicine*, 17, 323–9, 1995.

The research also contributed a chapter to the first programme book.

Framing, Salience and Product Images
Michael Bacharach, Andrew Colman and Diego Gambetta

Bacharach, M. and Gambetta, D., 'Signalling Identity', mimeo, *Institute of Economics and Statistics*, Oxford, 1996.

Bacharach, M. and Gambetta, D., 'Elements of a Theory of Quality Signals', mimeo, *Institute of Economics and Statistics*, Oxford, 1996.

Bacharach, M., Jones, M. and Stahl, D., 'Measuring Saliences in an Oddity Task and a Memory Task', mimeo, *Institute of Economics and Statistics*, Oxford, 1996.

Bacharach, M. and Stahl, D., 'The Variable Frame Level-n Theory of Games', mimeo, *Institute of Economics and Statistics*, Oxford, 1996.

Bacharach, M. and Bernasconi, M., 'The Variable Frame Theory of Focal Points: An Experimental Study', *Games and Economic Behavior*, 19, 1–45, 1997.

Bacharach, M., 'Showing What You Are by Showing Who You Are', Russell Sage Foundation Research Report, mimeo, *Institute of Economics and Statistics*, Oxford, 1997.

Bacharach, M., Jones, M. and Stahl, D., 'Saliences of Objects in an Oddity Task and a Memory Task', mimeo, *Institute of Economics and Statistics*, Oxford, 1997.

Colman, A.M., Wober, J.M. and Norris, C.E., 'Sight Bites: A Study of Viewers' Impressions of Corporate Logos in the Communications Industry', *Journal of the Market Research Society*, 37, 405–415, 1995.

Colman, A.M., 'Prisoner's Dilemma, Chicken, and Mixed-Strategy Evolutionary Equilibria', *The Behavioral and Brain Sciences*, 18, 550–1, 1995.

Colman, A.M. and Stirk, J.A., 'Stackelberg Thinking in Mixed-Motive Games: An Experimental Investigation', in C. Roland-Levy (ed.), *Social and Economic Representations*, 2, 1115–26, proceedings of the International Association for Economic Psychology XXIst Annual Colloquium, Paris: Académie de Paris, Université de René Descartes, 1996.

Colman, A.M., 'Focal Point Selection in Matching Games: Problems of Rational Justification', mimeo, *Department of Psychology*, University of Leicester, 1997.

Colman, A.M. and Bacharach, M., 'Payoff Dominance and the Stackelberg Heuristic', *Theory and Decision*, 43, 1–19, 1997.

Colman, A.M. and Wilson, J.C., 'Antisocial Personality Disorder: An Evolutionary Game Theory Analysis', *Legal and Criminology Psychology*, 2, 23–34, 1997.

Colman, A.M., 'Salience and Focusing in Pure Co-ordination Games', *Journal of Economic Methodology*, 4, 61–81, 1997.

Colman, A.M., 'Game Theory, Agent-Based Modelling and the Evolution of Social Behaviour' [review], *Complexity*, 3,3, 46–8, 1998.

Colman, A.M. and Stirk, J.A., 'Singleton Bias and Lexicographic Preferences among Equally Valued Alternatives', mimeo, *Department of Psychology*, University of Leicester, 1998.

Colman, A.M., 'Rationality Assumptions of Game Theory and the Backward Induction Paradox', in N. Chater and M. Oaksford (eds), *Rational Models of Cognition*, Oxford: Oxford University Press, 1998.

Colman, A.M., 'Modelling Imitation with Sequential Games', *Behavioral and Brain Sciences*, 21, 5, 686–71, 1998.

Colman, A.M. and Stirk, J.A., 'Stackelberg Reasoning in Mixed-Motive Games: An Experimental Investigation', *Journal of Economic Psychology*, vol. 19, no. 2, April 1998, pp. 279–93.

Gambetta, D., 'Model, Mimic and Dupe', Russell Sage Foundation Research Report, mimeo, *Institute of Economics and Statistics*, Oxford, 1997.

Pulford, B.D. and Colman, A.M., 'Overconfidence, Base Rates and Outcome Positivity/Negativity of Predicted Events', *British Journal of Psychology*, 87, 431–45, 1996.

Pulford, B.D. and Colman, A.M., 'Overconfidence: Feedback and Item Difficulty Effects', *Personality and Individual Differences*, 23, 125–33, 1997.

The research also contributed to: Bacharach, M., 'Common Knowledge', *The New Palgrave Dictionary of Economics and the Law*, ed. Newman, P., Macmillan: London, 1998.

Colman, A.M., 'Game Theory and Its Applications', *Social and Biological Sciences*, 2nd edition, Oxford: Butterworth-Heinemann, 1995.

Morals and Money: Green and Ethical Investing

Alan Lewis, Paul Webley, Adrian Winnett and Craig Mackenzie

Lewis, A., 'Markets, Morals and the Case of Ethical/Green Investing' in Earl, P. and Kemp, S. (eds), *Consumer Research and Economic Psychology*, Northampton Mass.:Elgar, 1998.

Lewis, A. and Mackenzie, C., 'Green and Ethical Investing: Can it Make a Difference?', in A. Warhurst (ed.), *Toward an Environment Research Agenda*, London: Macmillan, 1998.

Lewis, A. and Mackenzie, C., 'Support for Investor Activism among UK Ethical Investors', *Journal of Business Ethics*, 7, 1998.

Lewis, A. and Mackenzie, C., 'Morals, Money, Ethical Investing and Economic Psychology', *Discussion Paper*, University of Bath, School of Social Sciences.

Mackenzie, C., 'The Stewardship Process: A Case Study of Friends Provident Stewardship', *Discussion Paper*, University of Bath, School of Social Sciences.

Mackenzie, C., *Ethical Investment and the Challenge of Corporate Reform*, Ph.D. Thesis, University of Bath.

Mackenzie, C. and Lewis, A., 'Morals and Markets: The Case of Ethical Investing', in C. Roland-Levy (ed.), *Social and Economic Representations*, 2, 1153–65, proceedings of the International Association for Economic Psychology XXIst Annual Colloquium, Paris: Académie de Paris, Université de René Descartes, 1996.

Mackenzie, C. and Lewis, A., 'Morals and Markets: The Case of Ethical Investing', *Business Ethics Quarterly*, 8, 1998.

Mackenzie, C., 'Where are the Motives? Problems with evidence in the work of Richard Thaler', *Journal of Economic Psychology*, 18, 1, pp. 123–37, 1997.

Mackenzie, C., 'Lobbying the management to clean up its act', *Investment Adviser*, 1.12.97.

Mackenzie, C., 'Investing the Green Way Can Pay', *Investment Week*, 9.2.98.

Mackenzie, C., 'Ethical Accountability', *Investment Week*, 4.5.98.

Mackenzie, C., 'The Choice of Criteria in Ethical Investment', *Business Ethics: A European Review*, 7.2, 1998.

Webley, P. (1996). 'Role-playing on the Web', in C. Roland-Levy (ed.), *Social and Economic Representations*, 2, 1232–56, proceedings of the International Association for Research in Economic Psychology XXIst Annual Colloquium, Paris: Académie de Paris, Université de René Descartes, 1996.

Webley, P., Lewis, A. and Mackenzie, C., 'Ethical Investment: An Experimental Approach', *Discussion Paper*, University of Bath, School of Social Sciences.
Winnett, A. and Lewis, A., 'You'd have to be Green to invest in this: popular economic models, financial journalism and ethical investment', *Discussion Paper*, University of Bath, School of Social Sciences.

The project also contributed a chapter to the first programme book.

Public Attitudes to Taxation and Public Spending
Lindsay Brook, John Hall and Ian Preston

Besley, T., Hall, J. and Preston, I., 'Private Health Insurance and the State of the NHS', *IFS Commentary* No. 52, London: Institute for Fiscal Studies, 1996.
Besley, T., Hall, J. and Preston, I., 'Private and Public Health Insurance in the UK', *European Economic Review Papers and Proceedings*, 1998.
Besley, T., Hall, J. and Preston, I., 'The Demand for Private Health Insurance: Do Waiting Lists Matter?', *Journal of Public Economics*, 71, 1999.
Brook, L., Hall, J. and Preston, I., 'Attitudes to Taxation and Public Spending', in C. Roland-Levy (ed.), *Social and Economic Representations*, 2, 1141–52, proceedings of the International Association for Economic Psychology XXIst Annual Colloquium, Paris: Académie de Paris, Université de René Descartes, 1996.
Brook, L., Hall, J. and Preston, I., 'Attitudes to Tax and Spending', in R. Jowell *et al.* (eds), *British Social Attitudes*: the 13th Report, Dartmouth Publishing, 1996.
Brook, L., 'Attitudes to Spending on Welfare', *Insurance Trends*, July 1997.
Hall, J., Ridge, M. and Preston, I., 'How Public Attitudes to Expenditure Differ', in D. Corry (ed.), *Public Expenditure: Effective Management and Control*, London: Institute for Public Policy Research, 1996.
Preston, I. and Ridge, M., 'Demand for Local Public Spending: Evidence from the British Social Attitudes Survey', *Economic Journal*, 105, 644–60, 1995.
Hall, J., Emmerson, C. and Brook, L. 'Attitudes to Local Taxation and Spending', *Institute for Fiscal Studies Commentary* no. 68, February, 1998.
Hall, J. and Preston, I., 'Tax Price Effects on Attitudes to Hypothecated National Tax Increases', *Journal of Public Economics*, forthcoming.

The project also contributed a chapter to the first programme book.

Symbolic Meanings of Goods as Determinants of Impulse Buying Behaviour
Helga Dittmar, Jane Beattie and Susanne Friese

Dittmar H., Beattie J. and Friese S., 'Gender Identity and Material Symbols: Objects and Decision Considerations in Impulse Purchases', *Journal of Economic Psychology*, 16, 491–511, 1995.
Dittmar, H., Beattie, J. and Friese, S., 'Objects, Decision Considerations and Self-Image in Men's and Women's Impulse Purchases', *Acta Psychologica*, 93, 187–206, 1996.

Dittmar, H., Beattie, J. and Friese, S., 'Objects, Decision Considerations and Self-Image in Men's and Women's Impulse Purchases', in P. Ayton, J. Beattie, R. Beyth-Marom and P. Koele (eds), *Contributions in Decision Making*: II, North Holland, 1996.

Dittmar, H., Beattie, J. and Friese, S., 'The Role of Self-Discrepancies in Shopping Addiction', in C. Roland-Levy (ed.), *Social and Economic Representations*, 2, 1140, proceedings of the International Association for Economic Psychology XXIst Annual Colloquium, Paris: Académie de Paris, Université de René Descartes, 1996.

Dittmar, H., 'Social Psychology of Economic and Consumer Behaviour', in G.R. Semin and K. Fiedler (eds), *Applied Social Psychology*, Sage: London, 1996.

Dittmar, H., Beattie, J. and Friese, S., 'The Role of Self-Discrepancies in Ordinary and Compulsive Buying Behaviour', *Personality and Social Psychology Bulletin*, forthcoming.

Friese, S., 'Selbst, Identität und Konsum', in M. Neuner and L. Reisch (eds) *Konsumperspektiven: Verhaltensaspekte und Infrastruktur*, Berlin: Duncker & Humblot, 1998, pp. 35–54.

Friese, S., 'Addictive Buying', in P. Earl and S. Kemp (eds) *The Elgar Companion to Consumer Research and Economic Psychology*, London & Brookfield, Vermont: Elgar, 1998, pp. 12–17.

Friese, S., 'Addictive buying and self-concept: A theoretical account with some empirical evidence', in M.C. Campbell and K.A. Machleit (eds) *Conference Proceedings. Society for Consumer Psychology*, Austin, Texas, Society for Consumer Psychology, 1998, pp. 6–9.

The research also contributed to: Dittmar, H., 'Materialism', in P. Earl and S. Kemp (eds), *The Elgar Companion to Consumer Research and Economic Psychology*, London & Brookfield, Vermont: Elgar, 1998.

Dittmar, H., 'Ein symbolischer Interaktionsansatz zu der Verbindung zwischen Identitaet und materiellen Dingen', in U. Fuhrer (ed.), *Dinge Kultivieren: Persoenliche Dinge, Identitaet und Entwicklung*, Bern: Huber, forthcoming.

The project also contributed a chapter to the first programme book.

The Consistency or Inconsistency of Preferences under Risk and over Time

Robert Sugden, Robin Cubitt , Graham Loomes and Chris Starmer

Beattie, J. and Loomes, G., 'The Impact of Incentives upon Risky Choice Experiments', *Journal of Risk and Uncertainty*, 14, 149–162, 1997.

Cubitt, R.P. and Sugden, R., 'On Money Pumps', *Economics Research Centre Discussion Paper* No. 9509, University of East Anglia, 1995.

Cubitt, R.P., 'Rational Dynamic Choice and Expected Utility Theory', *Oxford Economic Papers*, 48, 1–19, 1996.

Cubitt, R.P., Starmer, C. and Sugden, R., 'Some Tests of the Validity of the Random Lottery Incentive System', in C. Roland-Levy (ed.), *Social and Economic Representations*, 2, 1176–87, proceedings of the International Association for Economic Psychology XXIst Annual Colloquium, Paris: Académie de Paris, Université de René Descartes, 1996.

Cubitt, R.P., Starmer, C. and Sugden, R., 'Dynamic Choice and the Common Ratio Effect: an experimental investigation', *Economic Journal*, 108, 1362–80, 1998.

Cubitt, R.P. and Sugden, R., 'The Selection of Preferences through Imitation', *Review of Economic Studies*, 65, 761–71, 1998.

Cubitt, R.P., Starmer, C.V. and Sugden, R., 'On the Validity of the Random Lottery Incentive System', *Experimental Economics*, 1, 115–31, 1998.

Loomes, G. and Sugden, R., 'Testing Alternative Stochastic Specifications for Risky Choice', *Economica*, vol. 65, 581–98, 1998.

Loomes, G., 'Probabilities vs. Money: A Test of Some Fundamental Assumptions about Rational Decision-Making', *Economic Journal*, vol. 108, 477–89, 1998.

Loomes, G. 'Some Lessons from Past Experiments and Some Challenges for the Future', *Economic Journal*, vol. 109, 1999.

Starmer, C., 'Explaining Risky Choices without Assuming Preferences', *Social Choice and Welfare*, 13, 201–213, 1996.

Starmer, C., 'The Economics of Risk', in P. Callow (ed.), *The Handbook of Environmental Risk Assessment*, Blackwell, 1997.

Starmer, C., 'Cycling with Rules of Thumb: An Experimental Test for a New Form of Non-Transitive Behaviour', *Theory and Decision*, forthcoming.

Starmer C., 'Experiments in Economics: Should We Trust the Dismal Scientists in White Coats?', *Journal of Economic Methodology*, forthcoming.

Starmer, C. and Sugden, R., 'Testing Alternative Explanations of Cyclical Choices', *Economica*, 65, 259, 347–62, 1998.

Sugden, R., 'Alternatives to Expected Utility', in S. Barbera, P. Hammond and C. Seidl (eds), *Handbook of Utility Theory*, Kluwer, 1997.

The Role of Beliefs about the Fairness of Wage Differentials in Wage Setting

Julie Dickinson and Lucia Sell-Trujillo

Dickinson, J., 'The Role of Beliefs about the Fairness of Wage Differentials in Wage Setting', *People Management*, November, 1995.

Dickinson, J. and Sell-Trujillo, L., 'Explanations for Pay Differentials: Rhetoric or Social Representations?', in C. Roland-Levy (ed.), *Social and Economic Representations*, 2, 1139, Proceedings of the International Association for Economic Psychology XXIst Annual Colloquium, Paris: Académie de Paris, Université de René Descartes, 1996.

The project also contributed a chapter to the first programme book.

Welfare Citizenship and Economic Rationality

Hartley Dean and Margaret Melrose

Dean, H. and Melrose, M., 'Fiddling the Social: Understanding Benefit Fraud', *Benefits*, 14, 17–18, September 1995.

Dean, H. and Barrett, D., 'Unrespectable Research and Researching the Unrespectable', in H. Dean (ed.), *Ethics and Social Policy Research*, University of Luton and the Social Policy Association, 1996.

Dean, H., 'What sort of a problem?', *New Review of the Low Pay Unit*, No. 37, p. 16, January/February, 1996.

Dean, H. and Melrose, M., 'Unravelling Citizenship: The Significance of Social Security Benefit Fraud', *Critical Social Policy*, 16, 3, 3–33, August 1996.

Dean, H., 'In Spite of Welfare: Understanding Social Security Benefit Fraud', in C. Roland-Levy (ed.), *Social and Economic Representations*, 2, 1127–38, proceedings of the International Association for Economic Psychology XXIst Annual Colloquium, Paris: Académie de Paris, Université de René Descartes, 1996.

Dean, H. and Melrose, M., 'Manageable Discord': Fraud and Resistance in the Social Security System, *Social Policy Administration*, vol. 31, no. 2, pp. 103–118, 1997.

Dean, H., 'Underclassed or Undermined? Young People and Social Citizenship', in R. MacDonald (ed.), *Youth, the Underclass and Social Exclusion*, Routledge, 1997.

Dean, H. 'The Politics of Fraud', Editorial, *Benefits*, 21, p. 1, 1998.

Dean, H. 'Undermining Social Citizenship: The Counterproductive Effects of Behavioural Controls in Social Security Administration', *Social Policy Paper* no 2, University of Hertfordshire Business School Working papers.

Dean, H. *Beating Fraud is Everybody's Business: Securing the Future – Response to the Green Paper*, 1998.

Melrose, M., 'Enticing subjects and disembodied objects', in H. Dean (ed.), *Ethics and Social Policy Research*, University of Luton Press/Social Policy Association, 1996.

The research contributed to: Dean, H. with Melrose, M. Poverty, *Riches and Social Citizenship*, Macmillan, Basingstoke, 1999.

The project also contributed chapters to both programme books.

Programme Discussion Papers
(available from *http://www.ukc.ac.uk/ESRC/*)

Manageable Discord: Citizenship and Welfare Fraud.
Hartley Dean and Margaret Melrose

Gender Identity and Material Symbols.
Helga Dittmar, Jane Beattie and Susanne Friese

Objects, Decision Considerations and Self-Image in Men's and Women's Impulse Purchases.
Helga Dittmar, Jane Beattie and Susanne Friese

A Simulation of Budgetary Decision-Making Based on Interview Data.
Edmund Chattoe and Nigel Gilbert

Asian Self-Employment in Britain: The Interaction of Culture and Economics.
Tariq Modood, Satnam Virdee and Hilary Metcalf

Can Sociologists and Economists Communicate? The Problem of Grounding and the Theory of Consumer Theory.
Edmund Chattoe

Why are We Simulating Anyway? Some Answers from Economics.
Edmund Chattoe

Reacting to the Housing Market Slump.
Clodagh Memery, Moira Munro, Ruth Madigan and Kenneth Gibb

Entrepreneurship and Innovation among GP Fundholders: Some Preliminary Evidence.
Christine Ennew, David Whynes and Teresa Feighan

Explaining Pay: The Perspective of Personnel Managers.
Julie Dickinson and Lucia Sell-Trujillo

The Demand for Private Health Insurance: Do Waiting Lists Matter?
Timothy Besley, John Hall and Ian Preston

What Drives Support for Higher Public Spending?
Lindsay Brook, John Hall and Ian Preston

Tax Price Effects on Attitudes to Hypothecated Tax Increases
John Hall and Ian Preston

Markets and Motives: Trust and Egoism in Welfare Markets
Peter Taylor-Gooby

Risk and the Welfare State
Peter Taylor-Gooby, Hartley Dean, Moira Munro and Gillian Parker

Public and Private Choice in Health Insurance
John Hall and Ian Preston

References

Adams, J. (1995) *Risk*, London, UCL Press.

Alaszewski, A. (1998) *Risk, Health and Welfare*, Milton Keynes, Open University Press.

Alhakami, A. S. and Slovic, P. (1994) 'A psychological study of the inverse relationship between perceived risk and perceived benefit', *Risk Analysis*, 14, 1085–96.

Allingham, M. G. and Sandmo, A. (1972) 'Income Tax Evasion: A Theoretical Analysis', *Journal of Public Economics*, I, 323–38.

Alm, J., McKee, M. and Beck, W. (1990) 'Amazing Grace: Tax Amnesties and Compliance', *National Tax Journal*, 43, 23–38.

Ames, C. (1984) 'Competitive, Cooperative, and Individualistic Goal Structures: A Cognitive-motivational Analysis', in Ames and Ames (eds) *Research on Motivation, Vol. 1 Student Motivation*, New York, Academic Press.

Andrews, K. and Jacobs, J. (1990) *Punishing the Poor: Poverty under Thatcher*, Basingstoke, Macmillan.

Anon. (1997) 'Pharmacists asked to move terfenadine products into the dispensary', *Pharmaceutical Journal*, 258, 581.

Appelbe, G. and Wingfield, J. (1997) *Pharmacy Law and Ethics*, Cambridge, The Pharmaceutical Press.

Arrow, K. J. (1972) 'Gifts and Exchanges', *Philosophy and Public Affairs*, 1, 343–62.

Atkinson, A. and Micklewright, J. (1988) *Turning the Screw: Benefits for the Unemployed 1979–1988*, London, STICERD, London School of Economics.

Avorn, J., Chen, M. and Hartley, R. (1982) 'Scientific versus commercial sources of influence on the prescribing behaviour of physicians', *American Journal of Medicine*, 73, 4–8.

Baldwin, S. (1994) 'The need for care in later life: social protection for older people and family caregivers', in S. Baldwin and J. Falkingham (eds), *Social Security and Social Change: New Challenges to the Beveridge Model*, Hemel Hempstead, Harvester Wheatsheaf.

Banks, J. and Tanner, S. (1996) 'Savings and wealth in the UK: evidence from micro-data', *Fiscal Studies*, 17, 37–64.

Barber, N. (1993) 'Drugs: from prescription only to pharmacy only', *British Medical Journal*, 307, 640.

Bardach, E. and Kagan, R. A. (1982) *Going By the Book: The Problem of Regulatory Unreasonableness.* Philadelphia, Temple University Press.

Barkema, H. G. (1995) 'Do Job Executives Work Harder When they are Monitored?', *Kyklos*, 48, 19–42.

Barlow, A. (1998) 'Family structuring, legal regulation and gendered moral rationalities; some empirical findings' paper given to Socio-legal Studies Association Annual Conference, Manchester Metropolitan University, 16 April (available from author at Law Department, University of Wales, Aberystwyth).

Barlow, A. and Duncan, S. (1999) 'New Labour's communitarianism, supporting families, and the 'rationality mistake', Centre for Research on Family, Kinship and Gender, University of Leeds, Working Paper 10.

Barter, G. and Cormack, M. (1996) 'The long-term use of benzodiazepines: patients' views, accounts and experiences', *Family Practice*, 13, 491–7.

Bartlett, W., Le Grand, J. and Roberts, J. (1998) (eds) *A Revolution in Social Policy*, Bristol, Policy Press.

Bauman, Z. (1988) *Freedom*, Buckingham, Open University Press.

Bauman, Z. (1993) *Postmodern Ethics*, Cambridge, Polity Press.

Bauman, Z. (1995) *Life in Fragments*, Oxford, Blackwell.

Bauman, Z. (1998) *Work, Consumerism and the New Poor*, Buckingham: Open University Press.

Baumol, W. J. and Oates, W. E. (1979) *Economics, Environmental Policy, and the Quality of Life*. Englewood Cliffs, NJ: Prentice-Hall.

Beatson, M. (1995) *Labour Market Flexibility*, Research Report No. 48, London, Department of Employment.

Beck, U. (1992) *Risk Society: Towards a New Modernity*, London, Sage.

Beck, U. (1992b) 'How modern is modern society?', *Theory, Culture and Society*, vol. 19, no. 2, pp. 163–9.

Beck, U., Giddens, A. and Lash, S. (1994) *Reflexive Modernisation*, Cambridge, Polity.

Becker, G. S. (1968) 'Crime and Punishment: An Economic Approach', *Journal of Political Economy*, 76, 169–217.

Becker, G. S. (1976) *The Economic Approach to Human Behavior*, Chicago, Chicago University Press.

Becker, G. S. (1996) *Accounting for Tastes*, Cambridge, MA, and London, Harvard University Press.

Becker, H. (1960) 'Notes on the concept of commitment', *American Journal of Sociology*, vol. 66, no. 1, pp. 32–40.

Beckman, R. (1997) *Housequake*, Leighton Buzzard, Rushmere Wynn.

Berridge, V. (1997) 'AIDS and the gift relationship in the UK' Ch. 2 in Oakley and Ashton, pp. 15–40.

Bissell, P., Ward, P. R. and Noyce, P. R. (1997a) 'Variations within community pharmacy: 1 Requesting over the counter medicines', *Journal of Social and Administrative Pharmacy*, 14, 1–15.

Bissell, P., Ward, P. R. and Noyce, P. R. (1997b) 'Variations within community pharmacy: 2 Responding to the presentation of symptoms', *Journal of Social and Administrative Pharmacy*, 14, 105–15.

Björnberg, U. (1992) 'Tvåförsörjarefamiljen i teori och verklighet', in J. Acker *et al.* (eds) *Kvinnors och Mäns Liv och Arbete*, Stockholm, SNS Förlag.

Björnberg, U. (1997) 'Single mothers in Sweden, supported workers who mother' in Duncan, S. and Edwards, R. (eds) *Single Mothers in an International Context: Mothers or Workers*, London, UCL Press.

Blair, T. (1995) 'The rights we enjoy reflect the duties we owe', *The Spectator Lecture*, London, Labour Party.

Blair, T. (1996) 'Battle for Britain', *The Guardian*, 29 January.

Blair, T. (1996a) Speech to the CPU conference, Cape Town, 14 October.

Blair, T. (1996b) in Radice, G. (ed.) *What Needs to Change: New Visions for Britain*, London, HarperCollins.

Blair, T. (1997) 'The will to win', speech to launch the Social Exclusion Unit at the Aylesbury Estate, Southwark, 2 June.

Blanchard, O. (1996) 'Theoretical Aspects of Transition', *American Economic Review*, 86, 117–22.

Blaxter, M. and Britten, N. (1996) *Lay Beliefs about Drugs and Medicines and the Implications for Community Pharmacy*, Report produced for the Pharmacy Practice Research Resource Centre, University of Manchester.

Blenkinsopp, A. and Bradley, C. (1996) 'Patients, society and the increase in self medication', *British Medical Journal*, 312, 629–32.

Bohnet, I. (1997) *Kooperation und Kommunikation. Eine ökonomische Analyse individueller Entscheidungen*, Tübingen, Mohr (Siebeck).

Bohnet, I. and B. S. Frey (1997) 'Rent Leaving', *Journal of Institutional and Theoretical Economics*, 153, 711–21.

Bonoli, G., George, V. and Taylor-Gooby, P. (2000) *European Welfare Futures*, Cambridge, Polity.

Borrie, Sir Gordon (1994) *Social Justice: Strategies for National Renewal, The Report of the Commission on Social Justice*, London, IPPR/Vintage.

Bourdieu, P. (1984) *Distinction: A Social Critique of the Judgement of Taste*, London, Routledge.

Bower, A. and Eaton, K. (1998) 'Auditing standards for responding to symptoms and quantifying the level of activity for this service in community pharmacies', *Pharmaceutical Journal*, 261, 828–30.

Bramley, G. (1989) *Housing Costs and Subsidies in Bristol*, York, Joseph Rowntree Foundation.

Breheny, M. and Hall, P. (1996) *The People – where will they go?*, London: TCPA.

Brehm, J. W. A. (1966) *A Theory of Psychological Reactance*, New York, Academic Press.

Brennan, G. and Buchanan, J. M. (1985) *The Reason of Rules. Constitutional Political Economy*, Cambridge, Cambridge University Press.

Britten, N. (1996) 'Lay views of drugs and medicines: orthodox and unorthodox accounts' in S. J. Williams and M. Calnan (eds), *Modern Medicine. Lay Perspectives and Experiences*, London, UCL Press.

Brockner, J., Tyler, T. R. and Cooper-Schneider, R. (1992) 'The Influence of Prior Commitment to an Institution on Reactions to Perceived Unfairness: The Higher They Are, the Harder They Fall', *Administrative Science Quarterly*, 37, 241–61.

Brody, E. M. (1981) 'Women in the middle and family help to older people', *The Gerontologist*, 21, 471–801.

Brook, L., Hall, J. and Preston, I. (1996) 'Public spending and taxation', in R. Jowell, J. Curtice, A. Park, L. Brook and K. Thompson (eds) *British Social Attitudes, The 13th report*, Aldershot, Dartmouth.

Brook, L., Preston, I. and Hall, J. (1998) 'What drives support for higher public spending', in P. Taylor-Gooby (ed.) *Choice and Public Policy: The Limits to Welfare markets*, Basingstoke, Macmillan.

Brown, P. (1992) 'Popular epidemiology and toxic waste contamination: lay and professional ways of knowing', *Journal of Health and Social Behaviour*, 33, 267–81.

Buchanan, J. M. (1987) 'Constitutional Economics', in J. Eatwell, M. Milligate and P. Newman (eds) *The New Palgrave: A Dictionary of Economics*, London, Macmillan, pp. 585–88.

Buck, N., Gershuny, J., Rose, D. and Scott, J. (1994) *Changing Households*, ESRC Research Centre on Micro-Social Change, University of Essex.

Burchardt, T. and Hills, J. (1997) *Private Welfare Insurance and Social Security: Pushing at the Boundaries*, York, Joseph Rowntree Foundation.

Burgoyne, C. and Millar, J. (1994) 'Enforcing child support: the views of separated fathers' *Policy and Politics*, 22, 2, 95–104.

Burkitt, B. and Ashton, F. (1996) 'The birth of the stakeholder society', *Critical Social Policy*, 16, 4, 3–16.

Burrows, R. and Ford, J. (1998) 'Self-employment and Home Ownership After the Enterprise Culture', *Work, Employment and Society*, 21, 1.

Burrows, R. and Loader, B. (eds) (1994) *Towards a Post-Fordist Welfare State?*, London, Routledge.

Bushnell, J. (1979) 'The New Soviet Man Turns Pessimist', *Survey*, 24, 1–18.

Cameron, J. and Pierce, W. D. (1994) 'Reinforcement, Reward, and Intrinsic Motivation: A Meta-Analysis', *Review of Educational Research*, 64, 363–423.

Carnes, S. A. *et al.* (1983) 'Incentives and Nuclear Waste Siting', *Energy Systems and Policy*, 7, 324–51.

Cebulla, A., Abbott, D., Ford, J., Middleton, S., Quilgars, D. and Walker, R. (1998) *A Geography of Insurance Exclusion-Perceptions of Unemployment Risk and Actuarial Risk Assessment*, Paper presented to Second European Urban and Regional Studies Conference, University of Durham, September.

CEC (Commission of the European Community, 1993) *Growth, Competitiveness, Employment*, White Paper, Bulletin, supp. 6/93, CEC, Luxembourg.

Chaney, D. (1996) *Lifestyles*, London, Routledge.

Clarke, K., Craig, C. and Glendinning, C. (1994) *Losing Support: Children and the Child Support Act*, London, Barnado's, The Children's Society, NCH, NSPCC, SCF.

Cole, I. and Furbey, R. (1994) *The Eclipse of Council Housing*, London: Routledge.

Coleman, J. S. (1990) *Foundations of Social Theory*, Cambridge, MA, Harvard University Press.

Collier, R. (1994) 'The Campaign against the Child Support Act: Errant Fathers and Family Men', *Family Law*, 384–7.

Consumers' Association (June 1994) 'Over-the-counter medicines. No prescription necessary', *Which?*, 38–41.

Consumers' Association (January 1996) 'Pharmacists in Crisis', *Which?*, 18–21.

Cook, D. (1989) *Rich Law, Poor Law: Different responses to Tax and Supplementary Benefit Fraud*, Milton Keynes, Open University Press.

Cooper, M. and Culyer, A. (1968) *The Price of Blood*. Hobart Paper No. 41, London, Institute of Economic Affairs.

Cooter, R. D. (1984) 'Prices and Sanctions', *Columbia Law Review*, 84, 1523–60.

Council for Mortgage Lenders (1998) *Housing Finance* No. 39: August.

Council for Mortgage Lenders (1998b) 'Will student debt damage the mortgage market?' *Housing Finance* 37.

Coward, R. (1998) 'Busybody's charter,' *The Guardian*, 9 June.

Crow, G. (1989) 'The use of the concept of strategy in recent sociological literature', *Sociology*, vol. 23, pp. 1–24.

CSO (Central Statistical Office, 1995) *Social Trends, no. 25*, London, HMSO.

Cuccia, A. (1994) 'The Economics of Tax Compliance: What do We Know and Where do We Go?', *Journal of Accounting Literature*, 13, 81–116.

Dake, K. (1992) 'Myths of nature: culture and the social construction of risk', *Journal of Social Issues* 48, 21–37.

Dake, K. and Wildavsky, A. (1991) 'Individual differences in risk perception and risk-taking preferences' in Garrick, B. J. and Gekler, W. C. (eds), *The Analysis, Communication and Perception of Risk*, New York, Plenum.

Davis, G., Wikley, N., Young, R. with Barron, J. and Bedward, J. (1998) *Child Support in Action*, Oxford, Hart Publishing.

Dawes, R. M. (1988) *Rational Choice in an Uncertain World*, San Diego and New York: Harcourt Brace Jovanovich.

Dawes, R. M., van de Kragt, A. J. C. and Orbell, J. M. (1988) 'Not Me or Thee but WE: The Importance of Group Identity in Eliciting Cooperation in Dilemma Situations – Experimental Manipulations', *Acta Psychologica*, 68, 83–97.

Daycare Trust (1997) *Childcare Disregard in Family Credit, Who Gains?* London, Daycare Trust.

Deacon, A. (1997) ' "Welfare to Work": Options and issues', in M. May, E. Brunsdon and G. Craig (eds) *Social Policy Review 9*, London, Social Policy Association.

Deacon, A. and Fairfoot, P. (1994) 'Investigating fraud ', *Poverty*, No. 87.

Dean, H. (1991) *Social Security and Social Control*, London, Routledge.

Dean, H. (ed.) (1995) *Parents' Duties, Children's Debts: The Limits of Policy Intervention*, Aldershot, Ashgate.

Dean, H. (1996) *Welfare, Law and Citizenship*, Hemel Hempstead, Prentice Hall/Harvester Wheatsheaf.

Dean, H. and Melrose, M. (1996) 'Unravelling citizenship: The significance of social security benefit fraud', *Critical Social Policy*, Issue 48.

Dean, H. and Melrose, M. (1997) 'Manageable Discord: Fraud and resistance in the social security system', *Social Policy and Administration*, vol. 31, no. 2.

Dean, H. with Melrose, M. (1998) *Poverty, Riches and Social Citizenship*, Basingstoke, Macmillan.

Dean, H. and Taylor-Gooby, P. (1992) *Dependency Culture: The Explosion of a Myth*, Hemel Hempstead, Harvester Wheatsheaf.

DeCharms, R. (1968) *Personal Causation: The Internal Affective Determinants of Behavior*, New York, Academic Press.

Deci, E. L. (1971) 'Effects of Externally Mediated Rewards on Intrinsic Motivation', *Journal of Personality and Social Psychology*, 18, 105–15.

Deci, E. L. (1975) *Intrinsic Motivation*, New York, Plenum Press.

Deci, E. L., Koestner, R. and Ryan, R. M. (1998) 'Extrinsic Rewards and Intrinsic Motivation: A Clear and Consistent Picture After All', *Mimeo*, Department of Psychology, University of Rochester.

Deci, E. L. and Ryan, R. M. (1985) *Intrinsic Motivation and Self-determination in Human Behavior*, New York, Plenum Press.

Deci, E. L. and Ryan, R. M. (1987) 'The Support of Autonomy and the Control of Behavior', *Journal of Personality and Social Psychology*, 53, 1024–37.

Dennis, N. and Erdos, G. (1993) *Families Without Fatherhood*, London, Institute of Economic Affairs.

Department of Health (1996) *A New Partnership for Care in Old Age: a Discussion Document*, Cm 3242, London, HMSO.

Department of Health (1997) *A New Partnership for Care in Old Age: a Policy Statement*, Cm 3563, London, HMSO.

Desvousges, W. H. and Smith, V. K. (1988) 'Focus groups and risk communication: the "science" of listening to data', *Risk Analysis*, 8, 479–84.

Dex, S. and McCullogh, A. (1997) *Flexible Employment, the Future of Britain's Jobs*, London, Macmillan Press.

DHSS (Department of Health and Social Security, 1985) *The Reform of Social Security*, Cmnd 9517, London, HMSO.

Diekmann, A. (1995) 'Umweltbewusstsein oder Anreizstrukturen? Empirische Befunde zum Energiesparen, der Verkehrsmittelwahl und zum Konsumverhalten', in A. Diekmann and A. Franzen (eds) *Kooperatives Umwelthandeln. Modelle, Erfahrungen, Massnahmen*, Chur and Zurich, Rüegger.

Disney, R. (1996) *Can we afford to grow older? A perspective on the economics of ageing*, Cambridge, Mass, MIT Press.

Disney, R. and Stears, G. (1996) 'Why is there a decline in defined benefit pension plan membership in Britain?' *Institute for Fiscal Studies Working Paper, No. 96/4*.

Disney, R. and Whitehouse, E. (1992) *The Personal Pension Stampede*, IFS Report Series, London.

Doling, J. and Ford, J. (1996) 'The New Home Ownership: The Impact of Labour Market Developments on Attitudes to Owning Your Own Home' *Environment and Planning A*, 28.

Douglas, M. and Wildavsky, A. (1982) *Risk and Culture: An Essay on the Selection of Technological and Environmental Dangers*, Berkeley, University of California Press.

Douglas, M. (1992) *Risk and Blame: Essays in Cultural Theory*, London, Routledge.

Douglas, M. (1986) *Risk Acceptability According to the Social Sciences*, London, Routledge & Kegan Paul.

Driver, S. and Martell, L. (1997) 'New Labour's communitarianisms' *Critical Social Policy*, 17, 3, 27–46.

Dryzek, J. S. (1992) *Discursive Democracy: Politics, Policy, and Political Science*, New York, Cambridge University Press.

DSS (Department of Social Security, 1998) *A New Contract for Welfare*, Cm 3805, London, HMSO.

DSS (Department of Social Security, 1998a) *New Ambitions for our Country: A New Contract for Welfare*, Cm 3805, London, Stationery Office.

DSS (Department of Social Security, 1998b) *Beating Fraud is Everyone's Business: Securing the future*, Cm 4012, London, Stationery Office.

DSS (Department of Social Security, 1998c) *The Future of Welfare*, London, HMSO.

DSS (Department of Social Security, 1998d) *Social Security Statistics, 1997*, London, HMSO.

Duncan, S. and Edwards, R. (1999) *Lone Mothers, Paid Work and Gendered Moral Rationalities*, London, Macmillan.

Duncombe, W. D. and Brudney, J. L. (1995) 'The Optimal Mix of Volunteer and Paid Staff in Local Governments: An Application to Municipal Fire Departments', *Public Finance Quarterly*, 23 356–84.

Easterling, D. H. and Kunreuther, H. (1995) *The Dilemma of Siting a High-Level Nuclear Waste Repository*, Boston, Kluwer.

Eisenberger, R. and Cameron, J. (1996) 'Detrimental Effects of Reward. Reality of Myth?', *American Psychologist*, 51, 1153–66.

Eisenberger, R. and Cameron, J. (1997) 'Rewards, Intrinsic Task Interest, and Creativity: New Findings', Paper presented at the Society of Experimental Social Psychology, Toronto.

Esping-Andersen, G. (1990) *The Three Worlds of Welfare Capitalism*, Cambridge, Polity.

Esping-Andersen, G. (ed.), (1996) *Welfare States in Transition*, London Sage (in association with UNRISD).

Evandrou, M. and Falkingham, J. (1995) 'Gender, lone parenthood and life-time incomes' in Falkingham, J. (ed.) *The Dynamics of Welfare*, London Prentice-Hall/ Harvester Wheatsheaf.

Evason, E. and Woods, R. (1995) 'Poverty, de-regulation of the labour market and benefit fraud', *Social Policy and Administration*, vol. 29, no. 1.

Evers, A. (1994) 'Payments for Care: a Small but Significant Part of a Wider Debate' , Ch. 2 in Evers, Adalbert and Ungerson.

Evers, A., Pijl, M. and Ungerson, C. (1994) *Payments for Care: a Comparative Overview*, Aldershot, Avebury.

Fehr, E. and Gächter, S. (1998) 'Cooperation and Punishment – An Experimental Investigation of Norm Formation and Norm Enforcement', Institute for Empirical Economic Research, University of Zurich.

Feld, L. P. and Kirchgässner, G. (1997) 'Public Debt and Budgetary Procedures: Top Down or Bottom Up. Some Evidence from Swiss Municipalities', Mimeo, Volkswirtschaftliche Abteilung, University of St Gallen.

Feld, L. P. and Savioz, M. R. (1997) 'Direct Democracy Matters for Economic Performance: An Empirical Investigation', *Kyklos*, 50, 507–38.

Field, F. (1996) *Stakeholder Welfare*, London, Institute of Economic Affairs.

Finch, J. (1989) *Family Obligations and Social Change*. Cambridge, Polity Press.

Finch, J. and Mason, J. (1993) *Negotiating Family Responsibilities*, London, Routledge.

Finn, D. (1997) 'The Stricter Benefit Regime and the New Deal for the Unemployed', paper given at the annual conference of the Social Policy Association, *New Politics: New Welfare?*, University of Lincolnshire and Humberside, Lincoln, 15–17 July.

Ford, J. (1998) *Risks*, London, Shelter.

Ford, J. (1999) 'Coping with risk in a flexible labour market' (this volume).

Ford, J. and Burrows, R. (1999) 'The Costs of Unsustainable Home Ownership', *Journal of Social Policy*, 28,3.

Ford, J. and Kempson, E. (1997) *Bridging the Gap? Safety nets for mortgage holders*, York, Centre for Housing Policy.

Ford, J. and Wilcox, S. (1994) *Affordable housing, low incomes and the flexible labour force*, NFHA Research Report 22, London, NFHA.

Ford, J. and Wilcox, S., (1998) 'Owner Occupation, Flexible Employment and Welfare' *Housing Studies*, 13,5.

Forrest, R., Leather, P., Gordon, D. and Pantazis, C. (1995) 'The future of home ownership', *Housing Finance*, 27, 9–15.

Forrest, R. and Murie, A. (1992) *Selling the Welfare State*, London, Routledge.

Forrest, R. and Kennett, T. (1996) 'Coping strategies, housing careers and house-hold with negative equity', *Journal of Social Policy*, vol. 25, no. 3, pp. 369–94.

Forrest, R., Leather, P., Gordon, D. and Pantazis, C. (1995) 'The future of home ownership', *Housing Finance*, 27, 9–15.

Foucault, M. (1977) *Discipline and Punish: The Birth of the Prison*, Harmondsworth, Penguin.

Foucault, M. (1984) *The Care of the Self*, Harmondsworth, Penguin.

France, A. (1998) ' "Why should we care?": Young people, citizenship and questions of social responsibility', *Journal of Youth Studies*, vol. 1, no. 1.

Frank, R. H., Gilovich, T. D. and Regan, D. T. (1996) 'Do Economists Make Bad Citizens?', *Journal of Economic Perspectives*, 10, 187–92.

Freeman, R. B. (1997) 'Working for Nothing. The Supply of Volunteer Labor', *Journal of Labor Economics*, 15, 140–66.

Frey, B. (1997) 'From the price to the crowding out effect', *Swiss Journal of Economics and Statistics*, 133, 325–50.

Frey, B. and Oberholzer-Gee, F. (1997) 'The cost of price incentives: an empirical analysis of motivation crowding out', *American Economic Review*, 87, 746–55.

Frey, B. S. (1992) *Economics as a Science of Human Behaviour*, Boston and Dordrecht, Kluwer.

Frey, B. S. (1997a) *Not Just for the Money. An Economic Theory of Personal Motivation*, Cheltenham, UK and Brookfield, USA, Edward Elgar.

Frey, B. S. (1997b) 'A Constitution for Knaves Crowds Out Civic Virtues', *Economic Journal*, 107, 1043–53.

Frey, B. S. (1998) 'State Support and Creativity in the Arts: Some New Considerations', Paper presented at the Association for Cultural Economics International, Barcelona.

Frey, B. S. and Bohnet, I. (1995) 'Institutions Affect Fairness: Experimental Investigations', *Journal of Institutional and Theoretical Economics*, 151, 286–303.

Frey, B. S., Pommerehne, W. W. and Gygi, B. (1993) 'Economics Indoctrination or Selection? Some Empirical Results', *Journal of Economic Education*, 24, 271–81.

Frye, T. and Shleifer, A. (1997) 'The Invisible Hand and the Grabbing Hand', *American Economic Review*, 87, 354–58.

Fukuyama, F. (1995) *Trust: The Social Virtues and the Creation of Prosperity*, New York, Free Press.

Gabe, J. and Bury, M. (1996) 'Risking tranquiliser use: cultural and lay dimensions' in Williams, S. J. and Calnan, M. (eds), *Modern Medicine. Lay Perspectives and Experiences*, London, UCL Press.

Gabe J. (1995) (ed) *Medicine, Health and Risk. Sociological Approaches*, Oxford, Blackwell.

Gallie, D. and Vogler, C. (1990) *Unemployment and Attitudes to Work*, Working Paper No. 18, Social Change and Economic Life Initiative, Nuffield College, Oxford.

Gambetta, D. (ed.) (1988) *Trust: Making and Breaking Co-operative Relations*, Cambridge, Cambridge University Press.

Garnham, A. and Knights, E. (1994) *Putting the Treasury First: The Truth about Child Support*, London, CPAG.

Giddens, A. (1990) *The Consequences of Modernity*, Cambridge, Polity.

Giddens, A. (1991) *Modernity and Self-Identity: Self and Society in the Late Modern Age*, Cambridge, Polity Press.

Giddens, A. (1992) *The Transformation of Intimacy*, Cambridge, Polity.

Giddens, A. (1994) *Beyond Left and Right*, Cambridge, Polity.

Giddens, A. (1998) *The Third Way: The Renewal of Social Democracy*, Cambridge, Polity.

Gillespie, (1996) 'Child Support: the hand that rocks the cradle' *Family Law* 162.

Glennerster, H. (1998) 'Priorities for welfare', *The Times Higher Education Supplement*, 7 August.

Glennerster, H. (1998) 'Welfare with the Lid On' in H. Glennerster and J. Hills (eds) *The State of Welfare: The Economics of Social Spending*, second edition, Oxford, Clarendon.

Glennerster, H. and Hills, J. (1998) *The State of Welfare* (second edition), Oxford University Press.

Goddard, E. and Savage, D. (1994) *People Aged 65 and Over: a Study Carried Out on Behalf of the Department of Health as Part of the 1991 General Household Survey*, London, OPCS.

Golding, P. and Middleton, S. (1982) *Images of Welfare: Press and Public Attitudes to Poverty*, Oxford, Martin Robertson.

Goldman, M. (1994) *Lost Opportunity: Why Economic Reforms in Russia have not Worked*, New York, Norton.

Gouldner, A. W. (1960) 'The Norm of Reciprocity: A Preliminary Statement', *American Sociological Review*, 25, 161–78.

Graetz, M. J. and Wilde, L. L. (1985) 'The Economics of Tax Compliance: Facts and Fantasy', *National Tax Journal*, 38, 355–63.

Grant, R. M. (1996) 'Toward a Knowledge-based Theory of the Firm', *Strategic Management Journal*, 17, 109–22.

Gray, A. and Jenkins, W. (1993) 'Public Administration and Government, 1991–92', *Parliamentary Affairs*, 46, 1, 17–37.

Green J. (1997) 'Risk and the construction of social identity: children's talk about accidents', *Sociology of Health and Illness*, 19, 457–79.

Gregg, P. and Wadsworth, J. (1995) 'A Short History of Labour Turnover, Job Tenure and Job Security, 1975–1993', *Oxford Review of Economic Policy*, 11, 1.

Grout, P. (1987) 'The wider share ownership programme', *Fiscal Studies*, 8, 59–74.

Güth, W. (1995) 'Shirking Versus Managerial Incentives of Chief Executive Officers (CEOs): A Note on a Possible Misunderstanding of Principal-Agency-Theory', *Journal of Institutional and Theoretical Economics*, 151, 693–98.

Güth, W., Schmittberger, R. and Schwarze, B. (1982) 'An Experimental Analysis of Ultimatum Bargaining', *Journal of Economic Behaviour and Organization*, 3, 367–88.

Hackman, R. J. and Oldham, G. R. (1980) *Work Redesign.* Reading, MA, Addison-Wesley.

Hahn, R. W. (1989) 'The Political Economy of Environment Regulation: Towards a Unifying Framework', *Public Choice*, 65, 21–47.

Hales, J. Shaw, A. and Roth, W. (1999) *Evaluation of the New Deal for Lone Parents: a Preliminary Assessment of the Counterfactual*, In house report 42, Social Research Branch, Department of Social Security.

Hamnett, C. (1989) *The north–south divide*, in owner occupation – in A. Lewis and J. Townsend (eds) The North–South Divide, London, UCP.

Hancock, K., Munro, M., Jones, C., McGuckin, A. and Parkey, H. (1991) *The impact of housing subsidies in Glasgow TTWA*, York, NFHA.

Handwerker L. (1994) 'Medical risk: implicating poor pregnant women', *Social Science and Medicine*, 38, 665–75.

Hanson, P. (1984) 'The Novosibirsk Report: Comment', *Survey*, Spring, 83–7.

Hantrais, L. (1998) *Interaction between Family Policies and Social Protection in the Context of Recent and Future Socio-Demographic Changes*, EC (DGV) Project SOC 97 100931.

Hargreaves-Heap, S., Hollis, M., Lyons, B., Sugden, R. and Weale, A. (1992) *The Theory of Choice*, Oxford, Blackwell.

Hey, J. D. (1991) *Experiments in Economics*, Oxford, Blackwell.

Heyman B. (1998) *Risk, Health and Health Care*, London, Hodder & Stoughton.

Higgins, E. T. and Trope, Y. (1990) 'Activity Engagement Theory: Implications of Multiply Identifiable Input for Intrinsic Motivation', in E. T. Higgins and R. M. Sorrentino (eds) *Handbook of Motivation and Cognition: Foundations of Social Behavior*, vol. 2, New York, Guilford, pp. 229–64.

Hirshleifer, J. (1985) 'The Expanding Domain of Economics', *American Economic Review*, 75, 53–68.

Holland J., Ramazanoglu C., Sharpe, S. and Thomson, R. (1992) 'Pleasure, pressure and power: some contradictions of gendered sexuality', *Sociological Review*, 40, 645–73.

Holmans, A. (1995) *Housing Demand and Need in England 1991–2011*, York, Joseph Rowntree Foundation.

Home Office (1998) *Supporting Families: A Consultative Document*, HOM/9/1998.

Hoorens, V. (1995) 'Self-favoring biases, self-presentation, and the self-other asymmetry in social comparison', *Journal of Personality*, 63, 793–817.

Hoorens, V. (1996) 'Self-favoring biased for positive and negative characteristics: independent phenomena?' *Journal of Social and Clinical Psychology*, 15, 53–67.

Hume, D. (1742) 'Of Independency of Parliament, Essays', *Moral, Political and Literary*, Vol. 1, London: University Press, pp. 117–18.

Hume, D. (1875), 'On the independency of Parliament' in *Essays, Moral, Political and Literary*, vol. 1, T. H. Green and T. H. Gross, (eds.), London, Longman.

Jensen, M. C. and Murphy, K. J. (1990) 'Performance Pay and Top-Management Incentives', *Journal of Political Economy*, 98, 225–64.

Jessop, B. (1994) 'The transition to post-Fordism and the Schumpeterian workfare state', in Burrows, R. and Loader, B. (eds) *Towards a Post-Fordist Welfare State?*, London, Routledge.

Johnson, P. and Falkingham, J. (1992) *Ageing and Economic Welfare*, London, Sage.

Jones, P., Cullis, J. and Lewis, A. (1998) 'Public versus private provision of altruism: can fiscal policy make individuals 'better' people?' *Kyklos*, 51, 3–24.

Jones, P. and Cullis, J. (forthcoming) 'Irrationality, preference endogeneity and social policy', *Journal of Social Policy*.

Jordan B., Redley, M. and James, S. (1994) *Putting the Family First*, London, UCL Press.

Jordan, B. and Redley, P. (1994) 'Polarization, underclass and the welfare state', *Work, Employment and Society*, vol. 8, No. 2.

Jordan, B., James, S., Kay, H. and Redley, P. (1992) *Trapped in Poverty? Labour market decisions in low income households*, London, Routledge.

Jordan, B., Simon, J., Kay, H. and Redley, M. (1992) *Trapped in Poverty?*, London, Routledge.

Jordan, W. (1998) *The New Politics of Welfare: Social Justice in a Global Context*, London, Sage.

Kagel, J. and Roth, A. E. (1995) *Handbook of Experimental Economics*, Princeton, Princeton University Press.

Kaplan, S., Newberry, K. and Reckers, P. (1997) 'The Effect of Moral Reasoning and Educational Communications on Tax Evasion Intentions', *Journal of the American Taxation Association*, 19, 38–54.

Karn, V. (1977) *Retiring to the Seaside*, London, Routledge.

Kazdin, A. E. (1982) 'The Token Economy: A Decade Later', *Journal of Applied Behavioural Analysis*, 15, 431–45.

Kelman, S. (1987) *Making Public Policy: A Hopeful View of American Government*, New York, Basic Books.

Kempson, E., Bryson, A. and Rowlingson, K. (1994) *Hard Times: How Poor Families Make Ends Meet*, London, Policy Studies Institute.

Kempson, E., Ford, J., and Quilgars, D. (1999) *Unsafe Safety Nets*, York, University of York, Centre for Housing Policy.

Kitzinger, J. (1995) 'Introducing focus groups', *British Medical Journal*, 311, 299–302.

Kohn, A. (1996) 'By All Available Means: Cameron and Pierce's Defense of Extrinsic Motivators', *Review of Educational Research*, 66, 1–4.

Kramer, R. M. and Tyler, T. R. (eds) (1996) *Trust in Organizations*, Thousand Oaks, Sage.

Kreuger, R. A. (1994) *Focus Groups: A Practical Guide for Applied Research*, Thousand Oaks, Sage.

Krska, J. and Kennedy, E. (1996) 'An audit of responding to symptoms in community pharmacy', *International Journal of Pharmacy Practice*, 4, 129–135.

Kunreuther, H. and Kleindorfer, P. R. (1986) 'A Sealed-Bid Auction Mechanism for Siting Noxious Facilities', *American Economic Review*, 76, 295–99.

Labour Party (1997) *New Labour: Because Britain Deserves Better*, General Election Manifesto, London, Labour Party.

Land, H. (1978) 'Who cares for the family?' *Journal of Social Policy*, 7, 357–84.

Land, H. and Rose, H. (1985) 'Compulsory altruism for some or an altruistic society for all?' in Philip Bean, John Ferris and David Whynes (eds) *In Defence of Welfare*, London, Tavistock.

Lane, D. (ed.) (1986) *Labour and Employment in the USSR*, New York, New York University Press.

Lane, R. E. (1991) *The Market Experience*, New York, Cambridge University Press.

Lash S., Szerszynski, B. and Wynne, B. (1996) *Risk, Environment and Modernity, Towards a New Ecology*, London, Sage.

Lash, S. and Urry, J. (1987) *The End of Organized Capitalism*, Cambridge: Polity.

Lash, S. and Urry, J. (1994) *Economies of Signs and Space*, London, Sage.

Lawler, E. E. (1990) *Aligning Organizational Strategies and Pay Systems*, San Francisco, Jossey-Bass.

Le Grand, J. (1997a) 'Afterword' in Oakley and Ashton (1997), pp. 15–40.

Le Grand, J. (1997b) 'Knights, knaves or pawns? Human behaviour and social policy', *Journal of Social Policy*, 26, 149–169.

Le Grand, J. and Bartlett, W. (eds) (1993) *Quasi-Markets in Social Policy*, London, Macmillan.

Le Grand, J. and Vizard, P. (1998) 'The NHS: Crisis, change or continuity?' in Glennerster, H. and Hills, J. (1998) *The State of Welfare* (second edition), Oxford, Oxford University Press.

Le Grand, J. Mays, N. and Mulligan, J. (1998) (eds), *Learning from the NHS Internal Market*, London, King's Fund.

Lea, S., Tarpy, B. and Webley, P. (1985) *The Individual in the Economy*, Cambridge, Cambridge University Press.

Leat, D. (1990) *For Love and Money: the Role of Payment in Encouraging the Provision of Care*, York: Joseph Rowntree Foundation.

Leat, D. and Gay, P. (1987) *Paying for Care: A Study of Policy and Practice in Paid Care Schemes*. London: PSI Research Report No. 661.

Leibfried, S. (1993) 'Towards a European welfare state?', in C. Jones (ed.) *New Perspectives on the Welfare State in Europe*, London, Routledge.

Lepper, M. and Greene, D. (1978) *The Hidden Costs of Reward: New Perspectives on the Psychology of Human Motivation*, Hillsdale, Wiley/Erlbaum.

Lepper, M. R., Keavney, M. and Drake, M. (1996) 'Intrinsic Motivation and Extrinsic Rewards: A Commentary on Cameron and Pierce's Meta-analysis', *Review of Educational Research*, 66, 5–32.

Lewis, A., Webley, P. and Furnham, A. (eds.) (1995) *The New Economic Mind*, Harvester Wheatsheaf, Hemel Hempstead.

Lister, R. (1998) 'From equality to social inclusion: New Labour and the welfare state', *Critical Social Policy*, 18, 2, 215–225.

Lively, B. T., Baldwin, H. J., Carlton, B. R. and Riley, D. A. (1981) 'The relationship of knowledge to perceived benefits and risks of oral contraceptives', *Drug Information Journal*, July/ December, 153–160.

Loomes, G. (1998) 'Probabilities versus money: a test of some fundamental assumptions about rational decision-making', *Economic Journal*, 108, pp. 477–89.

Lowy, E. and Ross, M. W. (1994) '"It'll never happen to me": gay men's beliefs, perceptions and folk constructions of sexual risk', *AIDS Education and Prevention*, 6, 467–82.

Luck, M. and Jesson, J. (1992) *Coping with Childhood Ailments, Coughs and Colds*, Birmingham, Birmingham Family Health Services Authority.

Luhmann, N. (1993) *Risk, a Sociological Theory*, Berlin, de Gruyter.

Lunt, P. and Disney, R. (1999) 'Interpreting Financial Service Adverts', in R. Elliott, *Interpreting Adverts*, Copenhagen, Copenhagen University Press.

Lunt, P. K. and Livingstone, S. (1992) *Mass Consumption and Personal Identity: Everyday Economic Experience*, Buckingham, Open University Press.

Lupton, D. (1996) 'Your life in their hands: trust in the medical encounter' in James V. and Gabe J., *Sociology of the Emotions*, Oxford, Blackwell.

Lupton, D. (1997) 'Consumerism, reflexivity and the medical encounter', *Social Science and Medicine*, 45, 373–81.

Maclennan, D. (1982) *Housing Economics: An Applied Approach*, Harlow, Longman.

Maclennan, D., Gibb, K. and More, A. (1991) *Paying for Britain's Housing*, York, Joseph Rowntree Foundation.

Maclennan, D., Meen, G., Gibb, K. and Stephens, M. (1998) *Fixed Commitments, Uncertain Incomes*, York, Joseph Rowntree Foundation.

Madden, J. Franklin (1998) *The Politics of Risk Society*, Polity (in association with IPPR), Cambridge.

Madigan, R. and Munro, M. (1999) Household strategies and housing ladders, *Sociological Review*, vol. 46, pp. 713–34.

Malpass, P. and Murie, A. (1995) *Housing Policy and Practice*, Basingstoke, Macmillan.

Mansbridge, J. (1994) 'Public Spirit in Political Systems', in H. J. Aaron, T. E. Mann and T. Taylor (eds) *Values and Public Policy*, Washington, Brookings, 1994, pp. 146–72.

Marsh, A. (1997) 'Making it work for lone parents' *The Guardian*, 31 December.

Marshall, T. H. (1950) 'Citizenship and Social Class', in T. H. Marshall and T. Bottomore (1992) *Citizenship and Social Class*, London, Pluto.

Mason, J. (1996) *Qualitative Researching*, London, Sage.

McGlone, F. (1987) 'Away from the dependency culture', in S. Savage and L. Robins (eds) *Public Policy Under Thatcher*, Basingstoke, Macmillan.

McGlone, F. (1999) 'Few lone parents find jobs through new deal' *Family Policy Studies Centre Newsletter*, autumn, 5.

McLaughlin, E., Millar, J. and Cooke, K. (1989) *Work and Welfare Benefits*, Aldershot, Avebury.

McRae, S. (1993) *Cohabiting Mothers: Changing Marriage and Motherhood*, London, Policy Studies Institute.

Means, R. and Smith (1998) *Community Care – Policy and Practice*, 2nd edn, London, Macmillan.

Mears, M. (1998) 'The Child Support Act revisited' *New Law Journal*, 148, 6828, 28.

Meen, G. P. (1996) 'Spatial aggregation spatial dependence and predictability in the UK housing market', *Housing Studies*, 10, 405–24.

Meikle, J. (1998) 'Luck be a lady to me', *Guardian*, 7 October, 19.

Menchik, P. and Weisbrod, B. (1987) 'Volunteer Labor Supply', *Journal of Public Economics*, 32, 159–183.

Mill, J. S. ([1861] 1958) 'Considerations on Representative Government', *Essays on Politics and Society* vol. 19 of the Collected Works, London, Forum Books.

Millar, J. (1996) 'Family obligations and social policy: the case of child support' *Policy Studies*, 17, 3, 181–219.

Moore, J. (1987) 'Welfare and dependency', speech to Conservative Constituency Parties' Association, September.

Morgan, D. (1996) *Family Connections*, Cambridge, Polity Press.

Morgan, D. L. (ed.) (1993) *Successful Focus Groups: Advancing the State of the Art*, Newbury Park, Sage.

Morgan, M. (1996) 'Perceptions and use of anti-hypertensive drugs among cultural groups', in S. J. Williams and M. Calnan (eds), *Modern Medicine. Lay Perspectives and Experiences*, London, UCL Press.

Muellbauer, J. (1990) *The Great British Housing Disaster and Economic Policy*, Economic Studies no. 5, London, Institute of Public Policy Research.

Mueller, D. C. (1995) *Constitutional Economics*, Cambridge: Cambridge University Press.

Munro, M. (1997) 'Rationality and choice in house purchase' in C. Roland Levy (ed.) *Social and economic representations*, 1, 473–86.

Munro, M., Madigan, R. and Memery, C. (1998) 'Choices in Owner Occupation' in: P. Taylor-Gooby (ed.) *Choice and Public Policy : the Limits to Welfare Markets*, London, Macmillan.

Murray, C. (1994) *Underclass: The Crisis Deepens*, London, IEA.

Murrell, P. (1991) 'Can Neoclassical Economics Underpin the Reforms of the Centrally Planned Economies?', *Journal of Economic Perspectives*, 5, 59–76.

NACAB (1995) *Security at Risk*, London, NACAB.

National Pharmaceutical Association, (October 1998) *NPA Newsletter*.

Nye, J. S., Zelikow, P. D. and King, D. C. (1997) *Why People Don't Trust Government*, Cambridge, MA, Harvard University Press.

Oakley, A. and Ashton, J. (eds) (1997) *Richard Titmuss's The Gift Relationship*, London, Allen and Unwin. London: LSE Books. Original edition with new chapters.

Oberholzer-Gee, F. (1998) *Die Oekonomik des St. Florianprinzips. Warum wir keine Standorte fuer nukleare Endlager finden*, Basel, Helbing and Lichtenhahn.

OECD (1994) *Integrating Environment and Economics: The Role of Economic Instruments*, Paris, Organization for Economic Cooperation and Development.

Offe, C. (1984) *Contradictions of the Welfare State*, Cambridge, Mass, MIT Press.

Offe, C. (1996) *Modernity and the State: East and West*, Cambridge, Polity Press.

Office for National Statistics (1997) *Population Trends 88*, London, HMSO.

Office for National Statistics (1998) *Social Trends*, no 28, London, HMSO.

Office for National Statistics (1999) *Population Trends*, March, London, HMSO.

O'Hare, M. (1977) 'Not On My Block You Don't: Facility Siting and the Strategic Importance of Compensation', *Public Policy*, 25, 409–58.

Oliver, M. (1990) *The Politics of Disablement*, London, Macmillan.

ONS, Office of National Statistics (1985) *Annual Abstract of Statistics*, London, HMSO.

ONS, Office of National Statistics (1997) *Social Trends, no. 27*, London, HMSO.

ONS, Office of National Statistics (1998) *Annual Abstract of Statistics*, London, HMSO.

OPCS (1996) *General Household Survey, 1994*, London, HMSO.

Oster, G., Huse, D. M., Delea, T. E., Colditz, G. A. and Richter, L. M. (1990) 'The risks and benefits of an Rx-to-OTC switch. The case of over-the-counter H2-blockers', *Medical Care*, 28, 834–49.

Osterloh, M. and Frey, B. S. (1998) 'Managing Motivation and Knowledge in the Theory of the Firm', *Mimeo*, Institute for Research in Business Administration and Institute for Empirical Economic Research: University of Zurich.

Pahl, J. (1989) *Money and Marriage*, London, Macmillan.

Parker, G. (1990) *With Due Care and Attention: a Review of Research on Informal Care*, 2nd edn. London, Family Policy Studies Unit.

Parker, G. (1993) *With This Body: Caring and Disability in Marriage*, Buckingham, Open University Press.

Parker, G. (1995) 'Community care – Which community? Who cares?', plenary lecture to the Department of Social Security Summer School, King's College, Cambridge. Leicester: Nuffield Community Care Studies Unit, 1995.

Parker, G. (1998) 'Inter-generational relationships and later life: families and household responsibilities in the UK', paper given at Nuffield Foundation conference 'Inter-generational Relationships and Later Life', Worcester College, Oxford.

Parker, G. and Clarke, H. (1997a) 'Will you still need me, will you still feed me? – Paying for care in old age', *Social Policy and Administration*, 31, 119–35.

Parker, G. and Clarke, H. (1997b) *Attitudes and Behaviour Towards Financial Planning for Care in Old Age*, Leicester: Nuffield Community Care Studies Unit Working Paper 58.

Parker, G. and Clarke, H. (1998) 'Paying for long-term care in the UK: policy, theory and evidence' in P. Taylor-Gooby (ed.) *Choice and Public Policy: The Limits to Welfare Markets*, London, Macmillan.

Parsons, E. and Atkinson, P. (1992) 'Lay constructions of genetic risk', *Sociology of Health and Illness*, 14, 437–55.

Payne, K., Ryan-Woolley, B. M. and Noyce, P. R. (1998) 'Role of consumer attributes in predicting the impact of medicines deregulation on National Health Service prescribing in the United Kingdom' *International Journal of Pharmacy Practice*, 6, 150–8.

Phillimore, P. and Moffat, S. (1994) 'Discounted knowledge: local experience, environmental pollution and health'. in J. Popay and G. Williams (eds), *Researching the People's Health*, London, Routledge.

Pommerehne, W. W. and Weck-Hannemann, H. (1996) 'Tax Rates, Tax Administration and Income Tax Invasion in Switzerland', *Public Choice*, 88, 161–70.

Pommerehne, W. W. (1985) 'Was wissen wir eigentlich über Steuerhinterziehung?', *Revista Internazionale di Scienze Economiche e Commerciali*, 32, 1155–86.

Portney, K. E. (1991) *Siting Waste Treatment Facilities: The NIMBY Syndrome*, New York, Auburn House.

Putnam, R. D. (1993) *Making Democracy Work*, Princeton, Princeton University Press.

Quilgars, D. and Abbott, D. (1999) *The Risks of Unemployment: Perceptions and Responses of Individuals and Families*, paper presented at international conference on 'Plant Closures and Downsizing in Europe: How do European Workers React to Job Insecurity and the Threat of Unemployment', Lenven, Belgium, January.

Rawls, J. (1972) *A Theory of Justice*, Oxford, Oxford University Press.

Reckers, P., Sanders, D. and Roark, S. (1994) 'The Influence of Ethical Attitudes on Taxpayer Compliance', *National Tax Journal*, 47, 825–36.

Reinganum, J. E. and Wilde, L. L. (1986) 'Equilibrium Verification and Reporting Policies in a Model of Tax Compliance', *International Economic Review*, 27, 739–60.

Renn O., Burns, W. J., Kasperson, J. X., Kasperson, R. E. and Slovic, P. (1992) 'The social amplification of risk: theoretical foundations and empirical applications', *Journal of Social Issues*, 48, 137–60.

Rentoul, J. (1989) *Me and Mine: The Triumph of the New Individualism?*, London, Unwin Hyman.

Ribbens-McCarthy, J., Edwards, R. and Gillies, V. (1999) *Moral Tales of the Child and the Adult: Narratives of Contemporary Family Lives Under Changing Circumstances*, Centre for Family and Household Studies Occasional Paper, Oxford, Oxford Brookes University.

Roberts, Y. (1998) 'Left holding the baby' *The Guardian*, 27 January.

Roth, J. A., Scholz, J. T. and Witte, A. D. (eds) (1989) *Taxpayer Compliance*, Philadelphia, University of Pennsylvania Press.

Rotter, J. B. (1966) 'Generalized Expectancies for Internal versus External Control of Reinforcement', *Psychological Monographs*, 80, Whole No. 609.

Rousseau, D. M. (1995) *Psychological Contracts in Organizations*, Thousand Oaks, Sage.

Rowlands, O. with Parker, G. (1998) *Informal Carers. Results of an Independent Study Carried Out on Behalf of the Department of Health as part of the 1995 General Household Survey*, London, The Stationery Office.

Rowlands, O., Singleton, N., Maher, J and Higgins, V. (1997) *Living in Britain: Results from the 1995 General Household Survey*, London, The Stationery Office.

Rowlingson, K., Whyley, C., Newburn, T. and Berthoud, R. (1997) *Social Security Fraud: The role of penalties*, London, Stationery Office.

Royal Commission on Long Term Care. (1999) *With Respect to Old Age: Long-Term Care – Rights and Responsibilities*, London, The Stationery Office.

Rummel, A. and Feinberg, R. (1988) 'Cognitive Evaluation Theory: A Meta-Analytic Review of the Literature', *Social Behavior and Personality*, 16, 147–64.

Runciman, W. B. (1966) *Relative Deprivation and Social Justice*, London, Routledge and Kegan Paul.

Ryan, R. M. and Deci, E. L. (1996) 'When Paradigms Clash: Comments on Cameron and Pierce's Claim that Rewards Do Not Undermine Intrinsic Motivation', *Review of Educational Research*, 66, 33–8.

Sachs, J. D. and Woo, W. T. (1994) 'Structural Factors and Economic Reforms in China, Eastern Europe, and the Former Soviet Union', *Economic Policy*, 11, 101–45.

Sachs, J. D. (1993) *Poland's Jump to a Market Economy*, Cambridge, MA, MIT Press.

Sainsbury, R. (1996) 'Rooting out fraud – innocent until proven fraudulent', *Poverty*, No. 93.

Saunders, P. (1990) *A nation of home owners*, London, Unwin Hyman.

Saunders, P. and Harris, C. (1989) *Popular Attitudes to State Services: A growing demand for alternatives*, Research Report 11, Social Affairs Unit, London, IEA.

Sevenhuijsen, S. (1998) *Citizenship and the Ethics of Care*, London, Routledge.

Shleifer, A. (1997) 'Government in Transition', *European Economic Review*, 41, 385–410.

Silva, E. and Smart, C. (1999) 'The 'new' practices and politics of family life' in Silva, E. and Smart, C.(eds) *The New Family*, London, Sage.

Slater, D. (1997) *Consumer Culture and Modernity*, Cambridge, Polity.

Slovic, P. (1987) 'Perception of risk', *Science*, 236, 280–85.

Slovic, P. Fischhoff, B. and Lichtenstein, S. (1990) 'Facts versus fears: Understanding perceived risk'. In Kahnemann D., Slovic P. and Tversky A., *Judgement under Uncertainty: Heuristics and Biases*, Cambridge, Cambridge University Press.

Smart, C. (1987) 'There is of course the distinction disclosed by natural law and the problem of paternity' in M. Stanworth (ed.) *Reproductive Technologies*, Oxford, Polity, 98–117.

Smart, C. and Neale, B. (1998) *Family Fragments?* London, Polity.

Solow, R. S. (1971) 'Blood and Thunder', *Yale Law Journal*, 80, 170–83.

Spencer, P. (1996) 'Reactions to A Flexible Labour Market' in *British Social Attitudes: The 13th Report*.

Steinberg, R. (1990) 'Labor Economics and the Non-profit Sector: A Literature Review', *Non-profit and Voluntary Sector Quarterly*, 19, 151–69.

Stigler, G. J. and Becker, G. S. (1977) 'De Gustibus Non Est Disputandum', *American Economic Review*, 67, 76–90.

Stigler, G. J. (1984) 'Economics – The Imperial Science?', *Scandinavian Journal of Economics*, 86, 301–13.

Survey of English Housing (1997) London, HMSO.

Swanson, G. (1992) 'Modernity and the postmodern', *Theory, Culture and Society*, vol. 19, no. 2, pp. 147–55.

Tang, S. H. and Hall, V. C. (1995) 'The Over-justification Effect: A Meta-analysis', *Applied Cognitive Psychology*, 9, 365–404.

Taylor, D. (1996) 'Citizenship and social power', in D. Taylor (ed.) *Critical Social Policy: A Reader*, London, Sage.

Taylor-Gooby, P., Dean, H., Munro, M. and Parker, G. (1998) '*Risk and the welfare state*', paper presented at the ESRC Economic Beliefs and Behaviour Programme conference on 'Decision making in theory and practice', University of Oxford, 1–2 July.

Taylor-Gooby, P. (1991) *Social Change, Social Welfare and Social Science*, Hemel Hempstead, Harvester Wheatsheaf.

Taylor-Gooby, P. (1994) 'Welfare outside the state', in R. Jowell, J. Curtice, L. Brook, D. Ahrendt (eds) *British Social Attitudes: The 11th report*, Aldershot, Dartmouth.

Taylor-Gooby, P. (1998) *Choice and Public Policy*, London, Macmillan.

Taylor-Gooby, P. (1999) 'Markets and motives: trust and egoism in welfare markets', *Journal of Social Policy*, 28, 97–114.

Taylor-Gooby, P. (1995) 'Comfortable, marginal and excluded: who should pay higher taxes for a better welfare state?' in Jowell *et al.* (eds) *British Social Attitudes. The 12th report*, Aldershot, Dartmouth Publishing Company.

Thaler, R. H. *The Winner's Curse. Paradoxes and Anomalies of Economic Life*, New York, Free Press, 1992.

Thomas, D. H. V. and Noyce, P. R. (1996) 'The interface between self medication and the NHS', *British Medical Journal*, 312, 688–91.

Timmins, N. (1996) *The Five Giants*, London, Fontana.

Titmuss, R. (1971). *The Gift Relationship* London, Allen and Unwin. See also Oakley and Ashton (1997) 1997 edn, Ann Oakley and John Ashton (eds), London, LSE Books.

Toulmin, S. (1990) *Cosmopolis: the hidden agenda of modernity*, New York, Free Press.

Townsend, P. (1979) *Poverty in the United Kingdom*, Harmondsworth, Penguin.

Travis, A. (1998) 'Straw plays Spock' *The Guardian*, 3 November.

TUC Economic and Social Affairs Department (1996) *Britain Divided – Insecurity at Work*, London, TUC.

Turner, B. (1992) 'Weber, Giddens and modernity', *Theory, Culture and Society*, vol. 19, no. 2, pp. 141–6.

Utting, D. (1995) *Families and Parenthood*, York, Joseph Rowntree Foundation.

Vaillancourt, F. (1994) 'To Volunteer or Not: Canada, 1987', *Canadian Journal of Economics*, 4, 813–26.

Vallacher, R. R. and Wegner, D. M. (1987) 'What do People Think they're Doing? Action Identification and Human Behaviour', *Psychological Review*, 94, 3–15.

Van Dijk, F. and van Winden, F. (1997) 'Dynamics of Social Ties and Local Public Good Provision', *Journal of Public Economics*, 64, 323–41.

Vuckovic, N. and Nichter, M. (1997) 'Changing patterns of pharmaceutical practice in the United States', *Social Science and Medicine*, 44, 1285–1302.

Waine, B. (1995) 'A disaster foretold? The case of personal pensions', *Social Policy and Administration*, vol. 29, no. 4, pp. 317–34.

Walker, R., Shaw, A. and Hull, L. (1995) 'Responding to the Risk of Unemployment', in: *Risk, Insurance and Welfare*, London, Association of British Insurers.

Ward, P. R. and Tully, M. P. (1998) *Self-Care and Pharmacy: Setting the Research Agenda*, Report to the Royal Pharmaceutical Society.

Warnes, T. (1992) (Migration and the life-course) pp. 175–87, in T. Chapman and T. Fielding (eds) *Migration Progress and Prospects*, London, Routledge.

Weisbrod, B. A. (1998) *The Non-profit Economy*, Cambridge, MA, Harvard University Press.

White, M. (1996) 'Labour Market Risk' in P. Meadows (ed.) *Work-in, Work-out?* York, Joseph Rowntree Foundation.

Whylie, C., McCormack, J. and Kempson, E (1998) *Paying for Peace of Mind: Access to Home Contents Insurance for Low Income Households*, London, Policy Studies Institute.

Wiersma, U. J. (1992) 'The Effects of Extrinsic Rewards on Intrinsic Motivation: A Meta-Analysis', *Journal of Occupational and Organizational Psychology*, 65, 101–14.

Wildavsky, A. (1988) *Searching for Safety*, Oxford, Transition Press.

Williams, G. and Popay, J. (1994) 'Lay knowledge and the privilege of experience' in Gabe, J., Kelleher, D. and Williams, G. (eds), *Challenging Medicine*, London, Routledge.

Williams, S. and Calnan, M. (1996) 'Conclusions: modern medicine and the lay populace in late modernity', in Williams, S. and Calnan, M. *Modern Medicine: Lay Perspectives and Experiences*, London, UCL Press.

Williams, S. and Calnan, M. (1996) 'The "limits" of medicalization? Modern medicine and the lay populace in late modernity', *Social Science and Medicine*, vol. 42, no. 12, pp. 1609–20.

Williamson, O. E. (1985) *The Economic Institutions of Capitalism. Firms, Markets, Relational Contradicting*, New York, Free Press.

Williamson, O. E. (1993) 'Opportunism and its Critics', *Managerial and Decision Economics*, 19, 97–107.

Winston, A. S. and Baker, J. E. (1985) 'Behavior Analytic Studies of Creativity: A Critical Review', *Behavior Analyst*, 8, 191–205.

Wintour, P. (1998) 'Nannying gives Labour pains' *The Observer*, 25 October.

World Values Study Group (1991) *World Values Survey, 1990–1993*. Ann Arbor, Inter-University Consortium for Political and Social Research.

Wynne, B. (1992) 'Misunderstood misunderstanding: social identities and the public uptake of science', *Public Understanding of Science*, 1, 281–304.

Young, H. (1997) Article on child benefit, *The Guardian*, 9 December.

Index

Conservative Party: administrations, 116; and paying for long-term care in old-age, 185–6; 'policies tying training and employment initiatives increasingly closely to social security and unemployment relief', 55; *see also* Major, J.; Thatcher, M.

Consumerism, 52

Consumers, x, xi, 17; complexity of, 148; 'discriminating scepticism' of, 3, 4; reflexivity of, 15; 'uncertain world' of, 131–48; views about risks and benefits of medicines, 138–48; Williams and Calnan (1996) on, 148

Consumption, 14–15, 116–18; cultural aspects of, 117–18; financial services in the new context of, 120–1

Consumption culture, 121–3

Cooter, R. D., 42

'Coping strategy', 3–4

Corporate bonds, 129

Cost–benefit analysis, 16, 71, 72, 78, 82; *see also* Consumers

Council housing, *see* Social housing

Council of Mortgage Lenders, 150

Creativity: 'institutional' and 'personal', 39, 50(n5)

Credit, 105, 110, 115, 123; *see also* Mortgages

Credit risk assessment, 99

Crime, 31–2, 41, 44; *see also* Fraud

Crowding theory, 33–49; consequences for policy, 43–9; ('crowding effects', 49; 'crowding-in effect', 43, 45); factors bolstering, 37–8; 'no such thing', 35–6 ('unwarranted conclusion', 36); 'crowding-out effect': 33, 35–7, 38, 39, 45, 49, 50(n5); (and environmental policy, 44; 'may be attributed to two psychological processes', 36–7; in old-age asylums, 36; reduction of self-determination, 36–7; violation of reciprocity, 37); 'crowding-out theory': 35, 36

CSA, *see* Child Support Act

Cubitt, R. P., 196–7

Cultural: attitudes, x; capital, 15, 117–18, 120–1, 124, 128, 129–30; expectations and preconceptions, xi; values, ix, x

Culture, 83; modern, 8; 'social capital' and, 40

Daily Mail, 78

Daily Mirror, 2

Dake, K., 132

Darling, A. M. (Social Security Secretary), 78

Dean, Professor H., 189, 197–8, 199; biography of, xiii; 'focuses on citizenship and social security', 13; survey (1990) of benefit recipients, 56

Deci, E.L., 35; Deci, Koestner, and Ryan (1998), 36

Demography, 5, 116; proportion at pensionable age (1961–91, with projection to 2021), 5

Dental treatment, 7–8

Department of Social Security, 102–3, 113(n4)

Dependency: in old age, 3; patterns of, 3

'Dependency culture', 52; attempted elimination of, 56–8, 114

Developed Economies, index for trust in, 40–1

Developing countries: index for trust in, 40–1

Dickinson, J., 197, 199

Disability, 7–8, 9, 55, 182

Discipline, 51–2; versus trust, 42–3

Discourse, 60, 135, 141, 147; popular, in relation to poverty, wealth and citizenship, 61–4; racist, 127; *re* risk, 132; 'social threat', 90

Discrimination, 15

Distrust: of financial services, 128–9; of insurance, 104, 109, 111, 129; of investment, 129; of markets, 95; of pensions, 129; of personal finance industry, 130; of private